THE SMALL BUSINESS VALUATION BOOK

THE
SMALL BUSINESS VALUATION BOOK

2ND EDITION

Easy-to-Use Techniques That Will Help You . . .

- Determine a Fair Price
- Negotiate Terms
- Minimize Taxes

LAWRENCE W. TULLER

Avon, Massachusetts

Published by
Adams Media, an F+W Publications Company
57 Littlefield Street, Avon, MA 02322. U.S.A.
www.adamsmedia.com

ISBN-10: 1-59869-766-8
ISBN-13: 978-1-59869-766-7

Printed in Canada.

J I H G F E D C B A

Library of Congress Cataloging-in-Publication Data
is available from the publisher.

This publication is designed to provide accurate and authoritative information
with regard to the subject matter covered. It is sold with the understanding that
the publisher is not engaged in rendering legal, accounting, or other professional advice. If legal advice or other expert assistance is required, the services
of a competent professional person should be sought.

—From a *Declaration of Principles* jointly adopted by
a Committee of the American Bar Association and a
Committee of Publishers and Associations

Many of the designations used by manufacturers and sellers to distinguish their
product are claimed as trademarks. Where those designations appear in this
book and Adams Media was aware of a trademark claim, the designations have
been printed with initial capital letters.

This book is available at quantity discounts for bulk purchases.
For information, please call 1-800-289-0963.

CONTENTS

PART I

BUSINESS VALUATION PRINCIPLES

CHAPTER 1

Exposing the Eight Myths of Business Valuations

Valuing a small, privately held business is very much like painting a picture. It is a creative endeavor, not a science. No single method or procedure for accomplishing this task exists. Generally accepted principles, such as those found in the accounting profession, do not apply to business valuations. It isn't until the brush has had time to do its work that the two parties to a transaction—the business owner on one hand and a business buyer, partner, lender, the IRS, or the courts on the other hand—negotiate the fair market value of a business.

As with an artistic endeavor, creativity plays a major role in business valuations. Such creativity occurs within the parameters of long-standing customs. Unfortunately, these parameters are not thoroughly understood by business owners. And any subject that is not thoroughly understood carries with it a mystique built on myths. This book dispels these myths. It takes the mystery out of business valuations by describing a variety of appraisal methods in clear, nonmathematical language.

Valuing small, privately held businesses requires a mindset significantly different from that of securities analysts or real estate appraisers. Securities analysts rely on mathematical formulas and statistical derivations to value traded securities, but these are largely minority interests and do not reflect the total value of a company; real estate appraisers relate the value of land and buildings to construction indexes, a grossly inappropriate method for valuing a growing concern.

Meaningful valuations of small, privately held businesses based on future cash flow discounted for risk are also at variance with the tax code and the courts. The IRS requires that specific formulas be used to value an estate or business interest for tax purposes, but these calculations determine value at a point in time, ignoring future benefits. Courts of equity attach random values to minority or majority business interests for divorce settlements and other legal remedies, but their randomness breeds inconsistency and pays little heed to the ongoing benefits generated by a business. None of these methods considers the total value of a going concern and the peculiar characteristics of closely held businesses.

Over the years, authors, accountants, lawyers, the IRS, the courts, and management consultants have tried to turn business valuations into a science with definitive, universally accepted methodologies. But all they have succeeded in doing is to cloak them in unfounded myths. Here are eight of the most insidious:

1. The only time a business owner needs to value his business is when he is ready to sell it or when his banker wants a valuation in support of a loan application.
2. A company's earnings determine how much the business is worth.
3. XYZ Corporation sold for $5 million, so my company must be worth the same amount.
4. The most logical way to value a company is to multiply its earnings by five.
5. Only companies that turn a profit are worth anything.
6. Business owners know the value of their companies better than any outsiders, including professional appraisers.
7. The best way to value a company is to multiply its annual revenue by two.
8. The market value of a company is in the eye of the beholder and not determined by fancy mathematical formulas.

Before tackling professional appraisal procedures—that is, the set of methodologies within which acceptable valuation parameters operate—we must dispel these myths.

When Selling a Business or Applying for a Loan

Banks view valuing your business as a crucial step in a loan application. Valuations are also required when you decide to sell the business. The necessity for reliable valuations in both situations seems obvious. Without an appraisal of a company's underlying assets banks can't know how much collateral supports the loan. And without a reasonably calculated market value, business buyers would not have any logical base from which to negotiate a purchase price.

However, if those are the only times you take a hard look at how much your business is worth, you are missing a key ingredient for managing the business.

Knowing the market value of your business helps in deciding when the time has come to retire and sell the entire company. Knowing the value of your business will guide you in restructuring the company to protect its assets from nefarious or frivolous lawsuits. Knowing how much each product line of your business is worth in the marketplace can be invaluable information for deciding whether to intensify marketing efforts for a product line or abandon it altogether.

A recent business valuation will prove the worth of the company for estate tax purposes. Whether a business survives or fades away with the demise of its owner, at the time of death it has some value. It may have hard assets (e.g., equipment, machinery, or real estate). It may have valuable patents or trademarks. Or it may have substantial customer goodwill, built up over years of profitable operation. All of these assets must be included in the taxable estate of the business owner.

Perhaps you have one or more business partners. Your partner could be a spouse or children, or partners might not be related to you at all. When the time comes to dissolve the partnership or to buy out one or more partners or to restructure your business, some type of buy/sell agreement must be in place. Such an agreement includes a method for determining the value of the business at the time of dissolution or buyout. To be certain the valuation meets with IRS approval, it should be updated periodically to reflect changes in the profitability and the acquisition or disposal of company assets.

Basing Value on Earnings

I cannot recall how many times I have argued with business buyers over the myth of a company's earnings determining how much the business is worth. Virtually all privately owned businesses try to show as little profit as possible. Preferably losses. Why? To minimize income taxes. So when potential buyers look at the financial statements or the books of account they see that earnings are low or nonexistent and the business appears to be a poor acquisition choice. But this is wrong. The value of a business is measured not by its earnings but by *how much cash it throws off.* A private company may show book losses but still generate substantial cash. Take for instance those cases where an owner pays himself a large bonus at the end of the year or pays personal expenses out of company funds or buys a new car with company funds. These expenditures represent a return of capital to the owner. Although they are recorded as expenses and hence reductions in profits, in reality the owner has benefited by positive cash flow from the business.

It's important to document these discretionary expenses. Some are deductible by the company for income tax purposes. Some are not. In any event, when the time comes to offer the business for sale, the fact that you have documented them as adjustments to recorded expenses will increase a buyer's confidence in your financial statements.

It is true, however, that when a court assigns a value to a business, as in a divorce settlement, earnings are important. It is much easier for lawyers and judges without accounting backgrounds, or business backgrounds for that matter, to understand the meaning of earnings as opposed to cash flow.

When Compared to Another Company

One of my clients—call him Mr. Brown—had a retail business that sold ice cream, party favors, and light sandwiches. He did about $4.5 million in annual sales. When Mr. Brown wanted to increase his line of credit, the local bank insisted that he determine the value of his business as a prerequisite to lending. I had consulted to this business for several years, so Mr. Brown asked me to do the valuation. Applying the normal capitalization calculation to my forecasted cash flow resulted in a value of about $3 million. My client was incensed. It seems that one of his friends had sold his auto repair business two years ago for $4.75 million. Mr. Brown insisted that his company was worth at least as much as that dingy auto repair shop, and in fact he argued that $5 million was a reasonable number for the bank to base its lending on. I tried to keep him from presenting this to the bank, but failed. The result? The bank turned down Mr. Brown's request for an increased credit line.

The prominent myth that two privately held businesses can have the same value has led more than one entrepreneur in the wrong direction. No two businesses are alike. Location, facilities, equipment, ownership philosophy, management ability, product lines, customer base, supply chains, and so on are unique to a given business. To assume that ABC Company is worth the same as XYZ Company denies these differences.

Comparing the worth of two businesses is like comparing the market value of two houses. Even if the houses have the same square footage and are located side-by-side, one may have a pool while the other doesn't. One may have landscaped gardens while the other doesn't. One may have new bathrooms or a new kitchen while the other doesn't. To determine a market price for these two houses, one must examine the interior as well as the exterior of both and then compensate with premiums or discounts for the differences. Exactly the same exercise must be done to appraise two seemingly comparable businesses. To assume that one company should be valued the same as another is a gross error.

This does not mean that comparative analyses are worthless. Just the opposite is true. As seen in Chapter 8, such analyses are crucial to the completion of a valuation. But they have to be interpreted properly.

Five Times Earnings

The five times earnings (FTE) myth seems to be the hardest one to disprove. Here is an example showing the rationale commonly used. A practicing management consultant for more than twenty years had performed many business valuations for lenders, business buyers, and business owners. Almost without exception he used the FTE method. On many occasions,

I pointed out the fallacy of such an arbitrary method. However, he consistently argued that the FTE method correctly assumed:

1. Lenders usually grant term loans to a small business for a maximum of five years.
2. Buyout partners frequently expect to receive full payment over no more than five years.
3. Business buyers reasonably expect a return of their investment in not more than five years.

Moreover, the adjusted earnings of his clients did, in fact, reflect actual cash flow.

If FTE is a myth, does it mean that this consultant's valuations were wrong and should not have been used? No. Each of these arguments has merit. However, it's important to understand that they ignore the basic tenets of business valuations.

- First, a business is worth only as much as the cash it generates.
- Second, cash generated today is worth more than cash generated next year or the following year.
- Third, the risk of achieving forecasted cash flows must be recognized.
- Fourth, business value should bear some similarity to actual prices paid for like businesses, adjusted for premiums and discounts as necessary.

Loss Businesses are Worthless

If it were true that only businesses turning a profit are worth anything, no dot-com would ever go public, no start-up business would ever be sold, and newer small businesses would have an awful time getting bank loans. As reiterated throughout this book, business value is based on future cash flow, not earnings. Small business owners are notorious for paying personal expenses out of company funds, causing book losses when actually the business generates substantial cash. Some of the most profitable companies began as loss-generating start-ups. The original Control Data Corporation comes to mind. Innovative companies such as Amazon.com operated in the red for many years, but then had a very successful public stock issue. Many other well-known companies survived substantial losses in the beginning to eventually become profitable, high-growth businesses. A small business that can credibly demonstrate the likelihood of substantial future growth, leading to significant cash flow, may have value far in excess of one that turns a steady profit but whose future signals unspectacular growth.

I once had a client whose manufacturing business had been losing money for five years. The business owner was an inveterate inventor, continually coming up with better mousetraps, as it were. Very few of these inventions panned out in the marketplace, however. One year he designed a new type of lens for use on airport runways that allowed light to penetrate fog much better than lenses then in use. He requested a five-year $2 million term loan from his bank to allow him to test the market and to get a production line up and running. His banker refused to grant the loan unless the entrepreneur could prove that his invention would cause the company's profitability to soar in the future. I performed a business valuation for my client, leaning heavily on airport industry growth statistics to validate our cash flow forecast. The bank bought the valuation and granted the loan, even though the business had been losing money for the previous five years.

Incidentally, the new lens was a market sensation. Several of the largest airports in the country ordered thousands of them. This entrepreneur's days of losses were over for good.

Every loss business does not have market value. But if the owner can show that future cash flow will be significantly greater than in the past, most lenders and business buyers would agree that the company is worth something.

Business Owners Know Best

If only it were true that business owners are in the best position to value their businesses, buying and selling private businesses, divorce settlements, and lender verifications would be a lot easier. Unfortunately, such is not the case. Owners who value their own businesses are very similar to homeowners who set selling prices for their own homes. If you have ever sold your home you understand the maxim that owners always believe that their properties are worth more than the market does. Any real estate agent will agree that homeowners are the worst judges of the market value of their own homes.

Having lived in our home for many years we decorated it to our taste, revamped bathrooms, modernized kitchens, added rooms, and so on. We had our home exactly as we wanted it and believed that others would be just as pleased with it. When we put it on the market, we got offers that were much lower than we thought the house was worth. We pulled it off the market after six months, frustrated that it hadn't sold.

Business owners experience the same situation. They also have lived with their businesses for many years, tweaking them here and there to meet their personal comfort levels. They recruited and trained personnel to do those things they wanted them to do in the way they wanted them done. Marketing programs, long-term strategies, facility layouts, and product designs, were uniquely configured to fit those particular businesses. Owners would argue that if decisions affecting these items had been different, their businesses would not have prospered as they had. Certainly, potential buyers must see this. But they don't. Buyers look at businesses with the same jaundiced eye that home buyers have when they look at houses. And in both cases, what they see is entirely different from what the owner sees.

Two Times Revenue

The multiple-of-revenue method is an attempt to standardize valuation procedures within an industry or profession. Characteristically, businesses that use this method are service companies that employ very few hard assets. For example, the hard assets of real estate agencies, accounting firms, business brokers, and law offices might be limited to office furniture and reference libraries.

The problem with basing valuations on a multiple of revenue is that multiplying factors range all over the lot, from less than one to double digits. Averages or medians for a given industry could be used, but that limits the multiple to companies that possess average and mean industry characteristics. Realistically it's very difficult to justify which multiple should be applied to a specific business.

In addition to lacking industry commonality, the multiple-of-revenue method ignores the fundamental parameters of business valuations. It does not recognize the value of future cash flow. Nor does it acknowledge the attendant risk in achieving future cash flows. Pragmatically, this method may be a convenient, simplistic approach to valuing a business, but it lacks the ingredients to make the resultant value credible.

There is one exception to this. Small professional practices (e.g., law firms, CPA firms, medical practices, architectural firms, and so on) and small personal services companies can reasonably be valued using the multiple of revenue method (see Chapter 15). Expenses recorded by these businesses reflect the owners' needs, not necessarily those of the business. This makes using pro forma financial statements to forecast cash flow virtually meaningless, leaving revenue as the most logical choice to represent business activity.

When the multiple of revenue method is used, you need to determine which multiplying factor makes sense. A multiple of two may not always be the right choice. In some cases a higher multiple will be warranted. In other cases a lower multiple makes more sense.

In the Eye of the Beholder

Of the eight myths, this one has the most merit. Professional business appraisers can calculate value with the discounted cash flow method, the capitalization of earnings method, or any other commonly used procedure The IRS and the courts may accept such a calculation as a reasonable estimate of business worth. However, from the perspective of a business buyer or a buyout partner, the value of intangibles frequently constitutes a far more meaningful appraisal of the business. This applies to start-up businesses as well as to going concerns.

Although a calculation of future cash flow discounted for risk is certainly a preferable way to go, in some cases it may be impractical. The eye-of-the-beholder method—if, in fact, this can be called a method—changes myth to reality and ends up being the only way to seal the deal.

However, despite the arbitrary assignment of value to intangible assets such as goodwill by the beholder, some calculation of future cash flow is the only logical base upon which to apply premiums or discounts. Yes, the worth of a business is nearly always in the eye of the beholder. But an acceptable calculation of value based on known facts and reasonable assumptions should also be used to determine the market worth of the company. Premiums and discounts can then be applied as necessary.

These eight myths distort the intent of business valuations to reflect fair market value and must be dispelled, the sooner the better. Misconceptions caused by myths are bad enough. But misunderstandings that emanate from a lack of business valuation standards cause even more confusion.

Lack of Business Appraisal Standards

Although valuations are most frequently used to establish prices for the purchase or sale of controlling or minority equity interests, at one time or another every small business will probably need to be valued for one of the following reasons:

- To determine buyout prices for partners/shareholders
- To minimize tax bases of estates and gifts
- To protect against random court valuations in divorce settlements
- To resolve disputes with minority shareholders
- To raise debt or equity capital at the most favorable terms
- To dispose of unprofitable product lines at the best price

Admitting to a lack of precision, the national Office of Advocacy (a business research group) estimates that 24.7 million businesses are operated for profit in the United States and almost 18 million operate with no employees other than the owner. Of the 24.7 million businesses, about 20,000 are considered large businesses. That means that small businesses represent about 99 percent of the total. Of this total, about 15 percent are corporations, with the balance being partnerships and sole proprietorships.

Every year, hundreds of thousands of closely held businesses change hands. Partial ownership changes can be counted in the millions. In one way or another, each of these transactions requires the valuation of a business or business interest.

With such a large demand, it seems inconceivable that there isn't a common body of knowledge from which appropriate valuation techniques can be drawn. Yet, such is the case. And this causes more than a little debate among business owners, investors, business advisers, bankers, and even professional appraisers.

Part of the controversy comes from the sheer complexity of the mathematical calculations used by securities analysts to value minority interests in traded securities. Part emanates from the misapplication of traditional real estate appraisal techniques to going concerns. Part stems from the indecisiveness of the Internal Revenue Service. And part derives from contradictory court rulings in divorce settlements, dissolution judgments, and shareholder disputes.

Although real estate appraisers, securities analysts, the IRS, and the courts apply their own special methods, the only broadly acceptable standard that can be applied to closely held businesses is one that reflects *fair market value*. Unfortunately, a workable definition of fair market value, applicable to all types and sizes of businesses, continues to elude even the most proficient business appraisers, as well as the IRS and the courts.

Four reasons stand out as the most likely explanation for the absence of standards that could fit into as neat a package as the American Institute of Certified Public Accountants' generally accepted accounting principles:

1. The lack of comparability between closely held businesses on one hand and easily measured publicly traded securities on the other
2. The absence of enforceable accounting rules that standardize financial reporting for closely held small businesses
3. The hesitancy by owners of closely held businesses to reveal buy/sell prices
4. The lack of acceptance by financial institutions of those valuation methods used by professional appraisers

Although this book does not proffer a unified set of valuation methods applicable to all businesses, it does set out principles that are in common use for most closely held companies. It also suggests specific methods that yield generally acceptable results for companies whose industry characteristics or unique features make them especially difficult to value, such as professional practices, micro businesses, real estate-based businesses, and start-up businesses.

Moreover, this book dispels any notion that beta and other esoteric theories used by securities analysts for valuing publicly traded securities can be effectively used for closely held companies. Rather than mathematical formulas, this book stresses the valuation process. Formulas that support fundamental valuation principles are important, but do not themselves provide a solution. It is to the *process* that we must look to develop creative yet meaningful techniques for establishing fair market value. And within the valuation process, the preparation of pro forma financial statements and cash flow projections is paramount.

Valuing a business is not easy. It requires a great deal of research, calculation, and interpretation. Several shortcut methods—such as the multiplication of current earnings or revenues by an arbitrary factor or the stipulation of values for buyout agreements—can be used under special circumstances to quantify a preliminary valuation. However, these methods should never be interpreted as depicting fair market value.

In the end, the fair market value of a business can only be satisfactorily determined by negotiation between the interested parties. Although the many valuation techniques described in this book should give you a good head start, it is the process itself that should be emphasized.

CHAPTER

The Basics

Because the art of business valuation is one of those ill-defined activities used in a wide array of circumstances, it breeds an army of self-proclaimed experts. Public accountants, real estate agents, bankruptcy lawyers, statisticians, securities analysts, insurance appraisers, taxing authorities, business brokers, management consultants, authors, and a variety of others get into the act, each purporting to offer the best, the most authoritative, and the most meaningful method for arriving at a company's market worth.

Most of the confusion surrounding business valuation methods stems from two conditions:

1. Various statutes, regulations, and court precedents dictate methods to match certain circumstances.
2. There are an unlimited number of purposes to which the results of a given business valuation can be applied.

The first condition we can do little about. Legislators, bureaucrats, and lawyers will continue to set rules that serve specific needs, and such rules must be followed if one is to stay in the game. Nevertheless, litigation of these rules has become a big business, as evidenced by the hundreds of cases concerning disputed valuations of businesses and business interests that have reached the courts; most of these have arisen because the proper valuation technique was not used within the context of a given law or business situation. Readers interested in pursuing these cases can easily track their favorite topic in a plethora of law journals and law reviews. Litigation is beyond the scope of this book, however, and will not be considered except in passing.

On the other hand, the second condition relating to the purpose of the valuation is critical in evaluating the pros and cons of different methods. In fact, to arrive at a meaningful valuation, one must have a clearly defined purpose in mind. Although accounting methods for valuing businesses and publicly traded shares can certainly serve as models, most authorities tend to agree that the choice of method should relate to the purpose of the valuation.

Although the focus of this book precludes a discussion of all or even a majority of the broad universe of reasons for valuations, the most common ones—and those that will be addressed in the following chapters—are valuations of businesses and business interests for:

- Selling a business, merging a business, acquiring a business or business line, divesting a business line or business interest, and forming joint ventures
- Structuring a buy/sell agreement for a partnership or a minority shareholder
- Dissolutions of a partnership or corporation
- Bankruptcy reorganizations

The type of business to be valued also has a major impact on the choice of method. Businesses with a majority of their assets in real estate, machinery, or equipment must of necessity include the appraised value of these assets as part of the total business valuation. And small retail businesses that own a relatively large inventory with well-defined market values should include that as part of the total picture.

On the other hand, service businesses usually do not have much in the way of either hard assets or inventory, and therefore they require a totally different approach. Professional practices (e.g., legal, health care, consulting, and investment advisory services) and personal service businesses (e.g., real estate agencies, insurance agencies, literary agencies, personal care businesses, and repair businesses) have unique goodwill characteristics and require yet another approach. Peculiar conditions also pertain to real estate–based businesses and start-up businesses.

Just as space precludes a thorough discussion of the multitude of reasons for making a business valuation, so does it restrict the examination of every variation in business type. Therefore, the following chapters limit discussions, somewhat arbitrarily, to business valuations useful for:

- Small manufacturing, retail, distribution, and service businesses
- Multibusiness entities
- Micro businesses
- Personal service businesses
- Professional practices
- Real estate–based businesses
- Start-up businesses

Terminology

Before getting into the basics of business valuation, it might be beneficial to clarify some of the most commonly used concepts and terms. Like other specialized disciplines, the field of business valuation has its own, somewhat unique vocabulary, much of it derived from the accounting profession and from the securities analysis and banking industries, with a few terms coined specifically for use in the valuation process. Terms that frequently cause the greatest confusion are examined below.

Fair Market Value

Valuing a closely held business is like forecasting the weather: Everyone wants an absolute, scientifically determined, accurate answer, but no one has come up with a way to achieve this goal. If there is one thing that everyone can agree on, however, it is that business valuation is an art, not a science. All the statistical, mathematical, and economic formulas concocted over the years cannot determine with certainty the value of a going business to a specific party over a future time period. The reasons are obvious:

- With the exception of federal, state, and municipal statutes that arbitrarily dictate the definition of value, the monetary value of anything is the amount of cash or property one party is willing to pay another party for it.
- The determination of monetary value includes not only measurable assets but also intangible assets and liabilities.
- Factors external to the business have a major impact on calculable values, and since these factors constantly change, any absolute numerical value is valid for only one point in time.

To further complicate the process, courts, taxing authorities, and others who have an inherent interest in arriving at an independent valuation, usually, for the assessment of judgments, fines, or taxes, widely use *fair market value* as an accepted standard. The generally accepted definition of fair market value is the cash or cash-equivalent price at which an asset would change hands between a willing buyer and a willing seller, both having the means to complete the transaction and neither acting under duress. In this definition, the market is assumed to be universal; that is, it represents all potential buyers and sellers of like businesses in the universe. Fair market value does not refer to a specific seller and a specific buyer, but merely to hypothetical parties involved in arms-length transactions in general.

Furthermore, the concept of fair market value assumes that economic and market conditions prevalent at the date of the valuation will continue. And the denominated price must be in cash or cash equivalents, as opposed to cash and nonmarketable assets or merely nonmarketable assets. In practice, the terms *market value* and *cash value* are used interchangeably with *fair market value.*

Fair market value serves as a basic starting point for various valuation purposes and, of course, as the final determinant when dictated by law. But excluding statutory valuation, fair market value is only one way to reckon the true value of a business. Several other commonly used definitions enter the calculation, depending on the party doing the valuation and the purpose to which it will be put.

Investment Value

Investors make judgments based on expected specific benefits—such as dividend flows, interest payments, and capital gains from appreciated assets—to be derived from a given investment over a specified time period. The worth of that investment is called *investment value* and represents individual investment requirements as opposed to a general, impersonal, and detached fair market value. Putting it another way, market value reflects the worth of a business in the general marketplace; investment value reflects the worth of a business to a particular investor or class of investors for their own reasons.

Investment value is predicated on the future return to the business owner or to an outside investor, and is measured by cash flow. Cash flow, in turn, may be cash flowing from the business to the investor—as in dividends, bonuses, profit sharing, or interest income—or it may be cash received in excess of the original investment when selling the business or business interest.

Expectations of the amounts of these future cash returns will vary with each investor, depending on the following:

- A business's future earning power
- Investor tax status
- The degree of risk in the investment or in an anticipated action that might affect the investment
- Potential interaction with other businesses owned or controlled by the investor
- Future government regulations affecting the preservation of earning power
- Marketability of the investment at a future date

Typically, but certainly not always, discounted cash flow methods are used to estimate future earning power. Since investment value measures an investor's personal requirements, it is unlikely that investment value will coincide with market value, which presumably reflects the consensus of unknown market participants. There is a relationship between the two, however.

For example, if a business seller determines that investment value (i.e., the worth of the business to the seller based on personal requirements) is greater than a calculated market value, then clearly the business should not be sold unless a particular buyer can be found whose investment requirements approximate the seller's. On the other hand, a serious seller using investment value and serious buyers using market value should, through negotiations, be able to arrive at a compromise price for the business.

Supply and demand forces, which in the end determine the price of a business, invariably invalidate hard and fast calculations of business value. Therefore, valuations should be considered as a starting point in making decisions, not an end in themselves.

Intrinsic Value

In contrast to investment value, the concept of *intrinsic value* focuses on determining worth based on perceived characteristics of the business, not the requirements of a particular investor. Theoretically, any number of analysts could come to similar conclusions through weighing the company's financial characteristics and then extrapolating similar projections of anticipated future events, such as future growth rate, future earnings and dividend policies, and the sale price of business assets.

Intrinsic value is most commonly used by securities analysts. When applied to publicly traded equity shares, the calculation of intrinsic value permits the analyst to assess the investment worth of a business before a similar determination under similar conditions is made by the marketplace at large (i.e., the investing public). In this manner, by getting a jump on the market, the analyst can help clients realize appreciation gains.

The analytic techniques used to arrive at intrinsic value include:

- Extrapolations and interpretations of a company's balance sheet and income statement ratios
- Discounted cash flow calculations based on earnings projections
- Assessments of the liquidation value of business assets

With these results in hand, securities analysts apply their own interpretation based on personal background and assessment of general market and industry trends. The result is an appropriate price for the shares regardless of the current market price. Obviously, if the intrinsic value is higher than the market price, buy orders should be issued. In the reverse case, the shares should be sold.

Going-Concern Value

The concept of *going-concern value* is not a measure of a valuation at all. It is an expression of the current status of a business. Public accountants express their opinion on a company's financial statements based on their going-concern standard; that is, based on the assumption that the business will continue in operation for an indefinite period of time. In contrast, the longevity of a company may be in question if it has a negative net worth, burdensome debt service payments, faltering markets, lawsuits threatening to force foreclosure, or an extended labor strike. Such a company would not be considered a going concern.

Although the going-concern concept is not a method of valuation, it does materially bear on the worth of a business. If future earnings and hence cash flow are jeopardized by negative conditions, statistical compilations such as discounted cash flows or financial statement ratio analyses based on current or historical data become meaningless. Also, liquidation value should be substantially enhanced when the business is viewed as being sold as a going concern rather than as a handful of assets at auction.

In most cases, the going-concern concept relates to the total value of the business, assuming it will continue to operate in its present form. It includes intangible assets that have no liquidation value, as well as goodwill, customer listings, technically skilled personnel, and in some cases management expertise. The exception—and isn't there always an exception—relates to the courts' interpretation of a going concern. Generally, unless intangible assets can be identified as yielding a definable future stream of income, such as patent royalties, a court will not consider them as part of its valuation.

Liquidation Value

Liquidation value refers to the value of individual business assets or groups of assets, not the business as a whole. When the focus is on the likely sale price of specific assets, future cash flow as a measure of investor or market worth has no meaning. The business is not viewed as an income generator, but merely as a group of assets, each of which has a value to someone. The fundamental assumption when arriving at liquidation value is that the company will cease to do business and therefore cannot be considered a going concern.

Typically, liquidation value has little meaning for investors or business sellers, both of whom view future cash returns as the justification for making the investment or continuing to operate the business. This method also has no relevance for statutory valuations that focus on market value. Conversely, financial institutions rely on liquidation value almost exclusively to determine the adequacy of loan collateral.

When estimating the liquidation value of assets, it's important to include all the costs associated with the liquidation as reductions from projected liquidation proceeds. In a *forced liquidation* all assets or major groups of assets are sold at one time, generally through the auction process. Associated costs might include:

* Auctioneer's fees
* State taxes
* Costs of moving equipment and machinery to the auction location
* Crane rentals
* Expenses of fixing up the assets prior to sale
* Out-of-pocket expenses of the auction house, such as travel expenses, advertising, telephone, and so on

Legal fees and mailing expenses might also be required to comply with state bulk sales laws.

In an *orderly liquidation*, assets are sold off in an orderly manner, one at a time, over a period as long as twelve months or more. Expenses of an auction house may not be involved, but additional advertising costs, fixing-up costs, taxes, sales commissions, and legal expenses are usually incurred. Also, since an orderly liquidation takes place over a period of time, normal operating expenses to keep the company going during this period must be reckoned as deductions from sale proceeds.

Once the assets are sold, it always takes several months to wind down a company's affairs and finally close the doors for good. Costs associated with these winding-down activities must be projected for both orderly and forced liquidations.

And finally, when a discounting calculation is used to estimate the liquidation value of a business, the estimated proceeds should be discounted from the time the net proceeds are expected to be received back to the valuation date at a rate reflecting the assumed risk. Clearly, the liquidation value of an entire business will be substantially less than the gross proceeds received from the sale of its assets.

Book Value

Book value is frequently confused with the worth of a business. This is an accounting term, used to designate either:

* For the business as a whole: the difference between total assets and total liabilities, including preferred stock with redemption features
* For individual assets or groups of assets: the net balance between the original asset cost and the current amount shown on the balance sheet, as in net book value of depreciated machinery and equipment

Book value reflects only those assets and liabilities recorded on the books, not contingent assets, contingent liabilities, or intangible assets, such as customer lists or client files, that, according to generally accepted accounting principles, cannot be recorded. Accounting standards require assets to be recorded at historical cost less accumulated depreciation or amortization, and liabilities, either short-term or long-term, to be recorded at actual amounts payable by contractual documentation. When referring to the business as a whole, *book value* is used synonymously with *net book value*, *owner's equity*, *shareholders' equity*, and *net worth*.

In owner-managed small businesses, it is quite common for the book value to be zero or negative, reflecting the withdrawal of cash and other property for the owner's use. We'll take a look a little later at acceptable valuation methods for dealing with this condition.

Other Relevant Terms

In addition to definitions of value, a few other terms should be clarified. Although pronouncements issued by the Financial Accounting Standards Board, the American Institute of Certified Public Accountants, the Securities and Exchange Commission, and the Internal Revenue Code set the standard definitions of terms for financial statement presentation and tax returns, these terms are at times confusing, conflicting, and misused.

Various professional appraisal organizations, many focusing exclusively on real estate appraisals, use these terms in a slightly different manner. Also, certain terms are unique to the appraisal profession and are seldom used in the accounting or tax fraternities. The following will be used in the balance of this book.

1. *Goodwill*—An intangible asset that arises as a result of the name or reputation of the company, the owner/manager, or company products or services; the company's location; customer loyalty; or similar conditions unique to a given business. Goodwill does not have a monetary value under generally accepted accounting principles (in this book cited as GAAP) and therefore is not recorded on a company's balance sheet unless it is paid for as a premium over book value in the acquisition of a going concern. However, goodwill does add economic benefit to a company and therefore, in some cases, must be reckoned with as part of the valuation process.

2. *Capitalization*—A term describing three different things: (1) the capital structure of a business enterprise, comprising the sum of long term debt and equity, (2) the accounting recognition of an expenditure as a balance sheet asset rather than an expense, or (3) the conversion of income into value as part of the valuation process by the

application of a *capitalization factor*, which is any multiplier or divisor used to convert income into value.

3. *Marketability Discount*—An amount or a percentage deducted from an equity interest to reflect the marketability of that interest. It is used primarily to discount market value to intrinsic or investment values.

4. *Control Premium*—An additional amount or percentage added to a valuation to reflect the benefits associated with owning the controlling interest in a business. This is in contrast to a minority discount, which reduces the pro rata share of the value of an entire business to reflect the absence of control.

5. *Discounted Cash Flow*—A stream of monetary sums to be paid or generated in the future reduced to its present value by the application of a *discount rate*. The discount rate frequently, but not always, incorporates the current market rate of interest. A discount rate may also be tied to a common, easily verifiable interest rate such as that paid on U.S. government securities. In theory, the riskiness of the cash flow determines the discount rate—the more risk, the higher the discount rate.

Cash Is King

Theoretically, the generally accepted definition of the value of a business interest is that it equals the future benefits, usually cash benefits, that will accrue to that interest, discounted back to a present value at an appropriate capitalization or discount rate. Discounted cash flow is a relatively simple concept, and since discount tables are embedded in standard spreadsheet software, the calculation is straightforward.

If this were the end of it, all you would have to do would be to come up with a forecasted cash flow and apply a discount factor, and then you would be finished. You wouldn't need to spend money on this book or any other. And you certainly wouldn't need to engage high-priced professional appraisers. But what is acceptable in theory seldom works in practice.

However, whether it is done by capitalizing future cash flow to its present value or by using one of many other methods, the measurement of future benefits denominated in *cash or cash equivalents* will, in nearly all cases, result in the most meaningful valuation. As in many other disciplines in which there are a multitude of experts, not everyone agrees with the cash approach. The accounting profession and securities analysts advocate variations on that approach.

The accounting profession prefers to measure future benefits in terms of company earnings. The value of a business interest is simply calculated as a year's current or projected earnings multiplied by some factor. Securities analysts look to the stock market to set the multiple, as in a stock's price/earnings (P/E) ratio, arguing that the market will always adjust price to the long-term health of the company. Although these approaches have merit for their simplicity, both fail to recognize the need to base value on the amount an investor or owner will receive in exchange for an investment, and to enhance comparative analyses of alternative investments. Let's look at fallacies in the accounting approach first.

When company earnings are stressed, the underlying assumption must be that all companies record business transactions in the same way, thereby allowing earnings comparisons between various investments. But we all know that that is not the case. Generally accepted accounting principles allow company management a wide range of choices for recording transactions. Various depreciation methods can be used. The recording of lease obligations varies with the type of lease. Special industries have been granted unique exemptions, such as booking depletion allowances in extraction industries or recording intangible inventory and progress payments in the aerospace and construction industries, respectively.

R&D expenses may be written off or capitalized under varying circumstances. The amortization of deferred charges, patents, organization expenses, goodwill, and other intangibles can vary among companies. Different forms of business combinations allow for a plethora of accounting variations. Clearly, with such a range of alternative recording choices, the reported earnings of a company bear little resemblance to anything investors might expect in future cash benefits.

The securities industry uses an even more misleading approach. Take publicly traded companies, for example. Theoretically, over a long period of time, the market price of a company's stock traded in an efficient market should reasonably reflect the long-term prospects of the company. However, at any point in time, such as when an investor wishes to make an investment or when a company wishes to issue more shares, the market may either overvalue currently traded shares through excessive optimism or undervalue the shares through unwarranted pessimism, neither based on factual information. In both cases, the current price/earnings ratio will not reflect future benefits to investors.

The securities analyst approach incorporates a second and even more potentially damaging error when it is applied to privately owned companies whose shares are not traded publicly and hence do not carry a price/earnings ratio. Some analysts would have us believe that since public Company ABC's shares trade at a multiple of fifteen, that multiple should also apply to private Company XYZ, which happens to be in the same industry. Clearly, even if the P/E ratio did reflect future investor benefits—which it does not—what rationale can be advanced for valuing Company XYZ the same as Company ABC merely because they are in the same industry?

A third approach occasionally advocated by champions of small, privately held companies is that business value should be determined by the replacement cost of Company LMN's assets. The theory underlying this argument presupposes that if an investor wanted to start up a company similar to Company LMN, sums equal to the replacement cost of LMN's assets would have to be expended. This concept clearly ignores the value of assets such as employees, customers, technical and management know-how, and so on, which are associated with a going concern. Furthermore, if a similar business were to be started from scratch, an investor would probably buy used equipment at prices similar to the liquidation value of LMN's assets. Because the replacement cost approach is meaningless except to the insurance industry, it does not deserve further consideration.

In the end, future cash flow must be considered the only viable nonstatutory basis for valuing a business or business interest. Cash or cash equivalents is the only meaningful measure of investment return. It is the only measure that can be applied consistently among companies. It is the only measure not influenced by regulatory or trade practices. And it is the only measure that applies equally well to large and small businesses, to those whose shares are publicly traded and those held in private hands, and to companies in any industry.

For many companies, the determination of future cash flow can be an exhausting exercise. Anyone familiar with the preparation of pro forma financial statements for business plans should be well aware of the machinations required to arrive at a detailed statement of cash flow. And a detailed statement of cash flow is mandatory for meaningful business valuations. Net income plus noncash depreciation and amortization, plus or minus changes in working capital—the accounting profession's definition of cash flow—won't do the trick. To get at true cash flow, the actual cash inflows and outflows must be analyzed.

The larger or more complex a business is, the more difficult the preparation of such a forecast becomes. The construction of an acceptable cash flow forecast for valuation purposes is complicated by the existence of companies with multiple product lines; a hierarchy of business entitles such as holding companies, captive insurance subsidiaries, foreign branches, and so on; more than one operating location; or heavy R&D programs. However, the use of the forecasting techniques and related cost/volume/price relationships described in Chapter 7 will reduce the amount of time and effort involved.

The Business Valuation Process

Regardless of the size or type of company, or of which valuation method is used, the business valuation process itself remains relatively constant. It comprises four major steps:

1. Forecasting the company's cash flow for a specified number of years
2. Estimating the cost of capital to be included in the valuation analysis
3. Determining the continuing value of a business beyond the valuation date
4. Analyzing and interpreting the results of calculations and assumptions

Valuation authorities continue to debate the virtues of using historical financial data as the basis for cash forecasts versus relying on prophetic judgments of future events. Advocates of historical data argue that the evidential nature of historical fact is more accurate than someone's dreams of the future. Opponents take the position that managers base current decisions on estimates of future events and are therefore well attuned to potentially changing conditions that would invalidate historical juxtapositions. Both arguments have merit, and in most cases historical facts are combined with future prognostications in order to arrive at cash forecasts generally acceptable to all interested parties.

Earnings

In many companies, the historical earnings trend is the most important financial variable in forecasting cash flow. Since earnings result from the net effect of sales revenues and associated expenses, this should be a fair measure of cash generation, assuming of course that known noncash expenses such as depreciation and amortization are excluded from the calculation. Except in rare instances, a company's future earnings should reflect either an upward or a downward trend from the current and prior years, thereby serving as a reasonable base to which incremental changes to reflect economic and business assumptions can be applied.

To be useful, however, the elusive accounting definition of earnings under GAAP must be understood by all parties. Furthermore, all parties must recognize the relationship between a given company's accounting practices and its ability to generate cash flows. In those situations in which some parties do not have free access to a company's accounting practices, which pragmatically includes nearly all investment decisions other than mergers and acquisitions, historical earnings may not be a reasonable measure of future returns.

For owner-managed companies, especially companies that maintain their accounting records under an election to be taxed as an S corporation, historical earnings records generally do not even come close to reflecting actual cash throwoff. In such cases, before earnings can be used as a meaningful starting point, a company's financial statements must be reconstructed to eliminate the effects of income and loss pass-throughs and cash distributions to shareholders.

Revenues

Not infrequently, historical revenue or sales is the best measure of future cash flow for service businesses or professional practices. Typically in these companies management decisions deliberately keep earnings at zero or close to zero for tax purposes. Owner/shareholder expenses may be paid from company accounts. Excessive salaries or bonuses may distort total expenses. Intercompany loans in the case of multiple entity ownership or shareholder/company receivables and payables not only drain cash but exaggerate expenses. All of these situations preclude the use of earnings as a measure of the ability of the business to generate future cash.

Revenues, on the other hand, reflect business level and the ability of the company to attract and service customers. Relatively constant or linear-trending revenues for three or four years should serve as a reasonable measure of the company's ability to generate sales in the future. If revenues serve as the basic measure, of course, expense estimates will have to take the place of historical records for developing a cash flow projection.

Assets

It's important to dispel the popular notion that assets in and of themselves create value. In the context of a going concern that is just not true. Much as we would like to believe that the machine that cost $1 million two months ago adds $1 million to the value of a business, the market doesn't see it that way. Business assets of any type—but primarily machinery, real estate, vehicles, receivables, inventory, patents, and so on—add to the worth of a business only to the extent that they can be used to generate actual cash flow or dividend benefits. Except in a liquidation, assets have no inherent value in and of themselves.

This may be a hard pill for small business owners/managers to swallow. Most of us like to think that the real estate housing our business or equipment and the machinery needed to produce our products are worth something to a business buyer or investor. Unless it can be shown that these assets create measurable benefits, however, they are useless as far as adding to the value of a business is concerned. An excellent case in point came about when the sole stockholder of a machine shop offered his company for sale.

Historical records showed the company losing money for the prior three years. Debts piled up. Bank loans went unpaid. But the owner had purchased three new computer-controlled machines for $1.2 million two years earlier, specifically to fill the production requirements of a large customer. When a potential investor offered to buy the business for $800,000, the owner merely laughed, quickly noting that the two new machines were worth more than that. The buyer backed out, and twelve months later the company's assets, including the two machines, were liquidated at auction for $500,000.

Cost of Capital

Most business valuation authorities would agree that cost of capital is the key external variable in the valuation process. It depends on two factors: the general level of interest rates in the marketplace and the amount of risk premium demanded by the market. *Risk* is the operative term that, in the valuation process, causes the greatest confusion.

Once a cash flow forecast has been prepared, the magnitude of expected returns is known. But that doesn't go far enough. All investments carry a measure of risk, however large or small, and such risk tempers expected returns. For purposes of this book, risk is defined as a measure of the uncertainty of attaining the expected future benefits that result from cash flow projections and other judgmental calculations.

When the uncertainty of realizing expected benefits is very high, the value attached to these benefits must be severely discounted. When the uncertainty is low or when it can be fairly determined that the expected returns or something close to the expected returns will be attained, then only a small discount need be applied.

Risk is reflected in a business valuation by ascertaining the cost of capital of an investment. Although various authorities define *cost of capital* in different ways to suit particular needs, a common definition for business valuations is the rate of return available in the marketplace on comparable investments, in terms of both risk and other characteristics, such as marketability. In other words, cost of capital is the expected rate of return required to induce an investor to purchase the right to a future stream of benefits generated by the business interest being considered. Cost of capital is inversely related to present value. As cost of capital increases, present value decreases, and conversely, as cost of capital goes down, the present value of a stream of benefits goes up.

It's important for owners of businesses or business interests to understand that the cost of capital is market-determined. This means that in any given situation, the cost of capital for investing in a business is completely beyond the control of the business owner. Granted, you can take measures to shore up your business and thereby decrease the risk associated with investing in it. This would tend to decrease the cost of capital and increase the company's value. But in the end, risk is in the eye of the beholder. It is perceived as independent of the assets or earnings of the business, and it has very little to do with actions taken or not taken by business owners.

The same market determination applies to an investment's marketability or liquidity. If the market perceives a business interest to be very illiquid—that is, if it perceives a resale of the interest as being very difficult to achieve—the value of the future benefits will be discounted more severely. Conversely, in cases where the marketability of a business or business interest is perceived to be high, as in many high-growth, technology-oriented industries, the discount applied to future benefits will be minimal.

Chapter 3 discusses in detail the application of one of the most widely used models for incorporating risk in business valuations, the capital asset pricing model. This model attempts to construct a method whereby factors can be introduced to measure the amount of premium an investor should expect as compensation for holding high-risk assets. A prime example is the approach used by venture capital firms when assessing the amount of equity participation required in exchange for an interest in a high-risk company.

Continuing Value Beyond Valuation Date

The valuation process also calls for a determination of the continuing value of the business beyond the valuation date. As previously described, when developing a cash flow forecast, a specific time period must be assumed in order to discount the cash stream to its present value. This in effect draws a curtain on the operations of the business at the end of the cash flow period.

But buyers of businesses or business interests do not expect a business to cease operations at that date, nor do they expect to liquidate its assets. Under the going-concern concept, a business is expected to have an indefinite life, well beyond the time period used in cash flow projections. If that is true, then some value must attach to the period beyond. This value is called *continuing value*.

Some valuation authorities try to quantify the impact of continuing value by slotting future earnings into a simplistic formula, such as:

$$\text{Continuing value} = \frac{\text{Net operating earnings}}{\text{Weighted average cost of capital}}$$

Net operating earnings represents the annual earnings of a typical year beyond the discounted cash flow horizon. Weighted average cost of capital is calculated by applying weighting factors to the relative amounts of debt and equity capital, taking opportunity cost, tax benefits, and after-tax benefits into account.

Although this simplistic approach may have merit when applied to publicly held companies with measurable dividend records, trackable share price trends, and published market capture rates, it does little for closely held companies without such readily available data.

A more meaningful approach to continuing value frequently involves the assessment of qualitative factors. Such factors as the caliber of management personnel, market position and competition, product diversity or lack thereof, vertical integration or lack thereof, employee education and training programs, new product research efforts, and a variety of other factors may affect the continuing value of a business far more than quantifiable cost of capital calculations. Since few of these qualitative factors can be numerically expressed, it is difficult, if not impossible, to include them in mathematical calculations.

In the end, the person making the valuation must add or subtract arbitrary amounts or percentages to or from cash flow benefits to reflect a company's continuing value. Typically, the smaller the company, the more relevant such long-term value is to an investor and therefore the more skewed the mathematical valuation calculation becomes.

Analyzing and Interpreting Valuation Results

Without question, formulas, theoretical models, cash flow projections, asset appraisals, and the assessment of qualitative factors are all important features of establishing business value for virtually any nonstatutory purpose. Each lends an air of authority to the valuation process by translating business conditions into numerical quantities that can then be manipulated at will. For publicly held companies, such manipulative steps are generally straightforward, using ratio analyses and industry comparisons. Results fit neatly into predetermined pigeonholes that meet generally accepted valuation and financial analysis standards.

Analyzing calculated results for privately held companies is a different story. Here, the variety of business structures, the absence of reliable financial data, unknown market positions of companies, discrepancies between the ongoing prospects of a small business and those of a firmly established large corporation, and a variety of other factors make the interpretation of quantifiable factors extremely personal. Nowhere is the phrase *value is in the eye of the beholder* more applicable than to owner-managed companies. When selling, buying, or merging such entities, the price is determined entirely through negotiations, with both parties weighing intangibles as much as or more than facts and figures.

Small professional practices provide an excellent example of businesses whose value, and hence future cash flow, depends as much or more on the personal relationship of owner and client (or patient) than on factual calculations of cost of capital, the present value of discounted cash flow, or statistically calculated risk factors. A buyer will weigh the likelihood of retaining the existing client base while attracting new clients through personal aptitude, not the actions or inactions of the seller in prior years.

The marketability of a purchased interest in a professional practice or personal service business must also be interpreted in light of the potential buyer base and the transferability of customers/clients. When the risk factor becomes very high, as in the case of buying service businesses of virtually any type, one must ask: How valid is any valuation based on projections factored down for risk? In truth, the downward risk factor may be greater than the entire discounted cash flow.

Such interpretive obstacles must be met, however; otherwise small, privately held businesses would never be sold. Yet they are sold, and willing buyers and sellers continue to negotiate prices based on perceived value rather than rigid formulas. Later chapters examine alternative methods for valuing businesses in unique situations and propose alternative methodologies to compensate for nonquantifiable benefits.

CHAPTER

Discounting Future Returns and Other Theoretical Methods

The theory behind discounting future cash or cash equivalents to a present value is that a dollar received today is worth more than a dollar to be received in the future: a bird in the hand is worth two in the bush, as it were. Regardless of a business's characteristics or the shrewdness with which one forecasts future events, most investors would agree that more risk is attached to the receipt of a dollar five years from now than to the receipt of a dollar tomorrow.

Wars, floods, fires, labor strikes, key personnel turnover, and many other events can and usually do prevent the timely receipt of expected future benefits. The longer the time period over which the benefits are to be received, the greater the likelihood that uncontrollable events will either delay their receipt or change the expected amount. By valuing future benefits in today's dollars, investors can at least partially quantify this future uncertainty.

Another way to explain the present value concept is in terms of investor opportunity. With $1,000 to invest today, you could lock in a risk-free return of 4.5 percent for the next ten years by buying U.S. Treasury ten-year notes. Earnings of $45 a year for ten years, or $450, plus a return of your original $1,000 principal would be guaranteed.

Contrast this choice with investing the $1,000 in the common stock of a privately owned company that promises to pay dividends of 4.5 percent per year. Excluding tax effects, the probability of actually receiving the 4.5 percent dividends for ten years and also getting your principal back would be substantially less than with the Treasuries option. To compensate for this increased risk, you would want more than a 4.5 percent return—perhaps twice as much. The return required to make the investment as valuable as 4.5 percent Treasuries can be calculated by discounting the future dividend stream to its present value.

The most difficult step in quantifying risk is establishing an appropriate discount rate. Although several theoretical models have been developed, none are straightforward. Most are too complex for small businesses. All make various assumptions that may or may not be applicable to a given situation. And results derived from statistical models must be tempered with personal judgment and nonquantifiable factors. Nevertheless, since professional appraisers and financial analysts use one or more models in virtually every situation, it might prove helpful to take at least a fleeting look at the most common one, the *capital market theory* (CMT).

The Capital Market Theory

The capital market theory is made up of a set of complex mathematical formulas that strive to identify how investors should choose common stocks for their portfolios under a given set of assumptions. Focused on publicly traded stocks, it has no direct bearing on valuing closely held companies; however, several intuitive segments of the theory are relevant. One of the easiest to understand is the determination of required rates of return for different levels of risk.

The capital market theory defines rate of return as the total return, including dividends, interest income, cash distributions, and the appreciation of an asset's market value. The concept can be expressed in the formula:

$$\text{Return} = \frac{\text{ending price} - \text{beginning price} + \text{cash distributions}}{\text{beginning price}}$$

Assume that you bought an equity interest in ABC Corp. for $100,000 and held it for five years. Annual dividends of $5,000 total $25,000 over the five-year period. In year 6, you sell the shares for $200,000. Your rate of return would be calculated as

$$R = \frac{\$200,000 - \$100,000 + \$25,000}{\$100,000} = 125\% = 25\% \text{ per year}$$

Of course discount factors could be applied to the five-year income stream to quantify risk. But the capital market theory approaches risk from a slightly different angle. It segregates risk into two components: market risk and investment risk.

Systematic risk is the term applied to market risk. It means the uncertainty of future returns caused by movements in the market as a whole. *Unsystematic risk* refers to uncertainty resulting from characteristics of the individual firm, the industry, and the type of investment (e.g., minority versus controlling, equity versus debt). *Total risk* is the sum of systematic and unsystematic risks.

The CMT approach, however, assumes that the required investment premium is limited to systematic risk. On the surface this makes little sense. In closely held companies, particularly small businesses, unsystematic risk associated with management skills, product line acceptability, market position, and so on deserves far more weight than stock market movements. However, since the capital market theory was developed to value publicly traded issues, it assumes that investors have the ability to hold widely diversified portfolios, thereby eliminating or minimizing the risk attached to any specific investment.

The *capital asset pricing model* (CAPM) is part of the larger capital market theory. Under CAPM, systematic risk is measured by a statistical factor called *beta*, which is a function of the relationship between the return on an individual security and the return on the market as a whole. The market return is measured by a market index, such as the Dow Jones Industrial Average or Standard & Poor's 500 Composite Stock Price Index. In other words, beta measures the volatility of a given security relative to market averages.

For those with a mathematical bent, the formula for calculating beta can be expressed using the following designations:

Observed return on Security A = OR
Average return on Security A over n time periods = AR
Observed return on S&P index = OSP
Covariance = $(OR - AR) \times (OSP - ASP)$

$$\text{Average covariance over } n \text{ time periods} = \frac{\Sigma \text{ Covariance}}{n} = AC$$

$$\text{Average variance of S\&P index over } n \text{ time periods} = \frac{\Sigma (OSP - ASP)}{n} = ASP$$

$$\text{Beta} = \frac{AC}{ASP} = B$$

The formula for the expected return then becomes:

$$EI = RF + B (MR - RF)$$

EI is the expected return on a specific investment, RF equals the rate of return on a risk-free security, (MR − RF) is equal to market risk premiums, and B stands for beta.

Before using this formula, it's important to recognize the underlying assumptions. They are:

- All investors are risk-averse (i.e., they require a premium kicker for an investment that does not have a guaranteed return).
- Investors will hold diversified portfolios.
- All investors have identical holding periods.
- All investors have identical expectations about rates of return and capitalization rates.
- No transactions costs will be incurred.
- There is no tax impact.
- The rate received for lending money is the same as the cost of borrowing money.
- The market has perfect divisibility and liquidity.

In practice, of course, none of these assumptions is true, certainly not for closely held businesses. Pragmatically, any mathematical calculation must of necessity be based on standard, assumed-perfect conditions, which is precisely why none are satisfactory for our purposes. Nevertheless, theoreticians like to talk about beta and the CAPM, so if for nothing else, it makes for interesting cocktail party discussions.

Having put the CAPM to rest, it's time to look at the practical side of valuing small businesses. And for that, we need to start with the mechanics for discounting future benefits to present value. Although *discounted cash flow* (DCF) serves the majority of valuation purposes, in some cases, notably in mergers and in selling/buying minority interests, some people find *discounted future earnings* (DFE) a more appropriate measure. The calculation of both is similar, however; the only difference is that one projects cash flow, the other earnings.

Discounted Cash Flow

Calculating discounted cash flow involves three steps:

1. Determining the period over which cash flow will be forecast
2. Forecasting a stream of future cash flows
3. Choosing a discount rate

Mathematically, a fixed discount rate yields a higher present value as cash flows increase. Conversely, if cash flow is held constant and the discount rate increased, the present value drops. The discount rate or capitalization rate (the two terms are used inchangeably) represents the cost of capital of an investment.

Although the calculation of present value can be done manually, the arithmetic gets very cumbersome. It's much easier to use the net present value function command in a spreadsheet program. Figure 3-1 illustrates three different results obtained by varying the capitalization rate and by changing the stream of cash flow.

The calculations in Figure 3-1 would be suitable for a company with no debt outstanding. But most companies have at least some debt obligations, and the present value of debt service should be factored into the calculation of present value for an equity investment. The easiest way to accomplish this is to deduct the present value of the cash paid to debtholders from the present value of total cash flow. Figure 3-2 presents an example of this calculation.

Forecast Period

The first step in calculating discounted cash flow is determining a meaningful forecast period. It should be noted that the further out one forecasts, the less the present value of cash generated in any one year. For example, using a discount rate of 8.5 percent, the present value factor for the first year out is 92.1 cents on the dollar. In year 2 it is 87.5 cents; in year 10, 58.2 cents.

FIGURE 3-1: Examples of Net Present Value Calculations

CASE I: Even Cash Flow for Ten Years, 8.5% Discount Rate

Year	Cash Flows	
1	$10,000	Annual interest rate (discount) 8.5%
2	$10,000	Net present value $60,473
3	$10,000	
4	$10,000	
5	$10,000	
6	$10,000	
7	$10,000	
8	$10,000	
9	$10,000	
10	$10,000	
TOTAL	$100,000	

CASE II: Even Cash Flow for Ten Years, 10% Discount Rate

Year	Cash Flows	
1	$10,000	Annual interest rate (discount) 10%
2	$10,000	Net present value $55,860
3	$10,000	
4	$10,000	
5	$10,000	
6	$10,000	
7	$10,000	
8	$10,000	
9	$10,000	
10	$10,000	
TOTAL	$100,000	

CASE III: Erratic Cash Flow for Ten Years, 8.5% Discount Rate

Year	Cash Flows	
1	$0	Annual interest rate (discount) 8.5%
2	$1,000	Net present value $54,433
3	$7,500	
4	$2,500	
5	$7,500	
6	$0	
7	$10,000	
8	$15,000	
9	$30,000	
10	$40,000	
TOTAL	$113,500	

FIGURE 3-2: Present Value of Equity Interest After Debt Service

STEP 1. Terms and Conditions of Loan

Loan principal	$50,000
Annual interest rate	9%
Term	120 months
Monthly payment	$633
Annual payments	$7,596

STEP 2. Present Value of Debt Service

Year	Annual Payments
1	$7,601
2	$7,601
3	$7,601
4	$7,601
5	$7,601
6	$7,601
7	$7,601
8	$7,601
9	$7,601
10	$7,601
TOTAL	$76,010
Present Value	$44,750

STEP 3. Present Value of Equity Interest After Debt Service Cash Flow

Year	Forecast
1	$10,000
2	$10,000
3	$10,000
4	$10,000
5	$10,000
6	$10,000
7	$10,000
8	$10,000
9	$10,000
10	$10,000
TOTAL	$100,000
Present Value	$60,473

Discount rate	8.50%
Present value of total cash flow	$60,473
Less: Present value of debt service	$44,750
Present value of equity interests	$15,723

There are no hard and fast rules dictating the right forecast period for all companies. Macroeconomic cycles, market trends, product/customer configuration, and several other factors determine the most meaningful forecast period for any particular business.

Industry cycles are especially important when setting the forecast period, since in most cases annual sales slow as the cycle trends downward and accelerates as it heads up. The most meaningful valuations are based on forecast periods that include at least one complete business cycle, peak to peak or valley to valley, and preferably two or more cycles, assuming each is three years or less. Some of the more widely known industry cycles are seven years for the aerospace industry, three to four years for residential construction, and ten years for nonresidential construction. Statistical compilations that track business cycles for your industry should be available from your trade association or the U.S. Department of Commerce.

Macroeconomic cycles also come into play. In the United States it is relatively easy to track gross domestic product (GDP), inventory and sales trends, money supply, and interest rates as significant measures of recession cycles or boom periods. Stock market trends also provided a key to national economic swings. Over the last thirty years, however, various changes in trading practices and the globalization of capital markets have practically invalidated this measure. On the other hand, average commodity prices remain a fairly reliable leading indicator.

Three economic indexes—leading, coincident, and lagging—derived from data submitted by private-sector businesses and public-sector agencies provide a broad measure of the direction the economy is heading. Although the federal government continues to publish national indexes, in recent years specific indexes for major metropolitan areas and for each of the fifty states are more popular, especially in business valuations. Properly adjusted using industry cycle indicators, these indexes can be helpful in assessing current and future national economic trends, particularly cyclical expansions and recessions. Figure 3-3 lists the indicators in each of three indexes published by The Conference Board and applicable to most geographic areas of the United States.

FIGURE 3-3: Indicators in The Conference Board Indexes

Leading Index
- Average weekly initial claims for unemployment compensation
- Stock prices of 500 common stocks (Stock Market Price Indexes and Dividend Yields)
- New private housing building permits issued (Housing Starts)
- Consumer expectations (Consumer Confidence Index and Consumer Statement Index)
- Vendor performance (percent of companies receiving slower deliveries)
- Real money supply (M2)
- Average weekly manufacturing hours (Average Weekly Hours)
- Interest rate spread

Coincident Index
- Employees on nonagricultural payrolls (Employment)
- Personal income less transfer payments in constant dollars (Personal Income)
- Industrial production index
- Manufacturing and trade sales in constant dollars

Lagging Index
- Average duration of unemployment (Unemployment)
- Inventory to sales ratio for manufacturing and trade in constant dollars (Inventory-Sales Ratio)
- Change in labor cost per unit of output in manufacturing (Unit Labor Costs)
- Consumer installment credit outstanding to personal income ratio
- Average prime rate charged banks (Interest Rates)
- Commercial and industrial loans outstanding
- Consumer price index for services (Consumer Price Index)

The concept underlying economic indexes is that recurring business cycles are caused by changes in the outlook for future profits, which is assumed to be the prime mover of the economy. Such an outlook is reflected in the leading index and in the ratio of the coincident index to the lagging index, which is itself a leading index.

Since the government began compiling these indexes, after World War II, the leading index has consistently declined for nine months and the coincident or lagging ratio for thirteen months before the onset of a recession. Also, the leading index predicts an expansion in the economy four months before it begins; the coincident or lagging index predicts an expansion two months before the official turn.

In some industries, macroeconomic cycles do not have much influence on a given company's sales. In others, such as most consumer goods industries and both residential and commercial construction, they do. For the same reasons as stated relative to industry cycles, the forecast period should take into consideration macroeconomic cycles.

Industries with long cycles create a difficult forecast hurdle. The further out one goes, the less reliable forecasts become. Typically, five years is about the maximum window for most companies. Even that can be too long for seasonal businesses or those subjected to erratic market forces, such as the toy industry. Still, anything less than five years usually doesn't provide sufficient data to value a business. Beyond five years, external economic factors increase the uncertainty geometrically, even for those industries with seven-to-ten-year cycles.

One way to resolve this issue is to calculate a weighted average of minimum, maximum, and most likely cash flows. Although some would argue, and rightly so, that even a most-likely scenario is fraught with error, at least the exercise of determining three levels of activity forces a person to think through the possible events that could influence the performance of the company.

In the example shown in Figure 3-4, the present value of the cash flows ranges from a minimum of $66,508 to a maximum of $99,976, obviously too wide a swing to make either or both immaterial. Several methods can be used to weight the two extremes with the most likely amount of $77,976. In the simplest calculation, merely assign arbitrary probability of occurrence factors to each of the three outcomes, as follows:

	Present Value		Probability		Expected Value
Minimum	$66,508	X	.35	=	$23,277
Most likely	$77,976	X	.50	=	$38,988
Maximum	$99,976	X	.15	=	$14,996
Weighted Average			1.00	=	$77,261

For many small businesses this is sufficient, and getting involved in a complex mathematical weighting formula won't yield any better results. In the end, a probability of occurrence must be assigned to each of the three outcomes, and it's safe to assume that no two people will view the chances of attainment the same way. Even this simplistic approach quantifies results, which for valuation purposes is necessary.

FIGURE 3-4: Most Likely Minimum and Maximum Forecasts

MOST LIKELY FORECAST
Assumptions:
1. 3% increase in sales through year 5 during upward cycle
2. 3% decrease in sales years 6 through 10 during downward cycle
3. Discount rate of 8.5%

Year	Sales	Earnings % of Sales	Net Income	Cash Flow	Discount Factor	Discounted Cash Flow
1	$100,000	10.00	$10,000	$11,000	0.921	$10,131
2	$103,000	9.50	$9,785	$10,763	0.875	$9,418
3	$106,090	9.25	$9,813	$10,795	0.837	$9,035
4	$109,273	10.20	$11,146	$12,260	0.795	$9,747
5	$112,551	8.40	$9,454	$10,400	0.754	$7,841
6	$109,174	9.30	$10,153	$11,169	0.716	$7,997
7	$105,899	8.70	$9,214	$10,135	0.680	$6,891
8	$102,722	8.60	$8,834	$9,718	0.645	$6,268
9	$99,640	9.40	$9,366	$10,303	0.613	$6,316
10	$96,651	7.00	$6,766	$7,442	0.582	$4,331
			TOTALS	$103,984		$77,976

MINIMUM FORECAST
Assumptions:
1. 1% increase in sales through year 5 during upward cycle
2. 3% decrease in sales years 6 through 10 during downward cycle
3. Discount rate of 8.5%

Year	Sales	Earnings % of Sales	Net Income	Cash Flow	Discount Factor	Discounted Cash Flow
1	$90,000	10.00	$9,000	$9,900	0.921	$9,118
2	$90,900	9.50	$8,635	$9,499	0.875	$8,312
3	$91,809	9.25	$8,492	$9,342	0.837	$7,819
4	$92,727	10.20	$9,458	$10,404	0.795	$8,271
5	$93,654	8.40	$7,867	$8,654	0.754	$6,525
6	$90,845	9.30	$8,449	$9,293	0.716	$6,654
7	$88,119	8.70	$7,666	$8,433	0.680	$5,734
8	$85,476	8.60	$7,351	$8,086	0.645	$5,215
9	$82,912	9.40	$7,794	$8,573	0.613	$5,255
10	$80,424	7.00	$5,630	$6,193	0.582	$3,604
			TOTALS	$88,376		$66,508

MAXIMUM FORECAST
Assumptions:
1. 5% increase in sales for all ten years
2. Discount rate of 8.5%

Year	Sales	Earnings % of Sales	Net Income	Cash Flow	Discount Factor	Discounted Cash Flow
1	$110,000	10.00	$11,000	$12,100	0.921	$11,144
2	$115,500	9.50	$10,972	$12,070	0.875	$10,561
3	$121,275	9.25	$11,218	$12,340	0.837	$10,328
4	$127,339	10.20	$12,989	$14,287	0.795	$11,358
5	$133,706	8.40	$11,231	$12,354	0.754	$9,315
6	$140,391	9.30	$13,056	$14,362	0.716	$10,283
7	$147,411	8.70	$12,825	$14,107	0.680	$9,593
8	$154,781	8.60	$13,311	$14,642	0.645	$9,444
9	$162,520	9.40	$15,277	$16,805	0.613	$10,301
10	$170,646	7.00	$11,945	$13,140	0.582	$7,647
			TOTALS	$136,207		$99,976

Forecasting Future Cash Flow

The cash flow forecast is the heart of the entire valuation process. Regardless of the theoretical intricacies of arriving at rates of return, present value, or continuing value, without a detailed cash flow forecast that recognizes all the variables of the business enterprise, no mathematical formula will yield acceptable results.

A cash flow forecast begins with historical financial data. Most companies prepare balance sheets and income statements periodically to meet bank loan requirements, but if you don't have recent statements, company tax returns will have to do. Historical financial statements may or may not be a true reflection of the future, but they represent the only summary data that can be verified.

Cash flow forecasting comprises eight elements:

1. *Economic assumptions.* Any cash flow forecast must be based on projected macroeconomic factors such as inflation rates and interest rates. Projected market conditions are also extremely important. The introduction of new competitive products, demographic changes, or government regulations could impact the continued growth or survival of the company and must be clearly stated as part of the forecast. Assumptions about sources of supply and results of upcoming labor contract negotiations should also be reflected.

2. *Sales forecast.* A sales forecast should recognize both volume variations and price changes. It should also incorporate probable shifts in product mix, market trends, new product introductions, and expected competitor actions. Companies that manufacture products to customer order forecast from the order book, order backlog, and production cycle rather than from historical shipments. The historical receivables turnover ratios can be a helpful guide to projecting cash receipts.

3. *Purchase forecast.* The purchase forecast should reflect the same variations in product mix as the sales forecast does. It should also reflect inflationary changes in the pricing of at least major items and preferably all purchases. Companies that stock inventory for resale should base purchasing time lags on historical inventory turnover. Those that buy materials to customer order should incorporate the same lag/lead time required by the production cycle.

4. *Payroll forecast.* Supervisory and direct labor payroll forecasts must include anticipated wage rate and salary increases. The projected number of employees should be used as the basis, in contrast to a straight extrapolation of historical payrolls. All fringe benefits should be included, taking into account expected increases in federal and state tax rates, worker compensation rates, group health insurance rates, and potential new pension plans. All salaries to the owner/manager should be excluded.

5. *Nonpayroll operating expenses forecast.* Forecasted expenses for utilities, lease payments, telephone, operating supplies, insurance, maintenance, professional fees, and so on should be based on historical averages. Such averages can then be factored up for expected inflation rates. Obviously, if facilities are added or deleted, historical data must be adjusted accordingly.

6. *Capital expenditures forecast.* If additional space and production machinery and equipment are needed to meet the sales forecast, these costs should be forecasted in the appropriate years. The capital expenditures forecast should, where relevant, include backup analyses of lease-versus-buy decisions. If external capital is needed to finance capital additions, it should be included as both cash receipts and cash expenditures; however, such new financing should be segregated from current outstanding loans.

7. *Taxes forecast.* Income taxes may or may not be forecasted depending on the structure of the company. For example, S corporations, partnerships, and limited partnerships do not pay income taxes. They pass income and losses directly to shareholders or partners for inclusion in personal tax returns. The same holds for proprietorships. C corporations, however, do pay taxes and should include a taxes forecast based on expected tax rates.

8. *Financing forecast.* The forecast of payments against current financing, payments of principal, interest, or dividends should be treated separately from other expenditures. Financing expenditures may or may not be included as deductions to arrive at free cash flow, depending on the purpose of the valuation. For example, if a business buyer anticipates new financing to liquidate existing loans and/or preferred shares, forecasted payments against current financing have no meaning. Conversely, for minority investors, current financing expenditures are as relevant as any operating expense in determining free cash.

It's important to note the differences between forecasting cash flow and forecasting net income or earnings. Although when properly constructed in sufficient detail, cash flow and net income forecasts can, and in fact must, reconcile, securities analysts and professional valuation appraisers tend to shortcut net income forecasts by relying on accounting definitions.

For example, instead of forecasting actual purchases, payroll, and operating expenditures during the periods in which the expenditures occur, the accounting approach merely considers total net changes in working capital accounts—namely increases or decreases in accounts receivable, inventory, prepaid expenses, accounts payable, accrued expenses, and so on. Instead of forecasting actual cash collections from sales, operating cash receipts are derived by adjusting reported net income for noncash items such as depreciation and amortization.

Public companies are required to maintain their accounting records according to generally accepted accounting principles (GAAP), but many small businesses, especially professional practices, service companies, contractors, and retail establishments, tend to either keep their records on the cash basis or use a hybrid of cash and accrual accounting. This makes forecast earnings based on accounting definitions virtually meaningless for valuation purposes. Therefore, except where specifically noted, business valuation techniques described in this book are based exclusively on cash flow, not GAAP-defined net income.

Choosing a Discount Rate

Theoretically, a discount rate should represent the expected return on alternative investments with comparable risk. However, the likelihood that two privately owned companies even in the same industry will be faced with the same market, personnel, management, and economic risks over a five-to ten-year period seems very remote.

Since discount rates theoretically reflect investment risk, a good starting point is the rate earned on a risk-free investment, such as U.S. Treasuries of comparable maturity. If the cash flow forecast covers five to ten years, start with U.S. Treasury ten-year notes. For shorter periods, market rates on one year Treasuries are more appropriate. Investments viewed as very long term could start with thirty-year bonds. To the Treasury rate, one must add an arbitrary premium for perceived risk. When buying and selling companies or equity interests, risk premium is usually determined through negotiation. However, one of the following established capitalization theories may be a good starting point.

One of the fascinating aspects of business valuation techniques is how little they change over the years. In the case of capitalization rates, one of the earliest quoted authorities is Ralph E. Badger (*Valuation of Industrial Securities*, Prentice-Hall, 1925). Badger classifies risk into four categories:

Class I, Low risk: 12 to 14.99 percent
Class II, Medium risk: 15 to 19.99 percent
Class III, High risk: 20 to 24.99 percent
Class IV, Very high risk: 25 percent and over

The assumption here is that a single year's earnings should be multiplied by a factor falling within a class range (i.e., 20 percent equals a factor of five). This is a clean, easily understood method that completely ignores discounting future benefits to present value. It has obviously stood the test of time, since it continues to be used under various circumstances.

Another highly respected valuation authority was Arthur Stone Dewing (*The Financial Policy of Corporations*, 5th Edition, The Ronald Press, 1953). Dewing's approach, like Badger's, applies a multiplier to a single year's net income. But Dewing expands his categorization to seven classes and goes further in defining the types of businesses falling into each class.

Category 1: Old established businesses, with significant hard assets and excellent goodwill: 10 percent, or ten times current year's income
Category 2: Well-established businesses requiring "considerable managerial care": 12.5 percent, or eight times earnings
Category 3: Strong, well-developed businesses making products whose sales and earnings are susceptible to general economic swings (i.e., recessions and booms) and requiring considerable managerial care but little specific knowledge by management executives: 15 percent, or seven times earnings
Category 4: Highly competitive businesses with low levels of hard assets and requiring average managerial care: 20 percent, or five times earnings
Category 5: Small, highly competitive businesses requiring little capital investment: 25 percent, or four times earnings

Category 6: Large or small companies requiring special managerial skills of one or more people, with little capital investment and in highly competitive fields where failure is a strong possibility: 50 percent, or two times earnings

Category 7: Personal service businesses whose success reflects the skill of the manager: 100 percent, or one times earnings

It's interesting to note that since Dewing's approach was developed, very little has changed. Most single-owner micro businesses, especially in the service area, still employ this very simplistic valuation approach in place of discounting formulas when buying or selling equity interests.

A more recent addition to valuation theory is advanced by James H. Schilt in his "A Rational Approach to Capitalization Rates for Discounting the Future Income Stream of Closely Held Companies," *The Financial Planner*, January 1982, and supported by Shannon P. Pratt in *Valuing a Business*, 4th Edition, McGraw-Hill, 2000. This approach does incorporate discounting of future earnings streams to present value. The risk premiums noted in the following are added to a risk-free rate, such as that paid by U.S. Treasuries, to determine a usable capitalization rate.

Category 1: Established businesses, good trade position, good management, stable past earnings, predictable future—6 to 10 percent

Category 2: Same as Category 1 except in more competitive industries—11 to 15 percent

Category 3: Companies in highly competitive industries, with little capital investment and no management depth, although with a good historical earnings record—16 to 20 percent

Category 4: Small businesses that depend on the skill of one or two people, or large companies in highly cyclical industries with very low predictability—21 to 25 percent

Category 5: Small personal service businesses with a single owner/manager—26 to 30 percent

It is interesting to compare these capitalization factors with the practice in venture capital firms that invest in small, high-tech start-up business ventures. Their general practice is to demand a 30 to 40 percent return on a five-year horizon. This is very close to Schilt's Category 4 of 21 to 25 percent plus the risk-free ten-year Treasury rate of 4 to 5 percent.

Many other theories for selecting discount rates or multiples of earnings pepper business valuation literature. All have merit; some are more convoluted than others; many relate entirely to valuing publicly traded common stocks. When all is said and done, however, the methods advanced by all four authorities, Badger, Dewing, Schilt, and Pratt, more than adequately serve the needs of most closely held companies.

To summarize the steps in calculating discounted cash flow:

1. Select an appropriate forecast period.
2. Develop a meaningful cash flow forecast. The development of a complete format and modeling technique for laying out a cash flow forecast is described in Chapter 7.
3. Choose a discount rate to reflect your perceived risk.

Continuing Value

Dealing with a company's *continuing value* is one of the most difficult problems encountered in business valuations. The larger and more diversified a company is, the more important continuing value becomes. Continuing value can be defined as the stream of benefits beyond the cash flow forecast period derived from a business investment on a going-concern basis.

Capital-intensive companies with diversified product lines; capable, ongoing management; and a solid position in the marketplace should, theoretically, continue to produce profits and cash flow in perpetuity. Smaller companies with unique product lines, ongoing research and development programs, financial strength, and solid marketing organizations should also continue to produce cash flow for an indefinite period. Only in companies whose continued success depends on the special managerial or technical skills of one or a few owner/managers may continuing value not be pertinent.

In most cases, however, although equity ownership may change, companies stay in business and continue to generate cash. That being the case, long-term earnings and cash flow become integral parts of the valuation process. The question is: How does one attach a numerical value to infinite earnings?

Several theories that deal with this problem have been advanced over the years, but nearly all of them rely on statistical sampling techniques that employ standard deviation calculations, linear analysis, or logarithmic projections. These have some value, and for those so inclined, any statistics textbook and most investment analysis books present myriad choices. For our purposes, however, the following simplified approach usually serves well for smaller businesses:

1. Arbitrarily choose a period long enough to make the end year insignificant for weighting investment options, such as fifty years, seventy-five years, or 100 years.
2. Assume that the cash flow from the last year in your finite forecast period will be typical for every year thereafter. In other words, multiply the last forecast year's cash flow times the number of years in the continuing period.

3. Assume that the same discount factor applies ad infinitum.
4. Calculate the present value of the continuing cash stream.
5. Add this present value to the sum of the annual present values derived within the forecast period.

Figure 3-5 presents a hypothetical cash flow forecast for ten years with an 8.5 percent discount factor and a continuing-value period estimated at fifty years.

FIGURE 3-5: Present Value of Ten-Year Cash Flow Forecast with Continuing Value

Month	Cash Flow ($000)	Discount Factor @ 8.5%	Present value
1	100.00	0.921	92.10
2	103.00	0.875	90.12
3	106.09	0.837	88.80
4	109.27	0.795	86.87
5	112.55	0.754	84.86
6	115.93	0.716	83.00
7	119.41	0.680	81.20
8	122.99	0.645	79.33
9	126.68	0.613	77.65
10	130.48	0.582	75.94
Continuing value	6523.87	0.233*	1520.52
TOTALS	7670.25		2360.39

*Average for fifty years based on 8.5% discount rate.

In this example, the continuing value represents 64 percent of the total present value. A range of 55 to 65 percent of the present value is not unreasonable for larger, well-established companies, since it can be expected that they will weather economic cycles and competitive pressures indefinitely. This obviously doesn't hold for small businesses, especially owner-managed companies. The annual failure rate for SBA-defined small businesses ranges between 65 percent and 75 percent, and to expect the remaining 25 to 35 percent of companies to be competitive over fifty years is a bit of a stretch.

One way to resolve this issue is to use a much higher capitalization rate for calculating the continuing value. If you are using an 8.5 percent rate for the forecast period, perhaps doubling or tripling this rate would allow for the extremely high risk that the longevity of a small business will not be as great as assumed.

Using the forecast numbers in Figure 3-5 but substituting a 25 percent capitalization rate for the extended fifty-year period results in a present value for this period of $525.87, or 38 percent of the total present value of

$1,365.77. Substituting a 35 percent rate yields a present value of $375.63, or just over 30 percent of the total value of $1,215.50.

For personal service businesses and small retail companies, however, even 30 or 38 percent is much too high. In these cases, a business buyer could argue strongly that using Dewing's definition of Category 5, which is four times the current year's earnings, or of Category 7, which is one times the current year's earnings, and ignoring both the discounting of a stream of cash benefits and continuing value might be more reasonable. While it's doubtful that many sellers would go along with it, this method can serve as a starting point for negotiations. In any event, the whole question of continuing value must be dealt with, even if the end result is a negotiated, arbitrary value.

The Excess Earnings Method

Originally devised in the 1920s to assess the goodwill lost by breweries with the advent of Prohibition, the *excess earnings method* continues to be used by the IRS for estate and gift tax purposes. It is also a popular method for determining the selling price of micro businesses and certain professional practices. This method is fraught with error, however, so it pays to stay alert to its major pitfalls.

The excess earnings method (EEM) was originally defined by the Internal Revenue Service. In 1959, the IRS enacted Revenue Ruling 59-60 (the Ruling), which was modified in 1965 by Revenue Ruling 65-193, for estate and gift tax purposes. Although the Ruling emphasized the importance of a company's earnings, it also specified that an appraiser should use a variety of other factors. In 1968, Revenue Ruling 68-609 offered a compromise approach, using a capitalization of earnings formula,. Here is a summary of the steps the Ruling calls for:

1. Determine a value for all net tangible assets, excluding intangibles.
2. Establish a normalized earnings level.
3. Estimate an appropriate capitalization rate applicable to that portion of the expected return based on or supported by net tangible assets.
4. Multiply the net tangible asset value by that rate to determine the amount of value generated by net tangible assets.
5. Subtract the amount in Step 4 from the normalized earnings from Step 2. The result is defined as excess earnings. Theoretically, this is the amount of earnings above a fair return on net tangible assets that could be expected.
6. Establish an appropriate capitalization rate to apply to the sum of excess earnings, presumably resulting from goodwill, and earnings from intangible assets, such as patents, leases, copyrights, and so on.

7. Add this value to that derived in Step 1 to arrive at a total business valuation.

Despite the theoretical fallacies in the excess earnings approach, its simplicity and ease of calculation give it merit. For example, assume the following conditions for a small, privately owned business that keeps its books as an S corporation:

- The value of net tangible assets, equipment, vehicles, furniture and fixtures, scales, building and land, and a few pieces of machinery, totals $100,000. This value should be established by an independent appraisal using the fair market value approach.
- Normalized—that is, before extraordinary items—current year's net income before taxes equals $30,000.
- Using industry statistics, we arrive at a return on net tangible assets of 15 percent.
- Based on normalized net income, we will use 30 percent to capitalize excess earnings.

The value of this business would be calculated as follows:

Net tangible asset value		$100,000
Normalized earnings	$30,000	
Less: Earnings attributable to net		
tangible assets ($100,000 @ 15%)	$15,000	
Excess earnings	$15,000	
Capitalized value of excess earnings		
($15,000/0.30)		$50,000
Total value of business		$150,000

Interestingly, even though IRS Ruling 68-609 still stands, the Service teaches its auditors to argue *against* the use of the excess earnings method, citing the arbitrariness of determining capitalization rates. It disturbs the IRS that such rates "have no foundation in fact."

Obviously, use of this method for buying and selling small businesses has strong appeal, since the only items to be negotiated are the rate of return on net tangible assets, which can usually be substantiated by industry statistics, and the capitalization rate for excess earnings. When using this approach, however, both buyers and sellers should be aware of the following common pitfalls:

Appropriate capitalization rates. As with any discounting calculation, arriving at appropriate capitalization rates is both the key to a meaningful valuation and the most difficult step on which to reach mutual agreement. Industry statistics may be skewed by very large companies, geographic discrepancies, or inaccurate or incomplete reporting. The parties to a transaction nearly always view risk factors for capitalizing excess earnings differently, depending on personal preferences and perceptions.

Realistic normalized earnings. Clearly, normalized earnings should reflect the future potential earnings of the business. Yet, users consistently ignore prior trends or potential future aberrations. They opt for current year's income, which may, and probably will, include at least a few unusual elements, such as the loss or gain of a major customer, new competitors entering the market, unusual one-time expenses, and so on, so that it is unreasonable to use this amount to project future earnings.

Low earnings. Some businesses traditionally generate low earnings relative to net tangible assets. This is particularly true in companies that have a high level of capital investment. In such a case, it is likely that excess earnings do not exist. The tendency then is to value the business at the liquidation value of its tangible assets. This is a grave mistake, since a going concern always has some earnings potential.

Owner/manager's salary. Revenue Ruling 68-609 specifically states that "If the business is a proprietorship or partnership, there should be deducted from the earnings of the business a reasonable amount for services performed by the owner or partners engaged in the business." For buying a business, this conflicts with the concept that the new owner(s) will establish their own salary levels and therefore are primarily interested in the future cash generation potential without regard to the seller's draw.

Failure to discount projected cash flow. By ignoring the present value of varying amounts of cash flow over a period of future years, the excess earnings method invariably overstates the value of the business. The simplistic approach of using one arbitrary capitalization rate in lieu of determining the present value of a stream of benefits penalizes the business owner(s) for estate and gift tax purposes as well as business buyers.

Although these pitfalls make the excess earnings method at best questionable and at worst totally meaningless, the IRS continues to use it for valuing estates and gifts. This does not mean, however, that business people must use it for business purposes. Other methods and offshoots of this method usually provide a more realistic value for all parties.

While on the subject of IRS methods, we would be remiss if we did not briefly look at the asset value method.

The Asset Value Method

The *asset value method* (AVM) assumes that all or a significant portion of a company's assets could be liquidated readily if so desired. This liquidation assumption makes this method a favorite of secured lenders for assessing the value of collateralized assets. Small businesses also frequently look to this method as a starting point from which to make plus and minus adjustments. In that case, book value, not liquidation value, is normally used as an expression of net asset value.

The IRS also applies the asset value method to valuations for Employee Stock Option Plans (ESOPs), special recapitalizations, and other situations involving tax impacts. It insists that nonoperating assets such as investments in securities or real estate be segregated and valued separately as adjustments to tangible assets. It states that, "In general, such nonoperating assets will command a lower rate of return than do the operating assets, although in exceptional cases the reverse may be true." The Ruling goes on to state, "In computing the book value per share of stock, assets of the investment type should be revalued on the basis of their market price and the book value adjusted accordingly."

The fundamental problem with using the asset value approach is that it looks at business assets as valuable in and of themselves, without regard to their impact on a going concern. In fact, however, businesses hold assets primarily as a means of generating future income and hence cash. Except in the rare case where an investment in a business is made for the express purpose of liquidating the company, the only real value in business assets lies in their ability to enhance the company's earning power.

In general, valuations with a view to mergers, the acquisition or sale of companies or equity interests, and other purely business purposes should employ other methods that more properly reflect future benefits to investors.

CHAPTER 4

Gathering Data

The accuracy of a valuation of a business or business interest depends directly on the amount of data that can be gathered from the company (and other sources) and the skill with which the data is assimilated and adjusted to meet specific purposes. If the valuation is to be used for tax purposes, the data-gathering process can usually be limited to tax returns and a modest amount of supplemental information. Information about publicly traded companies can be obtained from SEC filings and published annual reports, together with industry, trade, and economic statistics and trends. Public files are readily available and easily accessed, making the gathering of data for these purposes comparatively simple.

Closely held companies are another matter entirely. Seldom do they release financial statements, except when required by lenders and investors. Usually the statements are unaudited, compiled entirely by company personnel rather than by independent accountants. Generally accepted accounting principles may or may not be followed.

Many small businesses don't prepare financial statements at all, but submit bank-required financial data on bank forms. Managers use informal reports prepared by sales or production personnel. Accumulating relevant data and then assimilating it can be a time-consuming, frustrating, and in some cases futile exercise for an outsider. Nevertheless, to properly value a business, hard data must be used. The gathering of this data is called performing *due diligence*.

Due diligence normally takes place in three stages:

1. The initial stage comprises a tour of facilities and interviews with owners and perhaps key personnel.
2. The gathering and analysis stage involves accumulating and evaluating a wealth of company reports, trade statistics, and national economic indicators.
3. The concluding stage requires a final visit to the facility and a review of events that may have occurred since the analysis phase.

During any one of the three stages, data may turn out to be insufficient to warrant further investigation. Or you may uncover data that impels you to negotiate a purchase price or share value then and there, without completing the entire process. It pays to stay loose during the due diligence process, making decisions as you go based on information uncovered. Due diligence investigations normally begin with a tour of the company's facilities.

Initial Due Diligence

Although ideally one would like to obtain all financial statements and internal reports before visiting the facility, this hardly ever happens. Small business owners are known for zealously guarding financial and operating information from outsiders, believing it to be so proprietary that revealing even the most cursory data will somehow jeopardize their position. Time and again requests for financial data have been turned down based on the assumption that the requester will use the information to damage either the company or its owners.

Pragmatically, the only way to pry loose the information needed to even begin a valuation is to establish rapport with owners and other key managers. And this nearly always must be done on the premises, not by phone or letter. The extent of field work depends on many things, including the purpose of the valuation, the nature of the company's operation, and the size and complexity of the business.

In addition to establishing rapport with business owners and key managers, investigators should attempt to achieve four objectives during the initial visit:

1. Gain a broad overview of the business
2. Assess the general efficiency of the operation
3. Obtain information for preparing a personnel organization chart
4. Pick up at least three years' annual financial statements and the most recent interim statements

Experience has shown that this initial, firsthand contact with the company and its key personnel provides valuable insights for subsequent analysis of financial statements. Visualizing how one department melds with another, how customer orders are processed, how the facility is laid out, what the products look like, who is in charge of each activity, and the general temperament of owners and key managers makes the addition of qualitative judgments to ratio and risk analyses much more relevant.

Establishing the value of a business at a specified time requires going beyond financial statements. Financial statements based on historical cost data, accounting peculiarities, and reporting conventions very often indicate values that are at odds with observable performance. Facilities tours should establish a bridge between accounting records and reality that can then be used to adjust financial reports to reflect actual earning power.

Except in very unusual circumstances, pure extrapolation of reported historical performance to future periods misconstrues future benefits. Therefore, it is extremely important to identify those events and conditions that are likely to make the future different from the past, thereby affecting both the future earning power of the business and its cash flow. The fastest and most reliable way to ferret out such information is during a facilities tour.

During the tour, pay particular attention to the cleanliness of the operation. Even those businesses that by their nature involve messy processes, such as a foundry or a plating plant, can present an image of cleanliness. A well-maintained building, organized material flow and work patterns, trash in trash containers, and work areas swept clean at the end of a work shift give a clear indication that employees care and have pride in their work. Such attitudes tend to permeate the organization, giving customers the impression that the company conscientiously strives for high levels of product quality. Conversely, a dirty, messy work environment will most certainly indicate a lack of interest by management and probably quality shortcomings and customer dissatisfaction.

Also take a close look at how employees perform their jobs. Do they appear to be busy and at their work stations? Does the manager who leads the tour chat with the workers in passing? Is there an air of productivity? Or does it appear that employees walk around somewhat aimlessly or stand in small groups, smoking cigarettes and reading newspapers? Does the tour guide ignore the workers?

You can tell a great deal about the efficiency and productivity of a business simply by being observant on this first tour. A negative worker attitude indicates that something may be seriously wrong with the organization structure or that trouble is brewing in the labor relations area. This could signal a need to dig much deeper during the middle stages of the due diligence investigation.

An example of what can be learned during a plant tour occurred when a client asked me to review the facilities of a small company he was interested in buying. The company manufactured elbows, tees, unions, and other iron plumbing fittings. My client had already toured the plant several times, on each occasion observing on the shop floor only a fraction of the workers that were listed in the personnel reports. The plant manager explained the discrepancy by stating that the old building had a number of cubicles, alleyways, and small rooms where workers performed their jobs. Although none of these hideaways were visible during the tour, the manager assured the potential investor that all workers were present and accounted for.

I made an appointment with the president of the company for a tour of my own and observed a messy, dirty machining area with metal chips everywhere, cigarette butts on the floor, and a general sloppiness throughout the plant. When confronted with this observation, the president replied that such a condition was normal in this type of business and that no one could keep a clean shop when cutting metal. Further prying revealed that all janitors had been laid off the previous month as a cost-cutting move in response to a drop in incoming orders. In fact, I soon learned that 35 percent of the work force had been laid off just two weeks earlier. Obviously our personnel reports were outdated and the plant manager had not told the truth.

So it pays to be observant during the facilities tour. Notice the housekeeping. Do some mental arithmetic to count heads. It's possible to discover more at this time than in weeks or months of detailed due diligence. The facilities tour is also a good time to pick up sales literature and price sheets. Having established a rapport with the owner and conveyed your seriousness as an investor, you should have no difficulty getting the necessary financial statements, key reports, and other data required to perform the valuation.

If the company does not have financial statements, it will be necessary to prepare them from scratch, using tax returns and raw data. Accuracy is not crucial at this time, since adjustments can be made at a later stage if gross errors are subsequently uncovered. Figure 4-1 lists two categories of data to gather during this initial phase:

1. Information you must have to decide whether to proceed with the valuation
2. Information that may be helpful for future analysis but is not crucial for a preliminary go/no-go decision

---

FIGURE 4-1: Data to Gather for Preliminary Investigation

Decision Data
1. Listing of products or services offered for sale
2. Addresses of branch facilities
3. Sales for prior three years
4. Profit before tax for three years
5. Real estate owned or leased by the company
6. If leased, monthly rent and terms of lease
7. Number of employees
8. Either total monthly payroll or the average hourly rate and number of employees by function
9. Position of the company in the market (i.e., market share)
10. Listing of assets—inventory, receivables, machinery and equipment, real estate, and so on
11. Brief history of company
12. Company ownership structure
13. Unique characteristics of the company

Additional Data
1. Three years' financial statements, audited if possible
2. Tax returns for three years
3. Formal organization charts
4. Personal resumes of key employees
5. Any outstanding lawsuits or claims
6. Last year audited by IRS
7. Company financial forecasts for five years
8. Strategic plan
9. Description of distribution channels
10. Listing of competitors
11. Size of markets
12. Description of export program

Accumulating and Assimilating Data

For companies other than micro businesses, the second due diligence phase can be very time-consuming. At this stage, the addition of accountants, consultants, financial analysts, perhaps lawyers, or other professional advisers to assist in the manipulation and interpretation of the data is usually necessary. Time is of the essence for most buy/sell valuations. Prolonged investigations could open the door to bids from other investors; or the owner could become impatient and decide not to sell.

Most of the actual gathering of data should be performed by company personnel. They should know where to find it and who to contact outside the company to arrange for interviews. Figure 4-2 lists the information to request at the second stage in order to perform as exhaustive a financial and business analysis as possible in the shortest period of time.

FIGURE 4-2: Checklist for Due Diligence

A. Marketing
- Customer order backlog reports by customer and product line as of each quarter for the past three years and the current year to date
- Listing of orders received by customer and product line for each month for the past three years and the current year to date
- Listing of shipments by customer and product line for each month for the past three years and the current year to date
- Listing of outstanding customer contracts and outstanding customer bids: domestic, export, and international
- Listing and description of all manufacturer's rep organizations, agreements, and commission schedules
- Listing of buying sources: domestic, export, and international

B. Financial

- Detailed statements of income and balance sheets by quarter (including annual reports) for the past three years and the current year to date
- All supporting schedules to the above financial statements for the periods listed (e.g., manufacturing overhead detail accounts, selling, general, and administrative accounts; and detailed cost of sales). These schedules should be by major product line, if available, but as a minimum, there should be separate schedules for export and international.
- Aged accounts receivable by customer as of each quarter for the past three years and for each quarter of the current year to date
- Physical inventory summary or detailed breakdown of inventory among raw materials, work in process: material, labor, and overhead; and finished goods: material, labor, and overhead as of each year-end for past three years
- Aged accounts payable by vendor as of each quarter for the past three years and for each quarter of the current year to date
- Listing of accrued expenses as of each year-end for the past three years
- Federal and state tax returns for the past three years

C. Personnel

- All employment contracts or agreements, oral or written, including any severance or termination compensation arrangements with salaried, hourly, or collective bargaining unit employees
- All bonus, deferred compensation, stock option, profit sharing, or retirement programs or plans covering salaried, hourly, or collective bargaining unit employees
- If there is a pension plan, all documentation, including actuarial reports, tax returns, trustee reports, population census reports, funding requirements, unfunded liabilities, and so on, for the past three years
- Schedule of hourly wage rate and number of personnel at each rate, by work center, department, and geographic location
- Organization chart of salaried personnel, by location, showing function responsibility, tenure, age, salary, name, and title
- All documentation relating to employee insurance coverage

D. Contracts, agreements, appraisals, insurance, and litigation

- All contracts or agreements with vendors and customers
- All contracts or agreements with employees
- All contracts or agreements with collective bargaining units
- All contracts or agreements with other third parties
- All appraisals of real estate or machinery and equipment done within the last three years
- Listing of machinery and equipment
- All insurance claims outstanding
- All patents, copyrights, and license agreements
- All noncompete covenant agreements
- All lease or purchase agreements for machinery and equipment, autos, or real estate
- Legal descriptions of all real estate, including deeds, title reports, and title insurance documentation, together with documentation of any lien thereon
- Listing and description of all outstanding litigation or anticipated litigation
- Is union contract transferable? If yes, then description of mechanics of making transfer, such as required approvals

As a result of information uncovered during the initial phase, it may be possible to eliminate some of the data from Figure 4-2. Also, the smaller the business, the fewer of these items apply. This checklist can be used for a business of any size, however; just ignore those items that aren't relevant. Complete financial statements for the last three years, supplemented with monthly internal reports of orders received, shipments, order backlog, and number of employees, are the most important documents to obtain at this stage.

Interviewing Management Personnel

To the extent that management interviews were not conducted and organization charts obtained during the initial field trip, a second visit should be scheduled. Although company personnel can gather most of the factual data, an assessment of management capability and organization strength or weakness can be done only in person.

This time try to meet with each functional manager separately. Valuable insights into the interpersonal relationships among employees and the peculiarities of the company and its products and markets can be gained just by asking probing questions. Owners are sometimes reluctant to allow this type of privileged communication unless they are present at the interviews. That's all right, as long as you are free to ask the questions that need answers.

If an organization chart isn't immediately available, ask for one to be prepared that clearly identifies the lines of responsibility for all managers, supervisors, and other key employees. This is also a good time to ask about labor relations, employment contracts, personnel policies, and fringe benefit programs. Try to get a feel for management style: Is it beneficent or adversarial?

Interviews with the company's legal counsel and audit firm can also be helpful. Independent professionals tend to be hesitant about giving out hard information, but discerning their attitudes toward key employees might lead to areas that require further research. And you never know, some interesting facts could slip out.

Marketing

As qualitative inputs to a valuation appraisal, market conditions and marketing organizations are second only to the skills and technical abilities of key managers. The main questions needing answers in this area are:

- Is the marketing organization principally made up of salaried sales personnel or independent sales organizations?
- What are the predominant selling methods? Are they personal sales calls, telemarketing, catalogs, direct mail? Who is responsible for each?

- Does the company have a formal advertising program? If so, who does the art work, media copy, printing, mailings, and so on? Are they done in-house or by an advertising agency?
- Is there a process in place to measure advertising effectiveness?
- What is the size of each niche market served? What is the company's market share?
- Are competitors planning to introduce important new products this year or next?
- Does the company have a sales/order forecast for next year?
- What can be done to improve the marketing effort?

Answers to these questions won't always be readily available, but the chances are good that the marketing manager will at least have an opinion about most of them. This is the type of qualitative information that must be assimilated to give a valuation substance. Financial data is important, but without a clear understanding of the company's marketing program it's virtually impossible to judge the likelihood of receiving future returns.

Small businesses are particularly susceptible to ineffective marketing. Many times business owners do not have a marketing bent and completely misunderstand the relationship of modern marketing techniques to overall company performance. A good case in point was uncovered several years ago while performing a management assessment engagement immediately after a client purchased a small company.

During the due diligence phase, my client had not been allowed to interview key managers without the seller being present. The managers were tight-lipped and not at all helpful in clarifying a number of issues raised about slipping market share. As a result of the interviews, the client concluded that the slide had been due to ineffective marketing leadership and planned to replace the marketing manager as soon as possible after closing.

When interviewing this manager, I learned that when the business cycle had turned down three years earlier, his boss had forced a layoff of all salaried sales personnel and cut the number of independent sales organizations by 50 percent. All advertising had been terminated, and sales bonus programs were eliminated. These actions not only demoralized the remaining marketing staff but alienated several large customers, who subsequently established ties with two competitors.

At a time when business was slow, instead of bolstering marketing activities, the owner had done just the opposite. The decrease in market share was not a result of ineffective marketing management, but rather of the owner's shortsightedness. His failure to recognize these errors resulted in a sale price far below market value.

Production and Quality Control

Except for retail businesses, most companies engage in some form of production activity, whether actually manufacturing a product or performing services. All companies, including those in retail industries, have, or should have, some form of quality control activity. Smaller businesses tend to lump these activities into one department or place them under the supervision of one manager. Therefore, qualitative due diligence procedures can be performed for both production and quality control activities simultaneously.

Whether the company is a print shop, a publishing house, a computer software developer, or a manufacturing plant, the production manager has the responsibility for moving products through the shop and out the door on schedule at the lowest possible cost. This individual should be probed for answers to the following questions:

- What do the historical trends and current records show as promises kept to the customer or to the production schedule? This is an excellent measure of how effective production personnel have been in meeting schedules and could be a key indicator of pending problems.
- Does the company use just-in-time purchasing for buying materials, or is the raw material warehouse overstocked?
- If the company uses a standard cost system, what have been the historical variances from standards? Is the shop running at least 85 percent efficient against the labor standards? Manufacturing companies with an efficiency rating of less than 85 percent are probably headed for several loss years.
- How is labor productivity or facility utilization measured, and what has been the historical trend here? The answer to this question provides a clue to the adequacy of the number of direct labor employees. A downward trend indicates too many people on the payroll. Current productivity of less than 75 percent could point to shortcomings in first-line supervision.
- How good or bad are labor relations? What are the average number of grievances per week or per month? Have there been recent strikes or slowdowns?

The manager in charge of production must constantly balance customer order input, purchasing, material flow, scheduling of machines and labor, labor performance, customer demands, quality standards, equipment repair and replacement, and labor relations. Such a position, situated squarely in the middle of an organization chart, frequently gives this individual excellent insight into the interpersonal relationships among department heads.

This is the person to probe about potential interdepartmental conflicts that could damage the company's earning power.

Interviews with the person in charge of quality control should resolve the following issues:

- Who is responsible for entering customer and product design change orders, and is this activity being performed satisfactorily?
- Who is responsible for determining and approving new shop routings?
- What are the procedures for assuring compliance with engineering specifications and quality standards?
- Have quality rejects been increasing or decreasing?
- Have customer returns been increasing or decreasing? Is there increasing customer dissatisfaction with product deliveries or product quality? What is the field failure rate?
- Does the company have an up-to-date quality control manual?
- Are the current material and product scrap rates improving or deteriorating?
- Are inspections and testing performed on-line or at the finished product stage? Are inspectors responsible for maintaining quality standards, or are production personnel held responsible?
- Is the company using state-of-the-art quality assurance and testing methods? Are testing gauges and other equipment up to date and calibrated?

In addition to showing the level of control management has over production processes or service programs, negative answers to these questions provide a strong indication of potential customer dissatisfaction, which could severely damage the company's future earning power.

If markets demand a significant R&D effort, production and quality control managers should be queried about current development efforts, such as:

- What new product development programs are in process or on the drawing board?
- Are there long-term R&D programs, or does the company merely play catch-up with competition?
- Are those quality standards that have been written into the specifications more or less stringent than competitors'? No one should produce Cadillacs and sell them at Ford prices when the competition produces Fords.

Finance and Administration

Most small businesses either employ a bookkeeper, controller, or office manager to handle accounting, bank relations, insurance, and other administrative tasks or rely on outside professionals. This is usually the best place to gain insights into hidden factors that could lead to future changes in profits, costs, and cash flows. Moreover, the person responsible for finance and administration should be in the best position to answer questions about internal controls, collection patterns, supplier payment schedules, unprofitable product lines, and, most important, the various cost relationships that will be necessary for preparing pro forma financial statements and cash flow forecasts.

Asking the finance manager the right questions can cut down on the analytical time necessary to understand the company's financial statements and can also help you ferret out relevant internal reports that may be crucial to determining business or financial risk. Assistance in interpreting financial statements and foggy cost relationships frequently makes the difference between arriving at a valuation that points to a go decision and one that causes investors to back off.

Figure 4-3 offers a list of questions that cover the waterfront, grouped according to major topics.

FIGURE 4-3: Questions for Interviewing Finance Managers

A. Financial
- What are the internal controls over cash?
- Which customers are difficult to collect from, and why?
- Are there any accounts in dispute?
- What are the average days outstanding in payables, and is the payment policy thirty days, forty-five days, or longer? Why?
- How much was the inventory write-down last year?
- Is there obsolete or unsalable inventory?
- Is pension funding current?
- How good are bank relations?

B. Systems
- What types of systems are in use? Mainframes or PCs; purchased or customized software; integrated or stand-alone systems.
- Is there any programming talent in house? What are the capabilities of the data processing staff?
- In general, describe the functioning of the labor and production reporting, order entry, inventory control, production control, and accounting systems.
- What are the built-in internal controls in the systems?

C. Administrative
- What are the employee insurance programs?
- What are the mechanics of pension funding? Who is the trustee?
- What is the bonus or profit sharing program?
- Who is responsible for hiring, firing, and evaluating employees?
- Is there a company policy manual?

Internal Reports

Whether they produce formal monthly or annual financial statements or get by with once-a-year tax-return balance sheets and income statements, virtually all businesses create internal reports of one type or another. As a minimum, try to pick up recent sales statistics, payroll summaries, physical inventory valuations, and any other available internal reports. Although the most authoritative financial data comes from complete financial statements, it would be a big mistake to overlook the supplemental information available from informal, internal reports.

The best way to identify the types of internal reports in use is to ask the various department managers during field trip interviews. Although these reports vary widely, certain ones are necessary if the business is to operate. Others are often designed for the management of specific functional activities.

In the marketing area, the following reports are commonly prepared weekly or monthly:

- Customer orders received
- Order cancellations
- Shipments by customer and product line
- Customer order backlog
- Sales by territory or sales organization
- Industry statistics published by trade associations or other industry groups
- Historical pricing changes
- Sales discounts
- Customer returns

Nearly every marketing manager and many business owners periodically prepare forecasts of customer orders and shipments for three months to a year. These informal forecasts represents the expectations of those most in the know and serve as a viable source of data for preparing pro forma financial statements.

Production and quality control departments typically generate a series of specialized reports, most of little value to outsiders. However, the few that could be helpful for ratio and risk analyses are:

- Actual labor hours by week or month
- Production units completed at each work station
- Scrap and product failure statistics
- Production schedules by day or by week
- Delivery promises kept

- Number of direct labor and support employees by function
- List of major suppliers

The data contained in these dynamic management tools continually changes, so if it is to be of any forecasting value, the most current figures should be used. It might also be helpful to collect selected reports from prior periods to get a handle on trends.

Finance departments generally create too many reports rather than too few, making it necessary to selectively choose only those that include essential data. In addition to monthly or annual financial statements and tax returns, internal financial reports that might be helpful include:

- Gross margin by product line
- Gross margin by customer
- If a standard cost system is used, labor and material variance analyses would be helpful.
- Comparisons of actual expenses to budget by cost center

Annual budgets can also be helpful in understanding functional cost relationships, pricing and volume expectations, and capital expenditure requirements. You may not agree with the forecasted amounts, but this is a good base from which to start.

Contracts, Leases, Appraisals, Claims

All contracts and leases should be examined to determine their impact on a company's future earning power and asset values. Leases that cover equipment as well as real estate can materially affect future cash flow. If the company has not adhered to accounting and IRS lease-capitalization conventions, it's easy to miss rental payments that are buried in nonrent expense accounts. Furthermore, it may be necessary to adjust the financial statements if the company has long-term leases that cost less than the current market value.

Leases may include assets at far-flung locations, such as retail outlets or warehouses. In that case, company personnel should prepare a listing for each location. For a buy/sell valuation, all leases should be transferable and not subject to escalation clauses. Many leases do have such clauses, in which case adjustments to the financial statements are required.

Loan agreements must be scrutinized to verify that the company is not in default on restrictive covenants and, for buy/sell valuations, that the transaction itself won't create a default condition. Any covenants that restrict dividend payments should be highlighted. Also be alert for franchise and distributorship agreements that require the grantor's approval to transfer all or part of the company's equity interests. And verify that agreements are with the company, not the owner. Contracts that obligate the owner personally detract from the value of the business and would probably be sufficient reason to back off.

All customer and supplier contracts are extremely critical to the value of the business. Long-term contracts might tie a company to a supplier when better terms could be obtained elsewhere. Long-term customer contracts may specify prices that do not reflect changing cost structures. In both cases, cash flow forecasts would have to recognize these abnormalities in cost relationships.

Employment contracts with key employees could materially affect a business's value. If employees are performing well, such contractual ties enhance the value; reverse the situation and they detract. Also, check out the terms of any noncompeting covenants, either with employees or between the company and another business.

If patents, trademarks, or copyrights play important roles in the company's earning power, verify that they are still in force and will remain in force or be renewed during the entire forecast period.

Ask for copies of recent asset appraisals. Many companies undertake periodic insurance appraisals. Although the results are based on replacement cost, which usually overvalues the assets, such appraisals could be helpful in identifying owned assets.

Other types of contracts, agreements, and appraisals that might help in judging business value include:

- Real estate tax appraisals
- Union contracts (make sure they can be transferred with company ownership)
- Pension plan contracts
- Contracts in settlement of previous lawsuits, especially those dealing with employee discrimination suits, EPA settlements, and OSHA claims

As a final check, ask to see the IRS and state taxing authority settlement sheets for the last years that have been audited. If the company has never been audited, the risk of future unplanned cash payments escalates.

The company may be entitled to future payments against a legal judgment that never show up on the balance sheet. Or it may win an outstanding insurance claim. These are called *contingent assets*, and the only way to learn about them is to ask management personnel or the company's legal counsel. Of course, if such contingent assets exist, they increase the value of the company.

The reverse situation, *contingent liabilities*, is more common. Very few companies that have been in business for several years get by without some potential liability that has not been recognized in the books of account. A few of the more common include:

- IRS audit claims
- Product liability claims
- Employee discrimination lawsuits
- Compliance claims from federal or state regulatory bodies, such as the EPA or OSHA
- Warranties

It's crucial to ferret out all potential liabilities to avoid surprises in future years that could diminish the company's cash flow. Many investors arbitrarily increase valuation risk factors to cover contingent liabilities even though none have been uncovered during due diligence investigations.

Since it is seldom possible to accumulate everything during one visit, it may be necessary to return to the company's facilities a second or even a third time. Most investigations take at least two visits to accumulate all relevant data in a usable format. However, there is no better way to be certain that as much data as possible has been obtained than to be on the premises. Time and gain, those who try to accomplish due diligence investigations by phone, fax, or letter miss the boat completely, either paying too much for the business or erroneously dropping it as a viable investment.

It might appear that many of the areas covered in this chapter apply only to large companies or manufacturing businesses. While it's true that the size and nature of the business change the emphasis placed on each of the functional areas, most companies, large or small, must have basic marketing, production, and finance functions. Some won't have engineering or quality control departments, but all should be concerned about maintaining state-of-the-art management techniques and selling quality products and services. The smaller the company and the less complex the business, the fewer due diligence questions need to be researched. But all areas must be examined to determine whether or not they apply to a specific company.

Economic and Industry Data

So far we have been concerned exclusively with gathering data that relates to a specific company. The other half of the story is data that affects the entire country or industry. This data has an indirect but important bearing on a company's earning power. It's difficult to overstate the importance of accumulating appropriate national and industry data before laying out a cash flow forecast. As described in Chapter 3, one of the first forecasting steps involves the development of economic and business assumptions. And one of the most important assumptions has to do with national economic cycles and industry business cycles.

In fact, without a thorough understanding of a company's current positioning on both cycles, it's impossible to forecast sales with reasonable accuracy. Although marketing programs and selling techniques—as well as the market's acceptance of product lines—certainly affect sales levels, very few businesses are immune from cyclical trends. And to get a handle on cyclical trends, one must use national and industry data. To add credence to the importance of using cyclical data, bear in mind the clause in IRS Revenue Ruling 59-60 that states that "the economic outlook in general and the condition and outlook of the specific industry in particular" must be considered when valuing businesses for estate and gift tax purposes.

It goes without saying that it's necessary to choose only those cyclical indicators that apply to a given company. It does little good to worry about national unemployment rates for a company that employs two people. Or to be concerned with building permit trends for companies manufacturing motorcycles. Or to crank in aerospace industry statistics for ladies' garment stores.

However, certain national data can reasonably be applied to any company—interest rates, inflation rates, consumer spending, and perhaps business investment, to mention a few. This data should definitely be included during the gathering process, along with pertinent industry data.

Global economic conditions also affect an increasing number of companies. Those that import materials from abroad, that export products and services, or that have foreign subsidiaries or branches are affected by exchange rates, international financial conditions, and economic cycles in the markets they are involved with.

Stock market, commodity market, and currency market trends also affect many companies. To the extent that consumer or industrial buying habits are influenced by perceived capital market trends, statistics relating to these markets must be included.

The number of sources of national and international economic, financial, and trade data boggles the mind. One can only wonder how much the federal deficit could be reduced if the government were to eliminate only 25 percent of its statistical and data-gathering machinery.

At any rate, government data sources are voluminous. The *Federal Reserve Bulletin (www.federalreserve.gov), Statistical Abstract of the United States (www.census.gov), Survey of Current Business (www.bea.gov)*, and *The Economic Report of the President,* published by the Council of Economic Advisers *(www.gpoaccess.gov)* are the more popular sources. Eximbank puts out a wealth of data relating to international trade. The U.S. Department of

Commerce has offices in all major cities that are chock full of data, reports, government booklets, and a plethora of other information.

Many states and a few major cities also provide more localized economic and business data. California, New York, Texas, and Illinois all do excellent jobs, as do New York City, Los Angeles, and Chicago.

Major investment banks publish financial market statistics by the carload. Standard & Poor's, Mergent (née Moody's), Value Line Surveys, and Dun & Bradstreet compile valuable statistical tabulations. Money center banks like Citibank and Bank of America routinely circulate current economic trend information. The sources go on and on.

On the industry side, trade associations and trade magazines are invaluable sources of current data and statistical trends. The *U.S. Industrial Outlook* and *Standard & Poor's Industry Surveys* include data on most industries. And major securities houses like Merrill Lynch, Bear Stearns, and Goldman Sachs publish data on a wide range of industries. Once you start looking, you'll find an endless number of data sources. Just be certain to use only those indicators that relate to the company being valued.

CHAPTER

Restructuring Financial Statements

In an ideal world, the Financial Accounting Standards Board (FASB) and the Securities and Exchange Commission (SEC) would jointly issue a set of permanent accounting standards. In an ideal world, the Internal Revenue Service would not tinker with business structures or bookkeeping procedures. In an ideal world, public and privately held companies of all sizes, in all industries, and of all forms would willingly conform to one set of accounting rules for recording transactions and reporting financial results. In an ideal world, such uniformity would make the job of preparing pro forma financial statements and cash flow forecasts for business valuations a snap.

But we do not live in an ideal world. The FASB, the SEC, and the IRS seldom agree on anything. All three bodies regularly change their recording and reporting standards. Although publicly traded companies must comply with SEC regulations, privately held companies do pretty much as they please, as long as they don't violate IRS rules. This wide variation in accounting practices may serve the needs of small business owners, but it leaves potential investors in the dark. To make an intelligent decision about buying a minority or partnership interest, acquiring a going business, or investing venture capital, investors need to restructure a company's financial statements or, if necessary, create them from scratch or from tax returns to reflect the true condition of the business. This chapter sets out techniques and suggestions to help in achieving that end.

Assuming that a company has some type of financial statements available for inspection or can prepare them on request, adjustments will probably be necessary to reflect three conditions:

1. Adaptations in the way a company has elected to keep its accounts in order to bring them as closely as possible into line with generally accepted accounting principles
2. Eliminations of certain unusual or discretionary expenses—such as owners' draws, extraordinarily high management bonuses, or the use of company funds to pay owners' personal expenses—or such nonrecurring income as tax rebates from the carryover of prior years' losses, sales of hard assets, and one-time contract progress payments

3. Provisions to reflect expected future events that materially differ from past experience, such as the projected closing of a branch plant or the discontinuance of a product line

Such adjustments may affect only the income statement or only the balance sheet, or they may affect both. Some adjustments, such as revised depreciation methods, may be important for accounting purposes but have no bearing on prior or future cash flow and therefore will not be included in this discussion. Other adjustments, such as changes in the reserve for bad debts, may not have an immediate impact on cash flow but could in the future and therefore will be considered. And certain variations in bookkeeping practices, such as alternative inventory valuation procedures, may never have a direct impact on cash flow but do distort important financial ratios used to evaluate future income potential or tax liabilities. These adjustments are also relevant to the following discussions.

Transactions that cause the most difficulty and usually require adjustments include:

- Uncollected receivables
- Revenue recognition on long-term contracts
- Inventory valuations
- Leases
- Recording and writing off of intangible assets
- Unrecorded or unfunded pension liabilities
- Fixed assets written up or down to reflect purchase accounting for acquisitions
- Sales with contingent liabilities attached
- Intracompany pricing and borrowing
- Investments in affiliated companies
- Nonrecurring losses
- Owner/manager's expenses and compensation
- S corporation conversion

Receivables and Revenue Recognition

Many companies, especially smaller ones, refuse to write off any receivable unless a customer has actually gone out of business. Even accounts from companies in Chapter 11 bankruptcy may be carried at full value in the hope that at some indeterminable date they will be collected. Since beginning receivable balances form an integral part of a cash flow forecast (as described in Chapter 7), if collections are not forthcoming on a regular schedule, cash inputs in the first forecast year will be overstated.

The best way to learn about potentially bad receivables is to obtain an aged receivable listing (also called an aged trial balance of receivables) as part of the due diligence process (see Chapter 4). In most cases, a review of payment history should make actual customer confirmations unnecessary, but for large or very old accounts, investors may wish to contact the customer directly. If the company has recently been audited, it might also be a good idea to check with the audit firm about receivables confirmed during the audit.

Generally accepted accounting principles dictate that any suspect receivable not written off should be reserved against. If potential bad debts have been reserved against, that will take care of misstated cash collections next year. Even if a reserve for bad debts is not in use, investors should set one up for any questionable accounts. Promissory notes taken from customers in lieu of open accounts should also be reserved against if there is any question about their timely collection or if promised payment dates extend beyond one year.

Companies whose business involves progress payments, as with government contracts or construction projects, frequently record progress billings as a liability with an offsetting receivable called *unrealized sales*. Investors must be particularly careful to adjust for or reserve against unrealized sales that may never come to fruition. This could easily be the case, for instance, if a contractor experiences large cost overruns toward the end of a project without contractual rights to collect for them. Although customer billings may be recorded as liabilities, refusal by the customer to pay for these overruns would invalidate the offsetting unrealized sale.

Distortions in revenue recognition also occur when customers make payments on account prior to receiving the finished products. For instance, companies engaged in the production of components for government defense programs frequently have contracts that call for progress payments well in advance of the delivery of finished products. If scarce materials or large quantities of materials must be purchased, the contract may call for advance payments to provide the cash to buy the materials; however, finished products may not be delivered for a year or more. Other contracts call for progress payments against billings of labor hours incurred, overhead absorbed, and anticipated profit—again well in advance of the delivery of finished products.

When should the company recognize sales in its income statement? How should the company record inventory? What will be the impact on the cash flow forecast of customer payments received a year or more in advance of shipping products? And how should you forecast cash flow from new contracts whose terms may be different?

Accurate adjustments for variations in revenue recognition can be a nightmare, requiring educated estimates. It is not uncommon to forecast future cash flow based on historical average of progress payments and expenditures for materials and labor.

Using historical data to forecast future cash flow for percentage-of-completion contracts can be just as difficult. Once again, future cash flow will probably have to be based on some type of historical average of the relationship of cash inflows to payroll or purchased material expenditures. The most common procedure is to base future estimates on historical cash receipts/expenditures relationships for the entire company rather than by project.

Revenue recognition can also be a sticky problem when sales contracts call for future performance by the company, such as the delivery of services against maintenance contracts or publications against subscription contracts. Small companies engaged in these businesses frequently record sales when up-front cash is received, well in advance of incurring costs, performing services, or shipping products. This overstates income in early years and understates it in later years as costs are incurred to deliver the services or products.

As closely as possible, opening financial statements and forecasted cash flows should be adjusted in accordance with the accounting profession's matching principle, which states that costs and associated revenues should be matched in the time period during which they occur.

LIFO Versus FIFO Inventory Valuation

The *last-in, first-out*, or LIFO, inventory method permits companies to defer pricing gains that result from higher material costs during inflationary periods, by recording cost of sales at the most recent inventory acquisition prices. Ending inventory is then understated by the same amount that earnings are understated. The FIFO (*first-in, first-out*) method does the opposite. It records cost of sales at the earliest acquisition prices and inventory at the most recent prices. The IRS accepts LIFO as well as FIFO as valid inventory valuation techniques for tax purposes. Many companies now use LIFO in their financial statements.

The LIFO method benefits companies as long as sales continue level or increase, so that withdrawals from inventory are equal to or less than new purchases. When the reverse occurs, however, both earnings and ending inventory are misstated in the opposite direction. As inventories get reduced to a point at which prior years' cost layers with much lower prices are matched against current inflated sales prices, wide distortions in earnings can occur. The following simple example demonstrates the point.

Assume that a company begins the year with 100 clogs in inventory, each costing $10. It then buys twenty-five more clogs at $15, and later buys 100 more at $20. Further assume that it sells 110 clogs during the year. Figure 5-1 shows how these amounts flow to inventory and cost of sales under the LIFO method compared with the FIFO method and the adjustment to income that should be made as a result of the LIFO reserve.

The distortion that the LIFO method introduces into cash flow projections is even more important than the misstatement of earnings and inventory. Since both cost of sales and inventory are reported at fictitious prices that do not match the flow of actual costs, appropriate adjustments must be made to bring both in line with actual expenditures.

Leases

Although not as tricky to deal with as LIFO reserves, the recording of leases can be confusing. The Financial Accounting Standards Board (FASB) release "Accounting for Leases" holds that capital leases must be capitalized as an asset with an offsetting liability for future rental payments. Typically, a capital lease runs for the entire useful life of the asset and the lessee has responsibility for asset maintenance, insurance, property taxes, and other costs of keeping the asset in good working condition.

FIGURE 5-1: Calculations of Income Adjustment for LIFO Reserve

	Number of Clogs	Unit Price	LIFO Inventory	LIFO Cost of Sales	FIFO Inventory	FIFO Cost of Sales
Beginning inventory	100	$10	$1,000		$1,000	
Purchases	25	$15	$375		$375	
	100	$20	$2,000		$2,000	
Sales	100	$20		$2,000		
	10	$15		$150		
	100	$10				$1,000
	10	$15				$150
Total cost of sales				$2,150		$1,150
Ending inventory	15	$15			$225	
	100	$20			$2,000	
	100	$10	$1,000			
	15	$15	$225			
Total ending inventory	325		$1,225		$2,225	

TO ADJUST LIFO ENDING INVENTORY TO FIFO:
LIFO inventory	$1,225
Add LIFO reserve	$1,000
FIFO inventory	$2,000

TO ADJUST LIFO INCOME TO FIFO:
LIFO reserve	$1,000
Taxes @ 38%	$380
Adjustment to income	$620

According to the FASB, a lease must be treated as a capital lease if, at its inception, it meets one or more of the following criteria:

- Ownership of the asset will be transferred to the lessee at the end of the lease period.
- The lessee has a right to buy the asset at a price significantly below its fair market value.
- The lease term is equal to or greater than 75 percent of the asset's useful life.
- The present value of the minimum lease payments at the lease's inception is equal to or greater than 90 percent of the excess of the fair market value of the leased property over any investment tax credit claimed and expected to be realized by the lessor (assuming the IRS allows investment tax credits).

The present value is arrived at by discounting the lease payments at the lower of the lessor's implicit lease interest rate or the rate the lessee would have to pay for a loan of a comparable term, called the lessee's *incremental borrowing rate*. Minimum lease payments are defined as those payments that the lessee must make or can be required to make, including rent payments, residual value guarantees, and payments for failing to renew or extend the lease term.

Any lease not meeting at least one of these criteria is considered an operating lease. Operating leases are relatively short term, with the lessor retaining responsibility for the asset's maintenance, insurance, and taxes. Operating leases are not recorded on the balance sheet, and rental payments are written off as expenses when paid.

So far so good. Those are the rules. The problem arises when one tries to reconcile the FASB reporting requirements with cash flow forecasts. Here's why:

- The asset and the obligation must each be recorded on the balance sheet at an amount equal to the present value of the minimum lease payments.
- If the present value turns out to be greater than the assets fair value, which is generally the asset's purchase cost, then the fair value is recorded in place of the present value.
- The capitalized lease must be amortized at rates designated by the FASB depending on which of the criteria the lease falls under. This may or may not be consistent with a company's depreciation policy.

Since minimum lease payments include such noncash contingent items as residual value guarantees and penalties for failure to renew or extend the lease term, the annual reduction in the obligation cannot be considered as a cash outlay. Two adjustments must be made: (1) replace the present value minimum lease payment liability with an obligation equal to the sum of the total rental payments over the lease term; and (2) adjust the annual reduction of this liability to reflect the actual cash payments. Of course, the same adjustments must be made if the asset and obligation are recorded at fair value rather than at the present value of the minimum lease payments.

An even better way to deal with capital leases is to adjust them out of the balance sheet entirely and treat them as operating leases. That way cash expenditures for rental payments can be treated as expense items.

Intangibles

In many small businesses, intangible assets contribute more toward earnings, and hence cash flow, than tangible assets. Yet, both the accounting fraternity and the IRS hold to rules that do not permit all of these assets to be reported on balance sheets. The list of possible intangible assets is practically limitless; however, here are a few of the major ones:

- Goodwill
- Patents
- Copyrights
- Trademarks
- Customer/client lists
- Client files
- Noncompete covenants
- Employment contracts for key employees
- Licenses
- Franchises
- Organization costs for new branches, divisions, or subsidiaries
- Unpatented technical know-how

Companies are allowed to capitalize some of these assets, such as patents, copyrights, noncompete covenants, and organization costs, and then to amortize them over their useful lives. Purchased goodwill arising from a business acquisition falls into the same category, although amortization cannot be deducted for tax purposes.

A company could be substantially undervalued if intangible assets that have been developed internally rather than purchased have a significant bearing on its earning power. The rules state that costs of "developing, maintaining, or restoring intangibles which are unidentifiable, have indeterminate lives, or are inherent in a continuing enterprises" must be written off as incurred. This includes such valuable assets as employment contracts, customer/client lists, internally developed goodwill, client files, and unpatented technical know-how.

For many companies, these internally created assets may have been developed several years ago and written off to expense, yet they continue to add significant value to the business. Many professional practices, for instance, would be virtually worthless without an active client list. An accounting or tax practice could not exist without its client files. A computer software development company would be out of business without valuable technical know-how, much of which is unpatentable.

When you run up against companies that rely heavily on unrecorded or fully written-off intangibles, you must make adjustments for their estimated value to both the balance sheet and the income statement. Granted, if the expenses have already been written off, no further cash outlay will be necessary; however, if these assets are ignored, financial ratio analysis becomes virtually meaningless.

Pension Liability

Two types of unrecorded or underrecorded pension liability must be guarded against:

1. A liability that reflects the amount of pensions that will have to be paid to employees for past service to the company
2. A liability that reflects the amounts that employees earn for future service to the company

The former is called *past service costs*, the second, *future service costs*. Current accounting rules require companies to fully fund past as well as future service costs.

Typically, pension funds are managed by independent trustees: banks, insurance companies, and fund management firms. Companies make annual payments into a trust based on actuarial calculations of employees' ages, years worked, and probable retirement years. The trustee then invests these funds. The difference between (1) the value of the assets necessary for full funding, discounted to present value, that actuaries calculate and (2) the actual value of assets held in the trust represents the amount that must be contributed each year.

Investors may encounter one or a combination of several deficiencies in this practice:

- The company may not have paid sufficient amounts into the trusts in prior years and therefore must make up the difference in the future.
- Actuarial calculations may have assumed certain rates of return on trustee-invested assets that have not materialized, thereby understating trust assets and requiring makeup payments in the future.
- Trust assets may be more than actuarially necessary, thereby providing excess cash that can, by law, be returned to the company.
- Present value calculations used by actuaries to determine funding requirements may or may not reflect the true liability.

The biggest headache, however, arises as a result of FASB regulations that require the recording of all unfunded pension costs arising from past and future service. This could amount to a significant cash outflow in the next term as companies catch up on prior deficiencies.

Since unfunded or underfunded pension costs can add up to very large sums that must be expended in future years, it is essential to adjust the company's balance sheet to reflect the true liability and then, in the cash flow forecast, calculate the proper payments against it.

Another type of discrepancy frequently arises in very small businesses with few employees. In most cases, those companies that do have pension plans use one of the defined contribution plans sanctioned by the IRS as individual retirement plans. Both Simplified Employee Plans (SEP) and 401(k) plans are popular. Some are managed through a trustee, others by the company. When analyzing a company's financial statements, it's important to ascertain that prior year payments required by law have in fact been made. If not, balance sheets must be adjusted to reflect the proper liability.

Purchase Accounting Adjustments

Purchase accounting applies to the consolidated financial statements of companies that have acquired a going business through a stock purchase. Two major distortions must be guarded against. First, accounting rules stipulate that when a premium has been paid for the common shares of a going concern, such goodwill must be allocated to the assets of the subsidiary brought into the consolidation up to, but not exceeding, fair market value. To the extent that the premium exceeds a write-up of the acquired company's assets to fair market value, it must be classified as goodwill.

The purchase price is allocated first to the subsidiary's net current assets—which are generally receivables and inventory, less payables—and then to its fixed assets. The following example demonstrates how this works.

Assumptions:
1. Net assets on the books of the acquired company:

Receivables	$100,000
Inventory	150,000
Machinery & equipment	1,000,000
Less: Accumulated depreciation	(250,000)
Total assets	1,000,000
Payables	50,000
Accrued expense	50,000
Total liabilities	100,000
Net worth	900,000
Total liabilities and net worth	1,000,000

2. Fair market value of machinery & equipment	**3,000,000**
3. Purchase price	**1,200,000**

4. Allocation of purchase price:

Receivables	$100,000
Inventory	150,000
Payables and accrued expenses	(100,000)
Machinery & equipment	1,050,000
Total purchase price	$1,200,000

When the subsidiary's accounts are consolidated with the parent's, the new balance for machinery and equipment is $1,050,000 and accumulated depreciation is zero. The new machinery and equipment asset is then depreciated over a new useful life. Investors should be aware of this practice and make appropriate adjustments to the balance sheet and depreciation expense to reflect the true asset cost and useful life.

A second peculiarity arises from the requirement that the total unfunded pension costs of the acquired business be recorded as a liability. If the business has already complied with the new accounting rules, this may not be a problem. However, many small businesses have not yet recorded this liability, making it necessary to verify the accuracy of the pension cost resulting from an acquisition.

Intercompany Pricing and Investment

Accounting for intercompany transactions and investments in affiliated companies often causes more confusion about future earnings and potential cash flow than it should. Transactions between affiliated companies should, of course, be priced as arms-length transactions. Pragmatically, this seldom occurs in smaller companies.

For example, a business owner might create a separate entity to hold title to the real estate that houses the operating business. It could be a partnership, a limited partnership, or an S corporation. The holding company charges rents calculated in such a way as to minimize taxes, not necessarily to reflect an arms-length arrangement. The same holds true for intercompany charges for management fees. Pricing of intercompany sales/purchases tends to more equitably reflect market prices, but even here, tax considerations normally are the deciding factor.

As long as the investment is to be made in the parent company, none of these matters seriously affect the reliability of cash flow projections. However, adjustments to market prices are necessary for the independent valuation of a division or subsidiary branch operation.

The recording of investments in affiliates may create a different type of inconsistency. If you are looking at a branch operation, it doesn't make much difference how the parent has recorded its investment in the branch. It makes a big difference, however, when valuing the parent. The greatest distortion arises when the parent uses the cost method, as opposed to the equity method, to record its investment. Accounting rules permit parent companies to use the cost method when investments in affiliates represent less than 50 percent of total ownership. Above 50 percent, the equity method should be used.

Whereas the equity method includes a share of the subsidiary's earnings in the parent company's income statement, the cost method does not. When a subsidiary's earnings are significant relative to the total company's earnings, it might pay to adjust the parent's statements accordingly. However, this approach can backfire. The underlying assumption is that a dollar of the subsidiary's earnings is worth as much as a dollar of the parent's earnings. From an investor's perspective, this may not always be the case. For example, the subsidiary may be restricted by loan agreements or regulatory statutes from distributing earnings, and therefore may contribute nothing toward the parent's cash flows.

Nonrecurring Events

When analyzing historical financial statements, it's important to eliminate income or expense items, as well as assets and liabilities, that may have arisen as a result of extraordinary or nonrecurring conditions. Accounting standards define extraordinary events or transactions as those meeting *both* of the following criteria:

- The underlying event or transaction must be unusual; that is, it must have a high degree of abnormality and not be related to the ongoing business of the company.
- The underlying event or transaction must be infrequent, that is, it would not be reasonable to expect it to occur again in the foreseeable future.

Clearly, a large insurance settlement for a major fire that destroyed an entire factory would be extraordinary. A labor strike that forces the closing of a branch plant would be extraordinary. As would the sale of a division or subsidiary.

Profits or losses of a discontinued operation that arose prior to the operation's discontinuance would not meet the accounting definition of extraordinary but should be eliminated from financial statements before forecasting future benefits. The same holds true for a raft of other nonrecurring items that may not meet the definition of extraordinary but nonetheless have no impact on future earnings. Examples of such items include:

- Proceeds or expenditures from the settlement of a lawsuit
- Life insurance settlements from the death of a key employee or owner
- Any gains or losses on the sale of operating assets
- One-time radical swings in the price of purchased materials, as with major fluctuations in the price of oil or copper

To the extent to which it can be determined that these events are not likely to recur during the forecast period, their impact on historical balance sheet and income statement accounts should be eliminated prior to preparing a cash flow forecast.

Owner/Manager's Compensation and Expenses

As most owner/managers of small businesses know, tax laws make it difficult to withdraw significant amounts of cash from a business without the IRS treating them as dividends, thereby collecting taxes twice on the same income. First, dividends are not deductible to the corporation and therefore come from after-tax income. Second, dividends are taxed to the recipient as ordinary income. Business owners have found several ways around this obstacle:

- The corporation can elect to be taxed as an S corporation, so that all business income and losses are taxed to shareholders and cash distributions are essentially tax free.
- The owner/managers can pay wages to relatives (e.g., spouse, children, and so on) for services performed.
- The business can pay certain personal expenses of the owner/manager from company cash and treat them as business expenses.
- The owner/manager can borrow cash from the business.

From the perspectives of owner/managers, each of these tactics accomplishes the purpose of withdrawing cash without being taxed twice on the same income. From the perspective of a potential investor, however, all of them muddy the waters. Theoretically, whether investing in a minority interest—as in a partnership, limited partnership, or venture capital investment—or purchasing the entire company, prospective investors should adjust the company's financial statements for all such transactions that may have occurred during the periods preceding the acquisition date. In some cases the preceding three years should be adjusted. In others, adjusting the current year is sufficient.

Small businesses that elect to be treated as S corporations for tax purposes and that choose to keep their accounting records on the same basis present a peculiar set of problems for investors trying to identify the proper net worth from which to begin pro forma forecasts. Tax code provisions that affect the treatment of S corporation profits and distributions change periodically, so it pays to brush up on current regulations before beginning an analysis. The major areas that must be reconciled and adjusted currently include:

- Distributions to shareholders in excess of proportionate profit shares, which are treated as a return of capital, thereby reducing the company's net worth, loans to shareholders, dividends, or gains from the sale of property
- Retained earnings prior to the S election
- Corporate tax liability if the company was originally a C corporation
- The accumulated adjustments account and retained earnings when the accumulated adjustment account (which is treated similarly to partnership capital accounts) may not accurately reflect retained earnings
- Built-in gains tax to the corporation, which applies only for C corporations that switch to S corporations

In addition to adjustments that reconcile S corporation bookkeeping to generally acceptable accounting principles and reconstructions that result from owner/manager draws and company-paid expenses, adjustments may be required to reconcile the classes of stock permitted under the S election. Be aware that under certain conditions, the IRS treats S corporation stock warrants, rights, and call options as outstanding stock even though they have not been exercised. To the extent that the company keeps its books in compliance with IRS rules, the value of these near-stock obligations will have to be adjusted.

Impact of Inflation

Although the past decade has not witnessed any major inflationary spiral, it is certainly possible that high inflation rates could return in the future. Regardless of the current outlook, it would be foolhardy not to consider the impact of inflationary prices on the value of a business.

The major difficulty arises because sales and expenses are almost always stated in current dollars, whereas many of the assets used to generate income, such as a factory, production equipment, and inventory, may have been purchased at significantly lower price levels. Thus, an upward trend in profits may be more a function of inflationary pressure on prices than of management's ability to meet or beat competition.

Although the Financial Accounting Standards Board did issue rulings that required large corporations to disclose inflation-adjusted accounting in their financial statements, few continue to do so now that inflation is relatively constant. Very few closely held businesses ever revealed such adjustments.

When looking at a stream of future benefits from a closely held company, one must be constantly alert to the need for adjustments to reflect inflationary profits. Without such adjustments, inflation-driven profits feed on themselves, and when volume tapers off or prices stabilize, management can suddenly be faced with selling higher-cost inventory at lower prices. A forecasted 10 to 15 percent annual growth rate may be nothing more than an illusion, dissipating when the business cycle turns.

A few of the industries particularly susceptible to inflation-driven profits include:

- Food products
- Oil-based products
- All types of energy
- Lumber
- Rubber-based products
- Copper and other commodity-based products
- Financial services
- Health care service and products

In product-oriented businesses, those companies whose inventory represents a high percentage of sales and profits are the most sensitive to inflation-driven prices. In the services sector, when payroll represents a large percentage of sales and profits and employees are included in collective bargaining units, businesses such as hospitals, schools, transport firms, and building contractors become the most vulnerable.

CHAPTER

Ratio and Risk Analyses

As a prelude to developing pro forma projections and cash flow forecasts, it's important to form judgments about a company's health and its related potential of future earnings. To a very large extent, such judgments determine the probability of achieving the forecasted future benefits and thus the choice of an appropriate capitalization rate for calculating the present value of future cash streams. Once necessary adjustments have been made to asset, liability, income, and expense accounts, it's possible to begin interpreting financial statements through a series of financial ratios.

Financial ratios can yield relevant answers only if compared with a standard, however. In and of themselves, ratios may be interesting from an academic perspective, but unless relevant comparisons can be made, they don't bring new information to the valuation process. Comparisons may be against other companies' ratios, stock market averages, industry guidelines, lender policies, alternative investment opportunities, widely accepted standards, or—especially when valuing a closely held company—an investor's personal experience.

For example, most people are familiar with the current ratio (i.e., current assets divided by current liabilities) as a measure of liquidity. One widely accepted standard holds that a current ratio of 2-to-1 indicates that a company has sufficient liquid assets to meet its current obligations. This standard has merit when applied to larger companies where investors can be assured that generally accepted accounting principles are being followed. However, investors in small businesses with hybrid accounting systems usually draw on personal experiences that point to different standards to reflect prudent cash management, and hence liquidity. In some cases current ratios of 3-to-1 or even 4-to-1 would be expected.

Although ratio analyses can certainly be used to augment the valuation of a business, it should not be assumed that in and of themselves financial ratios can be used to make investment decisions. The fact is that in many instances, ratio analyses are more pertinent for avoiding investment losses than for determining future benefits. Lenders, for example, frequently look to indicators such as days sales in receivables, days inventory in payables, the quick ratio, and the debt-to-equity ratio to flag early warnings of debtor companies in trouble.

Many of these same ratios are necessary for preparing meaningful pro forma forecasts. Receivables to sales, payables to inventory, accrued expenses to operating expenses, purchases to sales, number of employees to sales, and many others are all useful ratios for quantifying the functional relationships that form the basis of forecasting.

Despite their wide use by securities analysts, investors, and lenders wanting to get a quick and easy fix on the health of a business, financial ratios can be very misleading, even when compared to valid standards. The reason is relatively simple. Ratios, like balance sheets, reflect the condition of a company at *one point in time*. Even income and expense ratios that span an entire accounting period reflect conditions prevailing only during that period.

Any number of events could cause a company's financial performance to go off track in one year. Floods, labor strikes, fires, significant R&D expenditures, the failure of a large customer, a leveraged buyout, and so on, could each cause a deterioration in financial performance for a given period.

When using ratio analyses to measure a company's health, it's necessary to apply the same ratios to the same company over several years, disregarding extraordinary events that cause distortions. Such an analysis will yield trends, either favorable or unfavorable, and provide a reasonable beginning for determining valuation risk factors.

Many common ratios are *quantitative* in nature; the facts they portray lend themselves to numerical analysis. They can usually be derived directly from financial statements. Less common ratios are *qualitative*, requiring interpretation and further analysis to be useful. As this chapter explores several ratios that fall into each category, it's important to bear in mind the purpose to which they will be put—namely, the valuation of a business as a going concern.

Here are the major quantitative ratios that can be especially useful for measuring the health of a company:

A. Debt utilization
- Total debt equity
- Long-term debt equity
- Total debt total assets
- Income before interest and taxes interest expense
- Income before fixed charges and taxes fixed charges

B. Liquidity
- Current assets current liabilities
- Cash plus cash equivalents minus inventory current liabilities
- Current assets short-term debt
- Fixed assets long-term debt

C. Profitability
- Gross profit sales
- Net income after tax sales
- Net income after taxes total assets
- Net income after taxes equity

D. Asset utilization
- Sales average receivables (turnover)
- Cost of sales average inventory (turnover)
- Sales fixed assets
- Sales total assets

As many qualitative measures as possible should be translated to numeric quantities. To accomplish this, analysts should draw on data from internally prepared reports. The most common qualitative measures of a company's health involve three sets of measurements:

1. Those that measure the effectiveness of cash management as shown by receivables collections and payments to suppliers
2. Those that measure production efficiency and labor utilization derived from production reports and payroll records
3. Those that measure the current status of customer relations as reflected in allowances granted, complaints, and returns

The following sections make use of a fictitious company, MAPAX Manufacturing Corp. (MAPAX), to demonstrate the use of financial ratio analysis. Chapter 7 also uses this company to demonstrate the economic assumptions and cost/volume/asset functional relationships used to prepare pro forma financial statements and cash flow forecasts.

A manufacturing company has been chosen as a demonstration model because it tends to have a more complex cost structure than other types of businesses and therefore can be used to demonstrate a greater number of ratios. Identical ratio analysis techniques, however, apply to retail, distribution, and service companies, provided similar account classifications are used.

Although the MAPAX model is certainly larger than many small businesses, do not be dissuaded by its size. This model was chosen because large numbers are easier to analyze and provide a much clearer picture than smaller ones. However, a company's size does not in any way change the usefulness of these ratios or the interpretation of their meaning. The identical principles and calculations apply to companies of any size—very small businesses as well as larger companies.

MAPAX Manufacturing Corp. manufactures two product lines, stoves and furnaces, both sold to the residential and commercial markets. The company also stocks a variety of resale accessories, some of which must be slightly modified to meet customer specifications. The stove and furnace business is a stable but growing industry. Although susceptible to both economic and industry cycles, its historical swings have been shallow, seldom more than 5 percent in either direction.

Figure 6-1 shows MAPAX's income statements and balance sheets for Year 1-2, Year 1-1, and Year 1.

FIGURE 6-1: MAPAX Manufacturing Corp. Financial Statements

MAPAX MANUFACTURING CORP.
STATEMENT OF INCOME

	Year 1-2	Year 1-1	Year 1
Sales	$10,914,750	$11,137,500	$11,250,000
Cost of sales:			
Material	5,588,352	5,702,400	5,760,000
Labor	849,430	866,765	875,520
Overhead	703,179	724,927	747,347
Total cost of sales	$7,140,960	$7,294,091	$7,382,867
Gross profit	$3,773,790	$3,843,409	$3,867,133
% of sales	34.6%	34.5%	34.4%
Operating expenses:			
Selling expenses	$584,788	$596,722	$608,900
Administrative expenses	520,297	530,915	541,750
Other expenses	20,000	20,000	20,000
Depreciation	468,000	532,000	585,000
TOTAL	$1,593,084	$1,679,637	$1,755,650
Net income before interest and taxes	$2,180,705	$2,163,772	$2,111,483
% of sales	20.0%	19.4%	18.8%
Interest	$597,500	$548,750	$517,000
Net income before tax	1,583,205	1,615,022	1,594,483
Taxes	601,618	613,708	605,904
Net income	$981,587	$1,001,313	$988,579
% of sales	9.0%	9.0%	8.8%

MAPAX MANUFACTURING CORP.
BALANCE SHEET

	Year 1-2	Year 1-1	Year 1
Cash	$622,852	$121,691	$1,000
Accounts receivable	1,364,344	1,392,187	1,406,250
Inventory	2,721,250	3,125,000	3,636,263
Prepaid expenses	5,000	5,000	5,000
Total current assets	$4,713,446	$4,643,878	$5,048,513
Buildings	2,000,000	2,000,000	2,000,000
Machinery & equipment	6,000,000	7,100,000	8,000,000
Delivery trucks	50,000	50,000	50,000
TOTAL	$8,050,000	$9,150,000	$10,050,000
Less: accumulated depreciation	(2,200,000)	(2,668,000)	(3,200,000)
Net fixed assets	5,850,000	6,482,000	6,850,000
Other assets	100,000	100,000	100,000
Total assets	$10,663,446	$11,225,878	$11,998,513

Bank note payable	$500,000	$250,000	$200,000
Accounts payable	580,440	666,559	775,614
Accrued expenses	200,000	200,000	200,000
Other current liabilities	50,000	50,000	50,000
Total current liabilities	$1,330,440	$1,166,559	$1,225,614
Long-term debt	4,400,000	4,200,000	4,000,000
Mortgage loan	1,150,000	1,075,000	1,000,000
Total Liabilities	$6,880,440	$6,441,559	$6,225,614
Common stock	$100,000	$100,000	$100,000
Retained earnings—beginning	2,701,419	3,683,006	4,684,320
Profit(loss)	981,587	1,001,313	988,579
Retained earnings—ending	3,683,006	4,684,320	5,672,899
Total net worth	$3,783,006	$4,784,320	$5,772,899
Total liabilities and net worth	$10,663,446	$11,225,879	$11,998,513

Debt Utilization Ratios

Debt utilization ratios measure the risk inherent in leverage financing. Too much debt impairs a company's liquidity by diverting to loan repayment cash that could otherwise be put to productive uses. Nonproductive interest expense damages a company's profitability. And during a business cycle downturn, companies with heavy debt service obligations tend to be the ones that don't make it through the trough. Clearly, the risk of receiving forecasted future cash benefits from a highly leveraged firm dictates the use of a very high capitalization premium.

Three debt utilization ratios offer insight into the amount of leverage employed by a company:

$$\text{Long-term debt to equity, expressed as} \quad \frac{\text{Long-term debt}}{\text{Net worth}}$$

$$\text{Total debt to equity, expressed as} \quad \frac{\text{Total debt}}{\text{Net worth}}$$

$$\text{Total debt to total assets, expressed as} \quad \frac{\text{Total debt}}{\text{Total assets}}$$

Companies with stable sales and earnings, such as utilities or railroads, can afford to employ more debt than those in cyclical industries, like automobiles, consumer electronics, and residential construction. The reason is obvious. When cyclical industries turn down, a company's cash flow shrinks and may not be sufficient to cover fixed interest and principal payments, let alone pay dividends to equity investors.

Using the numerical values from the MAPAX financial statements, these ratios yield the following results:

	Year 1-2	Year 1-1	Year 1
Long-term debt to equity	1.5:1	1.1:1	0.9:1
Total debt to equity	1.6:1	1.2:1	0.9:1
Total debt to total assets	0.6:1	0.5:1	0.4:1

The ratio of long-term debt to equity provides insights into the long-term capital structure of MAPAX. Generally, healthy manufacturing companies try to keep this ratio at 1:1 or less. Although MAPAX overshot the mark in Year 1-2, the three-year downward trend to 0.9:1 in Year 1 is a very healthy sign.

For some companies, especially those with high levels of short-term borrowings, the ratio of total debt to equity is a better measure of leverage. For MAPAX, the amount of short-term borrowings is minor compared with long-term debt, making the ratios and the trends very similar. If, however, short-term debt was high relative to long-term obligations and ratios of total debt to equity trended upward over three years, this would indicate that the company was probably suffering cash losses even if the income statement showed earnings.

Ratios of total debt to total assets indicate how efficiently a company has used its debt. Although each company has different capital needs, a 1:2 ratio would indicate that a company has in fact used its capital to create a reasonable level of assets for future cash generation. Once again, the MAPAX ratio looks high in Year 1-2 but is trending down to a reasonable level.

The ability of a company to cover its interest payments with earned income is measured by a ratio defined as income before interest and taxes to interest. In the case of MAPAX, this ratio yielded coverage of 3.7 times in Year 1-2, 3.9 times in Year 1-1, and 4.1 times in Year 1. The greater the number of times income covers interest payments, the more protection is afforded creditors. Ratios of 3 to 4 times show that MAPAX is probably not overleveraged and can easily support its debt service. Also, with the trend improving, investors in debt obligations could probably reduce the required capitalization premium.

Liquidity Ratios

Liquidity ratios demonstrate a company's ability to meet its current obligations, such as short-term notes, accounts payable, and accrued expenses. These ratios help to answer a common question in business valuations: Does a company have assets in excess of those required to meet operating needs, or do its assets fail to meet its needs?

The two most common liquidity ratios are the current ratio and the quick ratio, sometimes referred to as the acid-test ratio. These ratios are expressed as follows:

$$\text{Current ratio} = \frac{\text{Current assets}}{\text{Current liabilities}}$$

$$\text{Quick ratio} = \frac{\text{Cash and cash equivalents}}{\text{Current liabilities}}$$

Traditionally, lenders have regarded a current ratio of 2:1 as satisfactory and anything less than that as suspect. History has shown, however, that many companies whose business requires a longer receivables turnover or a longer inventory turnover have much lower current ratios but are just as safe for creditors.

The quick ratio is used to indicate a company's ability to quickly convert assets to cash to pay off current obligations in an emergency. A quick ratio of 1:1 is normally regarded as satisfactory. Some companies carry marketable securities, bank certificates of deposit, or other highly liquid assets, which are regarded as cash equivalents. In the MAPAX example, no marketable securities are carried, but receivables tend to be relatively short term. Therefore, the assets used to calculate the quick ratio are total current assets minus inventory. Over the three-year period, MAPAX's liquidity ratios were:

	1-2	1-1	1
Current ratio	3.5	4.0	4.1
Quick ratio	1.5	1.3	1.2

It should be noted that both the current ratio and the quick ratio measure a company's liquidity at a point in time and do not necessarily reflect its true need to finance short-term working capital requirements with short-term credits. During the course of a year, short-term borrowings could escalate significantly to purchase inventory that may be liquidated before the year ends, as in the toy industry.

Profitability Ratios

Profitability ratios indicate a company's ability to earn a *satisfactory* return on sales, total assets, and invested capital. Since the definition of satisfactory must be determined on a case-by-case basis, it would be wrong to assume that a company earning a 10 percent return on sales is worth more than one earning a 5 percent return, or that a company with an 80 percent gross profit margin will be a better investment than one turning a 30 percent gross profit. Comparisons with industry standards or with companies of similar size in similar businesses is the only reasonable way to interpret the values derived from profitability ratios.

Two profitability ratios are commonly used to measure the trend in a company's earnings potential: (1) gross profit margin as a percent of sales and, (2) net income as a percent of sales.

These ratios can normally be read directly from financial statements without additional analysis. Obviously, increasing ratios indicate improvements in operating expense control, pricing, product mix, or competitive advantage. Just as obviously, the reverse condition indicates deteriorating earning power. The following shows that MAPAX scores high in terms of absolute ratios. It has a 34 percent gross profit ratio and a 9 percent net income ratio, both of which are very respectable for manufacturing companies in stable, mature industries. However, the trend is not so good and indicates that something negative may be happening to MAPAX's cost structure or market position:

	1-2	1-1	1
Gross profit to sales	34.6%	34.5%	34.4%
Net income to sales	9.0%	9.0%	8.8%

Three other profitability ratios measure the return a company earns on invested capital: (1) return on owner's equity, (2) return on investment, and (3) return on total assets.

In the MAPAX example, these ratios were:

	1-2	1-1	1
Return on owner's equity	25.9%	20.9%	17.1%
Return on investment (adjusted for taxes on interest)	15.3%	13.9%	12.6%
Return on investment (unadjusted for taxes on interest)	17.9%	16.1%	14.5%
Return on total assets (adjusted for taxes on interest)	13.0%	12.3%	11.3%
Return on total assets (unadjusted for taxes on interest)	15.2%	14.1%	13.0%

Financial analysts will probably argue for the next 200 years about which of these ratios yields the most accurate picture of investment return. The arguments run as follows:

For return on owner's equity: The only true measure of a company's value is how much it returns to its owners.

For return on investment: The true measure of a company's value is how much it returns to all investors, both debtholders and equity investors.

For return on assets: The true measure of a company's value is the efficiency of its management, which can be measured only by the returns generated on assets employed.

All have merit, and the weight given to each of the three ratios is related to the capital structure of a company and to the purpose of the valuation, bearing in mind that ratio analyses should be used primarily to indicate the level of risk of an investment and the consequent capitalization rate.

Although the return on owner's equity is straightforward, the return on investment ratios and the return on assets ratios warrant an explanation. The theory applied to *return on investment* is that long-term debt represents as valid an investment as common shares. Therefore, by definition, the term *investment* as used in these ratios represents the sum of the average outstanding balances of long-term debt plus the average stockholder investment.

Furthermore, since debt is included in the ratio's denominator, interest expense must be added back to net income to arrive at the numerator. Arguments persist about the merits of adding back tax-affected interest expense or total interest. The answer can only be a matter of personal choice. The final point to clarify is that pragmatically, only interest on long-term debt should be used. Theoretically, short-term interest should be included; however, since it is virtually impossible to obtain an average interest expense on short-term debt, most calculations ignore the minor distortion caused by excluding it.

The *return on assets ratio*, sometimes referred to as the asset utilization ratio or assets employed ratio, uses average total assets as a denominator, on the theory that assets must be employed during the entire period to generate the income for the period. In addition, the same tax-affect versus non-tax-affected interest adjustments for the numerator applies here as in the return on investment calculation.

Asset Utilization Ratios

Asset utilization ratios measure the speed at which a company turns assets into sales, and hence cash returns. As with other financial ratios, to be meaningful, the trends in asset utilization ratios over several periods should be used. The speed with which inventory turns over this year may be a relevant measure for management to use in evaluating purchasing and production personnel, but it has little meaning in the broader context of analyzing the health of a business. Conversely, a trend might show that inventory turnover is slowing measurably, indicating obsolescence, slowing sales, or errors in recording transactions. These are all vital facts for determining risk. Four major asset utilization ratios are commonly used in the business valuation field:

- Receivables turnover
- Inventory turnover
- Fixed asset turnover
- Total assets turnover

Receivables turnover

Receivables turnover measures the number of times in a year that receivable balances are collected. Because it deals with the total receivables balance, distortions caused by individual customer accounts are ignored, except to the extent that they materially influence the total. The ratio may also be expressed as days-sales-in-receivables, meaning the number of days, on average, it takes to collect receivables.

The formula for calculated receivables turnover is:

$$\text{Turnover} = \frac{\text{Annual sales}}{\text{Average receivables}}$$

Since this ratio measures only credit sales, accounts of companies whose cash sales represent a significant part of the total should be adjusted to reflect only credit sales. A small percentage of cash sales won't make any difference in the average, however, and can be ignored. To get a true reflection of annual collection activity, average receivables should be used as the denominator. Ideally, an average of the sum of monthly averages gives the most reliable results, but available data usually limits the average to balances at the beginning and end of the period.

The MAPAX receivables turnover ratios for the three years are:

	Year 1-2	Year 1-1	Year 1
Receivables turnover	7.8 times	8.1 times	8.0 times
Receivables days sales	45.6 days	45.6 days	45.6 days

In this case the difference between years is so negligible as to be meaningless. A few conclusions that might be drawn from this are the following:

- MAPAX management does a terrific job of monitoring collections.
- The stability of the industry permits very little creative pricing.
- A significant portion of sales are made with advance payments or down payments and do not show up in receivables balances.

Regardless of the reason, historical receivables collections do not detract from the value of the company.

Inventory Turnover

Inventory turnover is normally calculated by dividing the annual cost of sales by the average inventory at the beginning and end of the period. Virtually the same conclusions that are drawn from receivables turnover can be drawn from this ratio. That is, the faster the turns, the more efficient the company and the less risk. Also, as with receivables, inventory turnover can be expressed as the number of times inventory turns during the year or the number of days sales that reside in inventory at the end of the year.

MAPAX inventory ratios came out to be:

	Year 1-2	Year 1-1	Year 1
Inventory turnover	2.8 times	2.5 times	2.2 times
Inventory days sales	156.3 days	175.9 days	200.0 days

The MAPAX inventory picture is quite different from that shown by receivables ratios. Inventory turns are definitely slipping, and days sales are correspondingly increasing. This could mean (1) that management has lost control of the purchasing function, (2) that production schedules are slipping, or (3) that for some unexplained reason, inventory obsolescence is increasing. With these results, an investor should certainly investigate further to learn the cause. If satisfactory answers aren't forthcoming, the risk premium probably should be significantly increased.

Asset Turnover

Asset turnover ratios measure the efficiency with which a company uses its assets to generate sales: the higher the turnover, the more efficient the company. Although both fixed assets and total assets are used in separate ratios, fixed asset turnover isn't relevant for companies without a significant hard-asset base. MAPAX, on the other hand, has a fairly large hard-asset base, and therefore both ratios should be calculated.

	Year 1-2	Year 1-1	Year 1
Fixed asset turnover	1.9 times	1.7 times	1.6 times
Total asset turnover	1.0 times	1.0 times	1.0 times

The slight deterioration in the fixed asset turnover is probably caused by increased accumulated depreciation and therefore can be ignored in judging risk. Also, a constant total asset turnover indicates that very little change occurs from year to year in assets other than those needed to directly support sales, such as receivables and inventory.

Risk Analysis

As stated previously, the whole purpose of ratio analysis is to use a numerical quantification of risk to determine the health of a company. In the parlance of business valuations, such a numerical quantification is referred to as *risk analysis*. The objective of risk analysis is to learn the uncertainty of the income flows to a company's various capital suppliers, one of whom, presumably, is a potential investor.

There are two broad classes of capital suppliers:

1. Those who loan the company money and receive a fixed return in the form of interest. Preferred shareholders are generally considered in this class when preferred dividend yields are stated and cumulative.
2. Those who contribute equity capital in return for the opportunity to receive dividends and investment appreciation gains through participation in the growth of the company

The higher the risk to one of these classes, the higher the cost of capital for that class.

Furthermore, as described in Chapter 3, the theoretical capital asset pricing model uses a factor called beta to measure systematic risk, which is risk measured by comparable market-determined share values. Although closely held companies do not have the luxury of measuring their stock values against the marketplace, making this source of beta calculations unavailable, several studies have shown a close correlation between beta systematic risk and risk measures that can be calculated directly from a company's financial statements. However, in the vast majority of closely held companies, analyses of nonsystematic risk that reflect the characteristics of a specific company produce more meaningful results than market-related beta calculations.

Two categories of nonsystematic risk quantify the uncertainty of income flows to various capital suppliers: *business risk* and *financial risk*. Ascertaining both types of risk involves the application to a company's financial statements of formulas that will quantify the uncertainty of income flows. The theory is that the greater the uncertainty of the company's earnings, the greater the uncertainty that capital suppliers will earn expected returns on their investments. Since this approach relies exclusively on a company's financial statements, only businesses that prepare such statements can use it.

Business Risk

Business risk assumes that the uncertainty of income is related to two factors: (1) changes in volume, pricing, and the product mix; and (2) the amount of relatively fixed operating costs.

Except for inflation price jumps and payroll increases, nearly all costs in small businesses are fixed. For companies with very few employees, direct labor hours may also be independent of volume.

The easiest way to quantify business risk is by using a very simple formula:

$$\text{Business risk} = \frac{\text{Standard deviation of operating income}}{\text{Mean of operating income}}$$

Standard deviation measures the dispersion of outcomes around an expected value, which, by definition, is the mean of a normal distribution. Statistics tells us that 68.26 percent of any series of outcomes should be within one standard deviation of the expected value, known as the *mean*. As a stand-alone measure, the *coefficient of variation of earnings* represented by the business risk formula is meaningless. The result must be measured against the distribution of earnings from other investments to determine whether the value is higher or lower.

Using hypothetical Cases 1 and 2 in Figure 6-2 (see page 98), this formula translates into, respectively,

$$\text{Case \#1: Business risk} = \frac{\$118,000}{\$144,000} = 0.165$$

$$\text{Case \#2: Business risk} = \frac{\$61,458}{\$298,000} = 0.042$$

Using standard deviations, the greater the coefficient of variance of earnings, the greater the risk to investors of not receiving expected returns. Therefore, Case 1, with a business risk of 0.165, carries nearly four times the risk of Case 2, at 0.042.

This method is particularly applicable to measuring business risk caused by sales fluctuations. Since many established small companies have little control over their sales volume and simply follow national economic and industry cycles, this formula may be the more valuable of the two measures.

A second method for arriving at business risk reflects both sales fluctuations and the impact of fixed operating costs on earnings. The formula for calculating this operating leverage is expressed as:

$$\text{Operating leverage} = \frac{\text{Percent change in operating income}}{\text{Percent change in sales}}$$

Dropping in the figures arrived at from the distributions in Figure 6-2, we get:

Case 1:

$$\text{Operating leverage} = \frac{92.85\%}{38.55\%} = 2.41 \ (2.4 \text{ rounded})$$

Case 2:

$$\text{Operating leverage} = \frac{10.32\%}{8.86\%} = 1.16 \ (1.2 \text{ rounded})$$

To interpret these relationships, in Case 1, a 1.0 percent change in sales results in a 2.4 percent change in operating income, and in Case 2, a 1.0 percent change in sales yields a 1.2 percent change in operating income. This clearly indicates that the operating leverage of XYZ Company, Inc. in Case 1 creates a greater business risk than that of ABC Company, Inc. in Case 2.

FIGURE 6-2: Examples of Business Risk Calculations

CASE 1
XYZ COMPANY, INC.

Year	Sales ($000)	Operating Income ($000)	Interest ($000)	Net Income ($000)
A	2,000	340	110	143
B	1,500	171	104	41
C	1,800	258	99	98
D	1,800	248	94	95
E	1,170	37	90	(33)
F	1,217	42	90	(30)
G	1,229	35	95	(37)
H	1,229	24	100	(47)

CASE 2
ABC COMPANY, INC.

Year	Sales ($000)	Operating Income ($000)	Interest ($000)	Net Income ($000)
A	2,000	340	110	143
B	1,500	177	104	45
C	1,800	270	99	106
D	1,800	267	94	107
E	2,100	360	90	168
F	2,016	330	90	148
G	1,814	262	95	104
H	2,177	375	100	171

Financial Risk

In addition to business risk, financial risk plays a role in determining the premium or discount necessary to attract investors. Financial risk calculations take the business risk concept one step further, reflecting the impact of a company's financing costs (i.e., interest expense) on common stockholders and hence potential investors. One way to calculate financial risk is through the use of the various debt utilization and liquidity ratios described earlier in this chapter. A second approach measures risk by calculating the degree of financial leverage. This is expressed by the formula:

$$\text{Degree of financial leverage} = \frac{\text{Percent change in operating income}}{\text{Percent change in net income}}$$

Using the distributions from Figure 6-2, we get:

Case 1:

$$\text{Degree of financial leverage} = \frac{92.85\%}{132.80\%} = 0.70$$

Case 2:

$$\text{Degree of financial leverage} = \frac{10.32\%}{19.70\%} = 0.52$$

On a comparison basis, in Case 2, a 1 percent change in net income results in approximately a 0.5 percent change in operating income, whereas in Case 1, a 1 percent variation yields a 0.7 percent change in operating income. Financing leverage therefore has less effect on shareholders in Case 2 than in Case 1.

Z Score

As previously stated, risk analysis tends to be more beneficial in preventing investors from picking losers than in providing information for picking winning investments. One well-known method for predicting when a company might be heading for bankruptcy was first introduced by Edward I. Altman in his article "Financial Ratios, Discriminant Analysis, and the Prediction of Corporate Bankruptcy," *Journal of Finance*, September 1968. Professor Altman, an authority on corporate distress predictive models, devised a formula that, when tested against a population of publicly held companies, was 95 percent accurate in predicting failure one year in advance and 72 percent accurate in predicting failure two years in advance.

The formula is expressed as:

$$Z = 1.2(X1) + 1.4(X2) + 3.3(X3) + 6(X4) + 1(X5)$$

Where:
X1 = working capital/total assets
X2 = retained earnings/total assets
X3 = income before interest and taxes/total assets
X4 = market value of equity/total liabilities
X5 = sales/total assets
Z = overall index

According to the model, if the resulting Z score is above 2.99, the company is considered to be healthy. Z scores below 1.81 indicate an unhealthy condition with a high probability of failure. Companies with Z scores between these two extremes are considered in the gray area and worthy of further analysis.

Subsequently, Professor Altman refined this formula and expanded it to seven categories in an effort to achieve greater accuracy. The new seven-step formula comprises:

1. A measurement of cumulative profitability, expressed as retained earnings/total assets
2. A measure of earnings stability during the last ten years, expressed as standard deviation of operating income/total assets
3. A measure of productivity of operating assets, expressed as income before interest and taxes/total assets
4. A measure of interest coverage and liquidity, expressed as income before interest and taxes/interest
5. The liquidity ratio, current assets/current liabilities
6. Another leverage ratio, expressed as market value of common stock/book value of equity
7. Total assets, to represent the size of the company

If you are interested in further information about the detailed weighting factors in this expanded model contact Zeta Services, Inc. (*www.zetascore.com*).

Qualitative Valuation Measures

Along with quantitative analytical methods that use data directly from a company's financial statements, a series of qualitative ratios and data can help bring performance analyses to the next level. The information required to thoroughly understand a company's internal operations and hence management proficiency is normally available only from internally prepared reports and records. When valuing closely held companies for purposes of mergers, business acquisitions, or the sale of entire businesses or minority interests, such data should be gathered during the due diligence stage.

Much of the qualitative information can be translated into numerical analyses; however, in many companies, non-numeric assessments prove just as valuable. The overall ability of management to control events, insistence upon timely and accurate reporting, and reputation with customers and suppliers are a few examples of unquantifiable information.

But here we are concerned solely with data that lends itself to numerical analysis. Such data may consist of several or all of the following:

A. Measures of cash management effectiveness
- Accounts receivable aging—a listing of customer accounts outstanding by due date (usually broken into thirty-day increments)
- Accounts payable aging—a listing of supplier accounts outstanding by due date (usually broken into thirty-day increments)
- Payables turnover—annual sales/average accounts payable
- Ratio of receivables to payables—average receivables/average accounts payable

B. Measures of production efficiency and the utilization of labor
- Sales per employee—annual sales/average number of employees
- Employee turnover
- Ratio of employee days absent to total days available for work
- Ratio of lost labor hours due to accidents to total labor hours available for work
- Ratio of rework labor hours to total labor hours
- Ratio of scrap cost to total material purchases
- Sales per square foot of space—annual sales/total square feet of production and administrative space
- Delivery promises kept

C. Measures of selling and customer service effectiveness
- Unusual allowances
- Ratio of customer complaints to sales
- Customer returns compared to unit shipments

Measures of Cash Management Effectiveness

Average accounts receivable and accounts payable balances taken from financial statements provide an overall indication of how effectively a company manages its cash. But there can be wide variations between months or in the collection practices for different classes of customers. There can also be variations in payment schedules to different classes of suppliers.

Quarterly aged listings of receivables and payables give an excellent picture of a company's uniformity in collection procedures or erratic behavior in paying suppliers. A lengthening of the age of receivables or a shortening in the age of payables indicates that management is losing control of cash.

Quick tests can also be performed with ratio analyses, although this seldom takes the place of a close scrutiny of individual accounts aging. The accounts payable turnover ratio can also be helpful in constructing a cash flow forecast, as described in Chapter 7. Comparisons of the monthly, quarterly, or annual ratio of accounts receivable to accounts payable is an excellent test to determine gross slippage in either collections or payment schedules.

Measures of Production Efficiency and the Utilization of Labor

These measures are useful primarily in manufacturing companies, to get a handle on the effectiveness of management control over the production process and related personnel. Most industry trade associations maintain statistics on average sales per employee, personnel turnover, lost time due to accidents, and rework and scrap ratios. Comparing a company's performance over a three-year period to industry norms gives a good indication of whether managers can control the production process or whether labor efficiency and productivity as well as material usage are out of control.

Delivery-promises-kept statistics can yield an especially provocative picture of customer satisfaction. If the lateness of deliveries increases, chances are good that customers have become dissatisfied, substantially increasing investment risk.

Measures of Selling and Customer Service Effectiveness

In addition to deteriorating promises-kept statistics, unusual allowances granted customers in the form of price discounts, or for warranty service, and product returns, usually mean that either product quality has slipped or competitive pressures are becoming more intense. In either case, questions should be raised about the future prospects of the company. Not infrequently, unusual allowances indicate that the company is not price-competitive and must rely on discounts and allowances to attract customers. Increases in customer complaints and returned goods also indicate something amiss in either the selling process or customer service, pointing to the need for further analysis.

CHAPTER

7

A Cash Flow Forecasting Model

Chapters 2 and 3 emphasized the fundamental role of cash flow forecasting in the business valuation process. Without a detailed cash flow forecast founded on economically sound assumptions, it is virtually impossible to arrive at a valuation acceptable to business buyers, sellers, or investors. Even IRS valuation methods call for abbreviated forecasts of future benefits.

This chapter lays out the steps involved in constructing a detailed cash flow forecast, fully integrated with a company's historical and pro forma financial statements. Such integration is essential to give forecasts the weight of authority. Stand-alone projections whose cash receipt and expenditure elements do not flow directly from pro forma financial statements are usually regarded as pure guesses, seldom holding up under close scrutiny by investors, the IRS, or the courts.

The diversity of industries, company forms, ownership configurations, capital structures, and market conditions makes any general set of forecasting rules and formats subject to modification. However, experience has shown that the format and procedures described in this chapter can be used effectively as the foundation for all valuations based on forecasts of future benefit streams, either cash flow or earnings.

The ten-step forecasting process can be summarized as follows:

1. Develop and evaluate a series of economic and business assumptions.
2. Prepare a sales forecast based on these assumptions.
3. Establish cost/sales/asset functional relationships from historical accounting records.
4. Forecast personnel requirements.
5. Set up historical balance sheet ratios for payables, receivables, and accrued expenses.
6. Project fixed asset needs.
7. Develop an R&D budget and new product introduction forecast.
8. Prepare pro forma balance sheets and statements of income.
9. Project new financing requirements.
10. Prepare a cash flow forecast.

The following sections make use of the fictitious company MAPAX Manufacturing Corp. (introduced in Chapter 6) to demonstrate types of economic assumptions and forecasting techniques that are applicable to nearly any company, regardless of industry or size. As explained in Chapter 6, the complex cost structures of manufacturing companies are ideally suited to demonstrate the complete line of analytic techniques. As the forecasting process unfolds, however, it will become clear that the same procedures apply to companies in distribution, retail, or service industries. Moreover, later chapters deal with variations specifically applicable to special and somewhat unusual circumstances.

To briefly review the background of MAPAX, the company manufactures two product lines, stoves and furnaces, both sold to the residential and commercial markets. It also stocks a variety of resale accessories, some of which must be slightly modified to meet customer specifications. The stove and furnace business is a stable but growing industry. Although susceptible to both economic and industry cycles, sales volume has seldom fluctuated more than 5 percent in either direction. New product development is not expected to be a major factor in the industry or at MAPAX during the forecast period.

Economic and Business Assumptions

As discussed in Chapter 3, the direction of economic and business cycles and the position on them are crucial to setting the forecast period. Companies will inevitably forecast stronger earnings and cash flows if they can look forward to a lengthy upward trend in both their industry cycle and the much broader national cycle; they could not if one or both cycles are trending downward. When the economic cycle trends in one direction and the business cycle in another, either for the entire forecast period or crossing over midway through it, forecasting performance is not as straightforward. Further analysis will then be required to determine specific indicators and conditions that may affect a company's earning power.

In the case of MAPAX, the following assumptions have been made:

1. The national economy as expressed by GNP will experience very slow growth during the balance of this decade. Year 9 will be the beginning of the next boom period. European and Japanese GNP growth will lag behind the slow U.S. recovery by two years. The stock market will anticipate the next cycle and, in turn, draw new foreign capital to U.S. markets. The economic recovery will be spurred by (1) the success of the new Independence Party in winning the presidency and control of Congress in Year 5, and (2) the new government's determination to immediately implement strong deficit-cutting policies. In anticipation of the next boom cycle, consumer confidence will begin building in Year 7.

2. The current slow-growth period will hold inflation in the range of 2 to 5 percent, with rates at the higher end beginning in Year 7.

3. With inflation held in check, interest rates will remain stable. The prime rate will hover in the 6 to 7.5 percent range.

4. New commercial construction will hold relatively steady during the decade, spurting in Year 5 and again in Year 9.

5. The commercial furnace industry, which experiences a five-to-seven-year business cycle, will be at its trough from Year 2 through Year 4 and will begin a slow upward climb in Year 5.

6. The residential and commercial stove industry experiences a three-year cycle. It is already on the upward curve and will reach its peak in Year 4–Year 5, after which it will decline for three years.

7. Unemployment in the stove and furnace industry will remain at about 7 percent throughout the decade, creating an adequate supply of technically qualified personnel.

8. Although foreign competition will accelerate in steel and cast iron materials and components, the market will not be flooded.

With these assumptions in place, the first steps can be taken to assemble a forecast. Two extremely critical rules must be highlighted before proceeding, however. First, accurate cash flow forecasts depend upon realistic pro forma balance sheet and income statement forecasts. For a cash flow projection to be meaningful and acceptable to third parties, it must interact 100 percent with related financial statements. If it becomes necessary to adjust financial statements that were initially prepared on a cash basis, a clear audit trail must be left to ensure that third parties can track the adjustments through the various steps to accrual payments.

Second, pro forma financial statements must be based on functional cost/sales/asset relationships. Since these relationships are different for each company, no standard formulas can be created. However, the *principles* of interacting costs at different sales volumes are uniform. To arrive at reasonable results, you'll have to play various "what-if" games, experimenting with different data in the functional relationships. This trial and error method is extremely time-consuming if done manually. A spreadsheet program makes it a snap, however. All functional relationships in the MAPAX forecast and the equations used to express them were developed by the author. You may need to modify them for use in your business.

Sales Forecast

The preparation of a sales forecast is the starting point in any financial forecast. More often than not, preparers are tempted to take a short-cut and extrapolate future sales by applying an incremental growth rate to current sales. This approach can be very misleading, however, and much better results will be obtained by building sales trends over the forecast period based on the economic and business assumptions previously discussed.

In the case of MAPAX, stoves and furnaces have conflicting business cycles. To recognize this condition and to reflect a projected improvement in the national economy into the next decade, the decision was made to use an eight-year forecast period—Year 1 through Year 9.

The first step was to forecast unit sales for each of the three product lines, stoves, furnaces, and accessories. The sales trends shown in Figure 7-1 follow the assumptions about industry growth and economic cycles for stoves and furnaces. Accessories relate primarily to furnaces and echo that growth trend.

Since all product lines are in stable, mature markets, major new competitors are not likely to enter or introduce radically new products that would disrupt MAPAX market shares. Therefore, the unit forecast can reasonably be assumed to reflect the general industry and national cycles. Accordingly, the growth rates used in figure 7-1 were:

Stoves: 5 percent growth for Year 2, Year 3, and Year 4
Level over the peak of Year 4 to Year 5
3 percent decrease for Year 6, Year 7, and Year 8
Strong 5 percent growth in Year 9, reflecting the beginning of the next boom cycle.

Furnaces: 1 percent growth through Year 4
3 percent growth from Year 5 through Year 9, reflecting the acceleration of the upward trend of a seven-year cycle

Accessories: The same growth rates as furnaces.

FIGURE 7-1:

MAPAX MANUFACTURING CORP.
SALES BY PRODUCT LINE

| | Actual | | | | ----Forecasted---- | | | | |
	Year 1	Year 2	Year 3	Year 4	Year 5	Year 6	Year 7	Year 8	Year 9
Units:									
Stoves	5000	5250	5512	5788	5788	5614	5446	5283	5547
Furnaces	1000	1010	1020	1030	1061	1093	1126	1160	1194
Accessories	7000	7350	7717	8097	8108	8102	8096	8110	8905
Unit price:									
Stoves	$920	$929	$938	$948	$957	$967	$1,015	$1,066	$1,119
Furnaces	$3,500	$3,535	$3,570	$3,606	$3,642	$3,679	$3,862	$4,056	$4,258
Accessories	$450	$455	$459	$464	$468	$473	$497	$521	$548
Dollars:									
Stoves	$4,600,000	$4,878,300	$5,173,437	$5,486,430	$5,541,294	$5,428,806	$5,529,239	$5,631,530	$6,208.762
Furnaces	3,500,000	3,570,350	3,642,114	3,715,321	3,865,048	4,020,809	4,348,505	4,702,909	5,086,196
Accessories	3,150,000	3,340,575	3,542,680	3,757,012	3,794,582	3,832,528	4,024,152	4,225,362	4,880.293
Total sales	$11,250,000	$11,789,225	$12,358,231	$12,958,763	$13,200,924	$13,282,143	$13,902,899	$14,559,800	$16,175,250

The next step involved projecting changes in unit pricing. Beginning with the current product line price structure, it was reasoned that because of the absence of new competition and the unlikelihood of new products being introduced, current pricing should hold through the entire cycle. Accordingly, unit price increases for all three product lines were conservatively estimated on the lower end of the inflation spectrum. Annual price increases of 1 percent were included through Year 6, and then prices were increased 5 percent for Years 7, 8, and 9 to reflect an expected strong economic recovery.

The final step was to multiply unit sales by unit prices for each year and lay out the totals in a product-line sales forecast. Structuring the forecast with this much detail makes playing what-if games very easy. Just substitute different product line growth rates and unit prices until the end result makes sound business sense. As will be seen in subsequent forecast segments, if functional relationships are clearly defined and forecast formulas set up to match these relationships, any number of what-if scenarios can be tested with virtually no effort and practically instantaneously.

Purchased Materials Forecast

Once a reasonable sales forecast has been developed, it's possible to construct a purchased materials forecast. Retail companies may find it helpful to build in monthly or seasonable time lags between sales and purchases. When forecasting in annual increments, however, short-term lag times become irrelevant. For this reason, most retailers should forecast purchases based on an historical relationship to sales and at their standard markup.

Manufacturing companies don't have that luxury. They usually find it necessary to stock some level of raw materials or components inventory to meet production schedules, to take advantage of volume discounts, or to ensure supplies of scarce parts or materials. Most manufacturing companies must also deal with production cycles—that is, the number of days, weeks, or months that it takes to manufacture the product from beginning to end. Such is the case with MAPAX, which experiences a long lead time to get the materials into the plant and six-to-nine-month production cycles.

To deal with these time lags, the MAPAX purchasing forecast in Figure 7-2 assumes that materials will be purchased in one year and be converted to sales the following year. In other words, it uses a one-year lag time. Furthermore, by using historical data, it was determined that on average, purchased materials for stoves and furnaces accounted for 40 percent of the sales dollar and purchased accessories 80 percent.

Using these assumptions, annual material purchases for stoves and furnaces were forecasted one year in advance at 40 percent of the following year's sales. Accessories were also forecasted one year in advance, but at 80 percent of the following year's sales. For instance, purchases of stove materials in Year 2 totaled approximately $2.1 million, which is about 40 percent of Year 3 stove sales of $5.2 million.

FIGURE 7-2

MAPAX MANUFACTURING CORP.
PURCHASED MATERIALS (in dollars)

| | Actual | | | | ----Forecasted---- | | | | |
	Year 1	Year 2	Year 3	Year 4	Year 5	Year 6	Year 7	Year 8	Year 9
Stoves	2,009,860	2,131,456	2,260,409	2,260,409	2,106,377	2,145,345	2,185,034	2,607,680	2,738,064
Furnaces	1,442,421	1,471,414	1,500,989	1,592,400	1,656,573	1,791,584	1,937,598	2,095,513	2,200,288
Subtotal	3,452,281	3,602,870	3,761,399	3,852,809	3,762,950	3,936,929	4,122,632	4,703,193	4,938,352
Accessories	2,752,634	2,919,168	3,095,778	3,095,778	2,974,042	3,122,744	3,278,881	4,099,446	4,304,418
Total purchases	6,204,915	6,522,038	6,857,177	6,948,587	6,736,992	7,059,673	7,401,513	8,802,639	9,242,771

It was further assumed that because of weak competition among suppliers, purchase prices would not radically change and that foreign competition, though increasing, would not make a major dent in pricing until after the turn of the century. Therefore, the same inflation rate assigned to finished-product selling prices was used for material purchases.

Since most of the materials and components will be put into production as soon as possible after arrival, the purchased-materials forecast leads directly to a forecast of direct labor.

Direct Labor Forecast

Although nonmanufacturing companies do not have production direct labor, distribution and retail companies may employ storekeepers, delivery-truck drivers, maintenance personnel, or custodians. To the extent that (1) these employees are paid by the hour, (2) their work efforts are directly tied to the level of activity, and (3) they can be hired and fired as volume shifts, the same relationships used in manufacturing forecasts will probably hold.

As can be seen in the direct labor forecast in Figure 7-3, four elements are necessary to begin the calculations:

1. Current number of direct labor employees
2. Approximate number of hours each employee works during a year. This is typically 1,944 hours after deducting holidays, vacations, and weekends.
3. Average hourly wage rate. If there are wide variations in wage rates between classes of employees, it might be better to segregate both numbers of employees and wage rates by class.
4. Average annual gross payroll

Various approaches can then be used to forecast the out years. You can take the ratio of the number of direct labor employees to sales dollars; you can relate the number of hourly employees to total employees; or, as in the case of MAPAX, you can relate total payroll dollars to purchases and work backwards.

FIGURE 7-3

MAPAX MANUFACTURING CORP.
DIRECT LABOR

	Actual				----Forecasted----				
	Year 1	Year 2	Year 3	Year 4	Year 5	Year 6	Year 7	Year 8	Year 9
Number of employees	51	52	53	53	53	53	53	58	60
Hours worked	1,944	1,944	1,944	1,944	1,944	1,944	1,944	1,944	1,944
Wage rate	$9,500	$9,785	$10,079	$10,381	$10,692	$11,013	$11,343	$11,684	$12,034
Payroll	$941,868	$989,146	$1,038,413	$1,069,566	$1,101,653	$1,134,702	$1,168,743	$1,317,372	$1,403,683
% of purchases	15.2%	15.2%	15.1%	15.4%	16.4%	16.1%	15.8%	15.0%	15.2%

The first step for MAPAX was to determine a constant ratio of payroll to purchases. The second step was to forecast annual wage rate increases of 3 percent, consistent with inflation projections. The third step was merely to divide the payroll dollars by the product of average wage rate times hours worked, yielding the number of employees required.

Since this resulted in minor fluctuations in the size of the work force that wouldn't be feasible in practice, it was assumed that once an approximate employment level was reached, which was judged to be fifty-three people, that level would be maintained through Year 7, with overtime hours filling any gaps to meet increased production schedules.

Cost/Sales/Asset Functional Relationships

As can be seen from the purchased-materials and direct-labor forecasts, functional relationships are the keys to forecasting. The amount and type of materials purchased is a direct function of the sales forecast. The timing of those purchases is a direct function of the purchasing lead time and the manufacturing lead time. Material price increases are a function of changes in the prices of finished products.

Similar functional relationships hold for direct labor. The number of direct labor employees is a function of the amount of work to be performed, which is a function of materials in inventory, which is a function of the sales forecast.

Further into the forecast we'll see that nearly all costs and set balances relate functionally to other costs, sales, or assets. For example, the number of shop supervisors is a function of the number of direct labor employees; however, it is more a *step* relationship than a direct one-to-one correlation.

Depreciation is a function of fixed asset costs and useful life. Accounts payable relates to inventory. Accounts receivable is a direct function of sales dollars. Financing requirements relate to incremental sales volume, changes in fixed asset capacity, and profit margins, which, in turn, relate to pricing decisions.

The final forecast schedule, the statement of cash flow, draws on all these functional relationships to determine cash inflows and outflows, which yield the net cash generated each year.

The biggest mistake normally made when preparing pro forma financial statements, especially cash flow forecasts, is to underestimate the direct impact of various costs and asset balances on each other. Investors and owners of small businesses generally have an easier time establishing reasonably accurate business valuations than their counterparts in large corporations, mainly because functional cost relationships can be determined more directly than in larger firms.

The MAPAX gross profit schedule laid out in Figure 7-4 demonstrates the functional relationships between material and labor cost of sales and sales dollars.

FIGURE 7-4

MAPAX MANUFACTURING CORP.
STATEMENT OF GROSS PROFIT (in dollars)

| | Actual | | | ----Forecasted---- | | | | | |
	Year 1	Year 2	Year 3	Year 4	Year 5	Year 6	Year 7	Year 8	Year 9
Sales	11,250,000	11,789,225	12,358,231	12,958,763	13,200,924	13,282,143	13,901,899	14,559,800	16,175,250
Cost of sales:									
Material	5,760,000	6,051,920	6,360,364	6,686,310	6,798,203	6,845,868	7,170,421	7,514,065	8,422,217
Labor	875,520	919,892	966,775	1,016,319	1,033,327	1,040,572	1,089,904	1,142,138	1,280,177
Overhead	747,347	777,376	808,535	900,391	927,403	991,625	1,021,373	1,136,441	1,267,250
Total standard cost of sales	7,382,867	7,749,188	8,135,674	8,603,020	8,758,932	8,878,065	9,281,699	9,792,644	10,969,645
Gross profit	3,867,133	4,040,037	4,222,556	4,355,743	4,441,992	4,404,078	4,620,200	4,767,156	5,205,606
% of sales	34.4%	34.3%	34.2%	33.6%	33.6%	33.2%	33.2%	32.7%	32.2%

To construct the cost of sales forecast, the actual Year 1 ratio of material cost of sales to sales for both stoves and furnaces was calculated to be 40 percent, with the ratio for accessories 80 percent. This yielded a combined material cost of sales of approximately 51 percent of sales. The material cost of sales was then forecasted for each product line, namely, stoves, furnaces, and accessories, for each year. The result was a combined ratio approximating the 51 percent achieved in Year 1.

The next step involved determining the ratio between labor cost of sales and material cost of sales that was actually achieved in Year 1. This turned out to be about 15.2 percent. Labor cost of sales could then be forecasted using this approximate ratio for each year. The percentage varied slightly in those years in which accessory sales were proportionately higher than normal.

The resulting gross profit as a percentage of sales held relatively constant for all years at 32.2 to 34.4 percent. It would have been more accurate to prepare a cost of sales forecast by product line, but for MAPAX's purposes the combined statements was close enough.

It should be noted that many companies include manufacturing overhead as a cost of sales component to reflect the true cost of producing the products. Certainly, this is more accurate and results in financial statements that more clearly reflect true gross profit margins. For cash flow forecasting, however, the allocation of overhead to product costs achieves nothing. Here we are interested in expenditures, not accurate product cost accounting. Whether overhead costs are written off in the year incurred or reside in year-end inventory is of no consequence for cash flow purposes.

Inventory Forecast

Once the cost of sales forecast has been completed, an inventory forecast can be constructed. This key schedule integrates expenditures for materials and labor (and overhead, if included in cost of sales) with accounting-oriented financial statements. The model presented in Figure 7-5 can be used for any type of business that carries inventory, not just manufacturing companies. Of course, for nonmanufacturing businesses, labor would probably be written off as incurred and not passed through an inventory account.

FIGURE 7-5

MAPAX MANUFACTURING CORP.
INVENTORY FORECAST (in dollars)

| | Actual | ----Forecasted---- | | | | | | | |
	Year 1	Year 2	Year 3	Year 4	Year 5	Year 6	Year 7	Year 8	Year 9
Beginning inventory:									
Material	2,093,750	2,538,665	3,008,783	3,505,595	3,767,872	3,706,662	3,920,466	4,151,557	5,440,131
Labor	1,031,250	1,097,598	1,166,852	1,238,490	1,291,737	1,360,062	1,454,192	1,533,031	1,708,266
TOTAL	3,125,000	3,636,263	4,175,635	4,744,085	5,059,609	5,066,724	5,374,658	5,684,589	7,148,397
Additions:									
Material	6,204,915	6,522,038	6,857,177	6,948,587	6,736,992	7,059,673	7,401,513	8,802,639	9,242,771
Labor	941,868	989,146	1,038,413	1,069,566	1,101,653	1,134,702	1,168,743	1,317,372	1,403,683
TOTAL	7,146,783	7,511,184	7,895,590	8,018,152	7,838,644	8,194,375	8,570,256	10,120,011	10,646,453
Cost of sales:									
Material	5,760,000	6,051,920	6,360,364	6,686,310	6,798,203	6,845,868	7,170,4212	7,514,065	8,422,217
Labor	875,520	919,892	966,775	1,016,319	1,033,327	1,040572	1,089,904	1,142,138	1,280,177
TOTAL	6,635,520	6,971,812	7,327,140	7,702,629	7,831,529	7,886,440	8,260,325	8,656,203	9,702,394
Ending inventory:									
Material	2,538,665	3,008,783	3,505,595	3,767,872	3,706,662	3,920,466	4,151,557	5,440,131	6,260,684
Labor	1,097,598	1,166,852	1,238,490	1,291,737	1,360,062	1,454,192	1,533,031	1,708,266	1,831,771
TOTAL	3,636,263	4,175,635	4,744,085	5,059,609	5,066,724	5,374,658	5,684,589	7,148,397	8,092,456

It might be helpful to briefly review the flow of costs through inventory. From an accounting perspective, the cost of all purchased material, parts, and components used in the finished product, along with the cost of labor used to make the product, should be charged to inventory accounts as incurred. The entry for purchases is a charge to inventory and a credit to accounts payable.

A similar entry is made for direct labor. Gross payroll is charged to inventory. Payroll checks written are credited to the bank account, and withheld amounts are credited to accrued expenses.

If products that use these materials and labor are not sold, the costs remain in inventory. When products are sold, either the actual material and labor costs associated with sold products or estimated amounts are deducted from inventory and charged to cost of sales.

Referring to Figure 7-5, it can be seen that forecasted material purchases from Figure 7-2 and direct labor payroll from Figure 7-3 are included as additions to inventory. Material cost of sales and labor cost of sales from Figure 7-4 are shown as deductions from inventory. The beginning inventory plus additions minus deductions yields an ending inventory which is then carried to the balance sheet forecast in Figure 7-9 (see page 121). The additions or inputs to inventory represent cash expenditures which are carried forward to the statement of cash flow in Figure 7-10 (see page 124).

Most of the errors made in cash flow forecasting result from mistaking the identity of material purchases and labor payrolls. It's important to reiterate the cost of sales does *not* represent cash outflows; expenditures are made only for inputs to inventory. The only exception to this rule occurs in retail businesses with very high inventory turnover, say less than one month. In this case, inventory accounts would not be used; instead, all monthly purchases would be charged directly to cost of sales for that month. These businesses do not include inventory accounts in their year-end balance sheets. If inventory accounts are used in the accounting records, regardless of the number of annual inventory turns, the cost of purchases should be recorded as inputs to inventory.

Operating Expenses Forecast

The forecast of operating expenses comprises several subforecasts such as personnel forecasts, fringe benefit forecasts, variable expense forecasts, and occupancy forecasts. The more detailed the analysis, the more accurate the forecast will be; therefore, larger companies or those with a more complex array of expenses should compile each of these forecasts separately. Smaller companies can get by with combining two or more as in the MAPAX forecasts in Figures 7-6 and 7-7 (see pages 115 and 117).

After the major expense elements have been forecasted separately for larger companies and combined for smaller ones, operating expenses should be departmentalized. Once again, larger companies may record expenses in many departments, while small businesses usually get by with three or possibly four groupings: manufacturing overhead expenses, selling expenses, administrative expenses, and R&D expenses. Since MAPAX does not incur significant new product development costs, unidentified R&D expenditures are scattered throughout the other three departments.

It usually works best to begin with departmental personnel forecasts. Figure 7-6 represents the personnel requirements for MAPAX.

FIGURE 7-6

MAPAX MANUFACTURING CORP.
PERSONNEL FORECAST (in dollars)

	Actual Year 1	Year 2	Year 3	Forecasted Year 4	Year 5	Year 6	Year 7	Year 8	Year 9
MANUFACTURING									
Shop Supervision:									
Clem	38,000	39,140	40,314	41,524	42,679	44,052	45,374	46,735	48,137
Marge	32,000	32,960	33,949	34,967	36,016	37,097	38,210	39,356	40,537
Stan	28,000	28,840	29,705	30,596	31,514	32,460	33,433	34,436	35,470
Mike	27,000	27,810	28,644	29,504	30,389	31,300	32,239	33,207	34,203
Holly				27,000	27,810	28,644	29,504	30,389	31,300
George						28,000	28,840	29,705	30,596
Agnes									30,000
John									30,000
TOTAL	125,000	128,750	132,612	163,591	168,499	201,554	207,600	213,828	280,243
Administrative:									
Mary	31,000	31,930	32,888	33,875	34,891	35,937	37,016	38,126	39,270
Roger	31,000	31,930	32,888	33,875	34,891	35,937	37,016	38,126	39,270
Harry	30,000	30,900	31,827	32,782	33,765	34,778	35,822	36,896	38,003
Joan	30,000	30,900	31,827	32,782	33,765	34,778	35,822	36,896	38,003
Sue				25,000	25,750	26,522	27,318	28,138	28,982
Eleanor								30,000	30,900
TOTAL	122,000	125,660	129,430	158,313	163,062	167,954	172,993	208,182	214,428
SELLING									
Mac	75,000	77,250	79,568	81,955	84,413	86,946	89,554	92,241	95,008
Roy	45,000	46,350	47,741	49,173	50,648	52,167	53,732	55,344	57,005
Mitsy	52,000	53,560	55,167	56,822	58,526	60,282	62,091	63,953	65,872
Ann	35,000	36,050	37,132	38,245	39,393	40,575	41,792	43,046	44,337
Clyde	30,000	30,900	31,827	32,782	33,765	34,778	35,822	36,896	38,003
Margaret				40,000	41,200	42,436	43,709	45,020	46,371
Ollie					50,000	51,500	53,045	54,636	56,275
TOTAL	237,000	244,110	251,433	298,976	357,946	368,684	379,744	391,137	402,871
ADMINISTRATIVE									
Bob	75,000	77,250	79,568	81,955	84,413	86,946	89,554	92,241	95,008
Marcia	75,000	77,250	79,568	81,955	84,413	89,946	89,554	92,241	95,008
Audrey	42,000	43,260	44,558	45,895	47,271	48,690	50,150	51,655	53,204
Gene	45,000	46,350	47,741	49,173	50,648	52,167	53,732	55,344	57,005
Barry	33,000	33,990	35,010	36,060	37,142	38,256	39,404	40,586	41,803
Ann	25,000	25,750	26,522	27,318	28,138	28,982	29,851	30,747	31,669
Pat	22,000	22,660	23,340	24,040	24,761	25,504	26,269	27,057	27,869
Clare	22,000	22,660	23,340	24,040	24,761	25,504	26,269	27,057	27,869
Ritchie	22,000	22,660	23,340	24,040	24,761	25,504	26,269	27,057	27,869
Dick	18,000	18,540	19,096	19,669	20,259	20,867	21,493	22,138	22,802
TOTAL	379,000	390,370	402,081	414,144	426,568	439,365	452,546	466,122	480,106

Some companies prefer to forecast personnel requirements by job category, such as management, clerical, technical, and so on. Others prefer to list the actual names of people currently employed and identify new hires by job classification. MAPAX management plans to rehire people who had worked for the company in prior years, so the actual names of new hires have been listed.

Given the functional relationships between overhead employees, nonpersonnel overhead expenses, and sales volume, Figure 7-6 shows new hires being added in Year 6 and Year 9 to reflect increases in production activity. The payroll for both shop supervision and manufacturing administrative personnel—typically those who work in production control, inventory control, production scheduling, timekeeping, and other departments—is considered a "step" cost that varies with production volume in *incremental steps* rather than directly, as direct labor does.

In the MAPAX case, it was assumed that salaries would increase 3 percent per year to keep up with inflation assumptions. Obviously, if merit increases are anticipated, they should be included. The same holds true for bonus or profit-sharing incentive programs.

As Figure 7-6 shows, sales personnel were added in anticipation of increased sales. This makes sense, since presumably they will be needed to generate these incremental sales. No new hires were anticipated for administrative personnel. This department should include office support employees, including those in accounting, engineering, and general management. If the valuation is to be used to set the selling price of a company or a minority interest, salaries of owner/managers should be omitted. Conversely, if it is to serve as a measure of fair market value for estate or gift tax valuations or for other statutory purposes, then by all means include these salaries. It doesn't make sense to increase the company's tax base by excluding them.

The next step is to forecast fringe benefits and nonpersonnel operating expenses as shown in Figure 7-7.

As previously mentioned, companies with a large number of employees or complex benefit structures should forecast fringe benefits in detail: payroll taxes, group insurance, pension cost, and so on. For most small businesses, however, the forecasting accuracy of annual cash flows can be nearly as good if the ratio of total fringe benefits to gross payroll is estimated. This should be done by department, however, not for the company as a whole. Although everyone may be included in the same benefit programs, departments with higher average salaries per employee will show a lower fringe benefit to gross payroll ratio.

In the case of MAPAX, the forecast included ratios established from Year 1 historical data. These ratios amounted to 40 percent for manufacturing overhead personnel and 25 percent for selling and administrative employees.

FIGURE 7-7

MAPAX MANUFACTURING CORP.
MANUFACTURING OVERHEAD FORECAST (in dollars)

	Actual			----Forecasted----					
	Year 1	Year 2	Year 3	Year 4	Year 5	Year 6	Year 7	Year 8	Year 9
Shop supervision	125,000	128,750	132,612	163,591	168,499	201,554	207,600	213,828	280,243
Fringe benefits									
Direct labor	376,747	395,658	415,365	427,826	440,661	453,881	467,497	526,949	561,473
Indirect labor	37,500	38,625	39,784	49,077	50,550	60,466	62,280	64,148	84,073
Administrative	122,000	125,660	129,430	158,813	163,062	167,954	172,993	208,182	214,428
Fringe benefits	36,600	37,698	38,829	47,494	48,919	50,386	51,898	62,455	64,328
Operating supplies	5,000	5,150	5,304	5,464	5,628	5,796	5,970	6,149	6,334
Maintenance	9,000	9,270	9,548	9,835	10,130	10,433	10,746	11,069	11,402
Utilities	12,000	12,360	12,731	13,113	13,506	13,911	14,329	14,758	15,201
Telephone	3,000	3,090	3,183	3,278	3,377	3,478	3,582	3,690	3,800
Insurance	10,000	10,300	10,609	10,927	11,255	11,593	11,941	12,299	12,668
Property taxes	8,500	8,755	9,018	9,288	9,567	9,854	10,149	10,454	10,768
Miscellaneous	2,000	2,060	2,122	2,185	2,251	2,319	2,388	2,460	2,534
TOTAL	747,347	777,376	808,535	900,391	927,403	991,625	1,021,373	1,136,441	1,267,250
% of direct labor	79.3	78.6	77.9	84.2	84.2	87.4	87.4	86.3	90.3
Direct labor	941,868	989,146	1,038,413	1,069,566	1,101,563	1,134,702	1,168,743	1,317,372	1,403,683

MAPAX MANUFACTURING CORP.
SELLING EXPENSE FORECAST (in dollars)

	Actual			----Forecasted----					
	Year 1	Year 2	Year 3	Year 4	Year 5	Year 6	Year 7	Year 8	Year 9
Salaries	237,000	244,110	251,433	298,976	357,946	368,684	379,744	391,137	402,871
Fringe benefits	59,250	61,028	62,858	74,744	89,486	92,171	94,936	97,784	100,718
Commissions	281,250	294,731	308,956	323,969	330,023	332,054	347,547	363,995	404,381
Telephone	12,000	12,360	12,731	13,113	13,506	13,911	14,329	14,758	15,201
Supplies	2,000	2,060	2,122	2,185	2,251	2,319	2,386	2,400	2,534
Samples	2,500	2,575	2,652	2,732	2,814	2,898	2,985	3,075	3,167
Auto expense	7,000	7,210	7,426	7,649	7,879	8,115	8,358	8,609	8,867
Sales literature	4,000	4,120	4,244	4,371	4,502	4,637	4,776	4,919	5,067
Advertising	2,900	2,987	3,077	3,169	3,264	3,362	3,463	3,567	3,674
Miscellaneous expense	1,000	1,030	1,061	1,093	1,126	1,159	1,194	1,230	1,267
TOTAL	608,900	632,210	656,560	732,001	812,796	829,310	859,721	891,534	947,746

MAPAX MANUFACTURING CORP.
ADMINISTRATIVE EXPENSES FORECAST (in dollars)

	Actual			----Forecasted----					
	Year 1	Year 2	Year 3	Year 4	Year 5	Year 6	Year 7	Year 8	Year 9
Salaries	379,000	390,370	402,081	414,144	426,568	439,365	452,546	466,122	480,106
Fringe benefits	94,750	97,593	100,520	103,536	106,642	109,841	113,136	116,531	120,026
Telephone	12,000	12,000	12,000	12,000	12,600	12,600	12,600	12,600	12,600
Office supplies	4,000	4,000	4,000	4,000	4,200	4,200	4,200	4,200	4,200
Maintenance	5,000	6,000	6,000	6,000	6,300	6,300	6,300	6,300	6,300
Insurance	18,000	18,000	18,000	18,000	18,900	18,900	18,900	18,900	18,900
Professional fees	25,000	25,000	25,000	25,000	26,250	26,250	26,250	26,250	26,250
Miscellaneous expense	4,000	4,000	4,000	4,000	4,200	4,200	4,200	4,200	4,200
TOTAL	541,750	556,963	571,601	586,679	605,660	621,656	638,132	655,103	672,582

Nonpersonnel expenses should be forecasted based on actual current experience. If different types of expenses are expected in the future or if an extraordinary event will cause unusual swings, then of course these conditions should be forecasted. In the case of MAPAX, however, it was assumed that the current expense structure would hold during the forecast period. Most expenses reflect annual increases of 3 percent based on expected inflation rates. A few of the less variable costs (e.g., most of the administrative expenses) were forecasted as step costs.

Annual totals from the manufacturing overhead, selling, and administrative expense forecasts then flow directly to the statement of income in Figure 7-8. Since MAPAX does not consider manufacturing overhead a direct product cost, annual totals of these expenses flow to cost of sales as period costs rather than to inventory. If your company absorbs overhead on direct labor, forecasted manufacturing expenses should flow to inventory, just as material purchases and direct labor do, not to cost of sales.

It should also be noted that companies using a standard cost system may record inputs and outputs from inventory as standard; in that case, variances between standard and actual costs are written off to cost of sales as variances. The material, labor, and overhead absorbed entries then reflect standard costs. To adjust a standard cost system to cash flow, it's necessary to add the variances to standard inventory input amounts for all three types of costs. MAPAX does not use a standard cost system; therefore, forecasted operating expenses flow to the statement of income as well as directly to the cash flow forecast.

Statement of Income Forecast

The statement of income summarizes the results of the previously described subforecasts following the same procedures used in the company's accounting records. Although it is clearly not a cash expenditure, depreciation expense based on current guidelines must be included to correlate pro forma statements with historical accounting-oriented financial statements.

For simplicity, MAPAX's taxes were forecasted at a straight 38 percent of pretax income for all years (see Figure 7-8). To the extent that the tax code sanctions special exclusions from or additions to income or expense items, these should be estimated and included as increases or decreases in the normal tax base. Also, state income taxes should be included.

FIGURE 7-8

MAPAX MANUFACTURING CORP.
STATEMENT OF INCOME (in dollars)

	Actual			----Forecasted----					
	Year 1	Year 2	Year 3	Year 4	Year 5	Year 6	Year 7	Year 8	Year 9
Sales	11,250,000	11,789,225	12,358,231	12,958,763	13,200,924	13,282,143	13,901,899	14,559,800	16,175,250
Cost of sales:									
Material	5,760,000	6,051,920	6,360,364	6,686,310	6,798,203	6845,868	7,170,421	7,514,065	8,422,217
Labor	875,520	919,892	966,775	1,016,319	1,033,327	1,040,572	1,089,904	1,142,138	1,280,177
Overhead	747,347	777,376	808,535	900,391	927,403	991,625	1,021,373	1,136,441	1,267,250
Total standard cost of sales	7,382,867	7,749,188	8,135,674	8,603,020	8,758,932	8,878,065	9,281,699	9,792,644	10,969,645
Gross profit	3,867,133	4,040,037	4,222,556	4,355,743	4,441,992	4,404,078	4,620,200	4,767,156	5,205,606
% of sales	34.4%	34.3%	34.2%	33.6%	33.6%	33.2%	33.2%	32.75%	32.2%
Operating Expenses:									
Selling expenses	608,900	632,210	656,560	732,001	812,796	829,310	859,721	891,534	947,746
Administrative exp.	541,750	556,963	571,601	586,679	605,660	621,656	638,132	655,103	672,582
Other expenses	20,000	20,000	20,000	20,000	20,000	20,000	20,000	20,000	20,000
Depreciation	585,000	585,000	585,000	585,000	585,000	585,000	585,000	585,000	585,000
TOTAL	1,755,650	1,794,173	1,833,161	1,923,680	2,023,456	2,055,966	2,102,854	2,151,637	2,225,329
Net income before interest and taxes	2,111,483	2,245,864	2,389,395	2,432,062	2,418,537	2,348,112	2,517,346	2,615,520	2,980,277
% of sales	18.8%	19.1%	19.3%	18.8%	18.3%	17.7%	18.1%	18.0%	18.4%
Interest	517,000	485,250	453,500	417,500	390,000	363,500	335,000	307,500	280,000
Net income before tax	1,594,483	1,760,614	1,935,895	2,014,562	2,028,537	1,985,612	2,182,346	2,308,000	2,700,277
Taxes	605,903	669,033	735,640	765,534	770,844	754,533	928,292	877,047	1,026,105
Net income	988,579	1,091,581	1,200,255	1,249,029	1,257,693	1,231,080	1,353,055	1,430,972	1,674,172
% of sales	8.8%	9.3%	9.7%	9.6%	9.5%	9.3%	9.7%	9.8%	10.4%

Seeing how costs flow into an income statement makes it easy to understand why the accounting procedure that defines cash flow as net income plus noncash expenses (i.e., depreciation) does not yield an accurate cash flow:

- Material and labor cost of sales are determined through ratio analysis. Actual cash expenditures for purchases and direct labor payroll are recorded as inputs to inventory, not to cost of sales.
- When depreciation is added back to net income, the tax effect of the depreciation deduction is completely ignored.
- The actual tax rate may be more or less than a straight 38 percent depending on adjustments to income based on tax code provisions. In the case of MAPAX, such adjustments are assumed to be negligible.

One final point about the statement of income: It may be that the final business valuation will be used for several purposes, some of which may require a forecast of future earnings rather than cash flow. Depending on the circumstances, forecasted earnings may be net income after taxes, before taxes, or before taxes and interest. Because of this, it's better to keep these different definitions of earnings separate in the pro forma statements.

Balance Sheet Forecast

From an accounting perspective, the statement of income records transactions that occur over a period of time. Balance sheet accounts, however, reflect asset and liability amounts as of a *specific* point in time. Income accounts are dynamic, balance sheet accounts static.

The cash flow forecasting procedure recognizes both: cash flow created over a period of time by a series of income statement transactions and positive or negative cash flow created by collecting the prior year's balance sheet assets or setting up new balance sheet amounts for the current year-end. This combination of dynamic transactions and static account balances yields the amount of cash remaining in bank accounts at the end of a period.

The whole purpose of preparing forecasts for business valuations is to arrive at the amount of net cash flowing into or out of a company's bank accounts. Forecasts show the flow of cash receipts and expenditures over a given period that results in net cash balances. Therefore, the balance sheet bank account is a dynamically derived amount, not static as other balance sheet accounts are.

Referring to the MAPAX balance sheet forecast in Figure 7-9, the following sections describe the functional relationships used to arrive at non-cash balance sheet amounts, beginning with accounts receivable.

Accounts Receivable

Sales flow into accounts receivable as inputs, and collections flow out. During the course of a year the receivables balance will constantly fluctuate up or down based on these two flows. For forecasting purposes, however, we must arrive at a balance as of a point in time, namely the end of the year. Since it is impractical to forecast each sale and collection transaction for the entire year, an approximation of the accounts receivable balance at year-end can be calculated by assuming a functional relationship to sales expressed in terms of the number of days sales that have not been collected. This relationship is referred to as *receivables days sales* or *receivables turnover*.

In the case of MAPAX, historical data shows that on average, the accounts receivable balance represents about forty-five days sales. The forecasted year-end balance is then calculated as:

$$\text{Accounts receivable} = \frac{\text{Current year sales}}{365 \text{ days}} \times 45 \text{ days}$$

The simplified calculation translates to annual sales times a factor of 1.5.

FIGURE 7-9

MAPAX MANUFACTURING CORP
BALANCE SHEET (in dollars)

	Actual				Forecasted				
	Year 1	Year 2	Year 3	Year 4	Year 5	Year 6	Year 7	Year 8	Year 9
Cash	1,000	785,445	1,648,017	1,727,882	3,231,740	4,495,068	5,813,453	6,183,520	7,076,719
Accounts receivable	1,406,250	1,473,653	1,544,779	1,619,845	1,650,116	1,660,268	1,737,737	1,819,975	2,021,906
Inventory	3,636,263	4,175,635	4,744,085	5,059,609	5,066,724	5,374,658	5,684,589	7,148,397	8,092,456
Prepaid expenses	5,000	5,000	5,000	5,000	5,000	5,000	5,000	5,000	5,000
Total current assets	5,048,513	6,439,733	7,941,881	8,412,336	9,953,579	11,534,994	13,240,779	15,156,892	17,196,081
Buildings	2,000,000	2,000,000	2,000,000	2,000,000	2,000,000	2,000,000	2,000,000	2,000,000	2,000,000
Machinery & equipment	8,000,000	8,000,000	8,000,000	9,000,000	9,000,000	9,000,000	9,000,000	9,000,000	9,000,000
Delivery trucks	50,000	50,000	50,000	50,000	50,000	50,000	50,000	50,000	50,000
TOTAL	10,050,000	10,050,000	10,050,000	11,050,000	11,050,000	11,050,000	11,050,000	11,050,000	11,050,000
Less: accumulated depreciation	(3,200,000)	(3,785,000)	(4,370,000)	(4,955,000)	(5,540,000)	(6,125,000)	(6,710,000)	(7,295,000)	(7,880,000)
Net fixed assets	6,850,000	6,265,000	5,680,000	6,095,000	5,510,000	4,925,000	4,340,000	3,755,000	3,170,000
Other assets	100,000	100,000	100,000	100,000	100,000	100,000	100,000	100,000	100,000
Total assets	11,998,513	12,804,733	13,721,881	14,607,336	15,563,579	16,559,994	17,680,779	19,011,892	20,466,081
Bank note payable	200,000	150,000	100,000	0	0	0	0	0	0
New bank note	0	0	0	0	0	0	0	0	0
Accounts payable	775,614	815,255	857,147	868,573	842,124	882,459	925,189	1,100,330	1,155,346
Accrued expenses	200,000	200,000	200,000	200,000	200,000	200,000	200,000	200,000	200,000
Other current liabilities	50,000	50,000	50,000	50,000	50,000	50,000	50,000	50,000	50,000
Total current liabilities	1,225,614	1,215,255	1,207,147	1,118,573	1,092,124	1,132,459	1,175,189	1,350,330	1,405,346
Long-term debt	4,000,000	3,800,000	3,600,000	3,400,000	3,200,000	3,000,000	2,800,000	2,600,000	2,400,000
Mortgage loan	1,000,000	925,000	850,000	775,000	700,000	625,000	550,000	475,000	400,000
Total liabilities	6,225,614	5,940,255	5,657,147	5,293,573	4,992,124	4,757,459	4,525,189	4,425,330	4,205,346
Common stock	100,000	100,000	100,000	100,000	100,000	100,000	100,000	100,000	100,000
Retained earnings—beginning		5,672,898	6,764,479	7,964,734	9,213,763	10,471,456	11,702,535	13,055,590	14,486,562
Profit/(loss)		1,091,581	1,200,255	1,249,029	1,257,693	1,231,080	1,353,055	1,430,972	1,674,172
Retained earnings—ending	5,672,898	6,764,479	7,964,734	9,213,763	10,471,456	11,702,535	13,055,590	14,486,562	16,160,734
Total net worth	5,772,898	6,864,479	8,064,734	9,313,763	10,571,456	11,802,535	13,155,590	14,586,562	16,260,734
Total liabilities and net worth	11,998,513	12,804,734	13,721,881	14,607,336	15,563,580	16,559,994	17,680,779	19,011,892	20,466,080

Inventory

Since a subforecast inventory schedule was prepared using material purchase and direct labor payroll, no further calculation is necessary for the balance sheet forecast. Just bring in the year-end balances from the inventory forecast (Figure 7-5).

Prepaid Expenses and Other Assets

Generally the amounts in these accounts either are very small and therefore immaterial in relation to total cash flow or change very little from one year to the next. In either case, it should be safe to assume constant balances, as in the MAPAX forecast. If either of these conditions is not true in your company, then obviously a separate subforecast schedule should be used to track the ins and outs.

Fixed Assets

If major changes in facilities space or production/delivery machinery and equipment are not planned and significant disposals are not anticipated, these balances remain constant throughout the forecast period. Of course, major additions or disposals must be forecasted. For MAPAX, it was determined that furnace production would reach capacity in the Year 3–Year 4 period. To meet the increased sales volume in Year 5–Year 9, new machinery costing $1 million would have to be added in Year 4.

Accounts Payable and Accrued Expenses

The majority of transactions flowing through trade payable accounts are related to material purchases. This functional relationship allows the accounts payable balance to be forecasted as a percentage of purchases. In the case of MAPAX, material purchases make up the majority of inventory at any point in time, so the use of that functional relationship is justified. This leads to a choice: forecast payables either as a percentage of purchases or as a percentage of inventory. MAPAX chose the latter.

MAPAX's policy was to pay supplier invoices on a forty-five-day schedule to coincide with receivables turnover. For forecast purposes, accounts payable balances were derived from the following formula:

$$\text{Accounts payable} \;=\; \frac{\text{Inventory}}{365} \times 45 \text{ days}$$

As with accounts receivable, the simplified calculation translates to year-end inventory times a factor of 1.5.

Accrued expenses usually include employer-paid fringe benefits, unpaid interest and property taxes, and various other items that have been booked as expenses but not yet paid. To the extent that the accrued expense balance varies significantly from year to year, the same functional analysis should be made as for accounts payable, only this time the balance should be calculated as a percentage of operating expenses. In the case of MAPAX, however, historical accrued balances varied slightly year to year, but not enough to warrant a separate analysis. Therefore, balances were held constant over the forecast period. The same was true for other current liabilities.

Debt

Forecasting debt balances can be a tricky exercise, especially for companies with low profit margins or severely fluctuating cash needs. Of course, current debt service payments are easy to project, and the company should plan to pay off current bank notes as soon as cash balances permit.

New debt requirements are determined from the cash flow forecast. For those years in which sales volume does not generate sufficient internal cash to meet obligations, additional short-term borrowings should be forecasted. Large purchases of fixed assets may also be financed externally, necessitating the inclusion of additional long-term debt. To the extent that new short- or long-term debt is necessary, separate headings on the balance sheet forecast should be used to identify it. Interest expense on all outstanding debt should, of course, be included in the statement of income forecast.

That brings us to the statement of cash flow, the main forecast schedule for determining future cash benefits reckoned in the valuation process.

Cash Flow Forecast

All the previous subforecast schedules and pro forma financial statements have been based on generally accepted accounting principles. This is not the case with the statement of cash flow. The format used in the MAPAX forecast in Figure 7-10 will not be found in any accounting literature and probably not in any business valuation literature. Yet, over many years of experimenting with various formats, this one has proven the most useful in showing the cost/sales/asset functional relationships that generate or use cash and that simultaneously interact with GAAP-prepared balance sheets and statements of income. This format can also be easily adapted to computer-based spreadsheet formulas.

Cash Receipts

Cash receipts is probably the easiest place to begin. All cash receipts originate from one or a combination of six sources:

1. Collection of prior period accounts receivable balances
2. Current period sales
3. New loans or other debt financing
4. Sale of business assets
5. Sale of equity interests
6. Settlement of claims or refunds

All current period sales are assumed to be collected except those residing in accounts receivable at the end of the period, which is why ending accounts receivable are deducted from operating receipts. Since the main purpose of this forecast is to establish a stream of future benefits to a potential investor, no sale of equity interests should be shown.

MAPAX does not need additional debt financing to reach its forecasted volume or to purchase new equipment, nor does the company plan to sell any fixed assets. Therefore, these two line items in Figure 7-10 remain zero throughout the forecast period. Of course, the amounts included as sales and beginning and ending accounts receivable flow directly from the statement of income (Figure 7-8) and the balance sheet (Figure 7-9).

FIGURE 7-10

MAPAX MANUFACTURING CORP.
STATEMENT OF CASH FLOW (in dollars)

	Actual		----Forecasted----					
	Year 2	Year 3	Year 4	Year 5	Year 6	Year 7	Year 8	Year 9
CASH RECEIPTS								
Beginning receivables	1,406,250	1,473,653	1,544,779	1,619,845	1,650,116	1,660,268	1,737,737	1,819,975
Sales	11,789,225	12,358,231	12,958,763	13,200,924	13,282,143	13,901,899	14,559,800	16,175,250
Ending receivables	(1,473,653)	(1,544,779)	(1,619,835)	(1,650,116)	(1,660,268)	(1,737,737)	(1,819,975)	(2,021,906)
Cash receipts from operations	11,721,822	12,287,105	12,883,696	13,170,654	13,271,991	13,824,429	14,477,563	15,973,319
New bank loans	0	0	0	0	0	0	0	0
Other cash receipts	0	0	0	0	0	0	0	0
Total cash receipts	11,721,822	12,287,105	12,883,696	13,170,654	13,271,991	13,824,429	14,477,563	15,973,319
CASH EXPENDITURES								
Beginning payables	775,614	815,255	857,147	868,573	842,124	882,459	925,189	1,100,330
Purchases	6,522,038	6,857,177	6,948,587	6,736,992	7,059,673	7,401,513	8,802,639	9,242,771
Ending payables	(815,255)	(857,147)	(868,573)	(842,124)	(882,459)	(925,189)	(1,100,330)	(1,155,346)
Material cash expenditures	6,482,398	6,815,284	6,937,160	6,763,441	7,019,338	7,358,783	8,627,498	9,187,754
Direct labor	989,146	1,038,413	1,069,566	1,101,653	1,134,702	1,168,743	1,317,372	1,403,683
Operating expenditures								
Beginning accrued expenses	200,000	200,000	200,000	200,000	200,000	200,000	200,000	200,000
Manufacturing expenses	777,376	808,535	900,391	927,403	991,625	1,021,373	1,136,441	1,267,250
Selling expenses	632,210	656,560	732,001	812,796	829,310	859,721	891,534	947,746
Administrative expenses	556,963	571,601	586,679	605,660	621,656	638,132	655,103	672,582
Other expenses	20,000	20,000	20,000	20,000	20,000	20,000	20,000	20,000
Ending accrued expenses	(200,000)	(200,000)	(200,000)	(200,000)	(200,000)	(200,000)	(200,000)	(200,000)
Total operating expenditures	1,986,549	2,056,696	2,239,071	2,365,858	2,462,590	2,539,227	2,703,078	2,907,579
Taxes	669,033	735,640	765,534	770,844	754,533	829,292	877,047	1,026,105
Machinery purchases	0	0	1,000,000	0	0	0	0	0
Financing expenditures								
Bank note								
Principal	50,000	50,000	100,000	0	0	0	0	0
Interest	12,750	8,500	0	0	0	0	0	0
Long-term loan								
Principal	200,000	200,000	200,000	200,000	200,000	200,000	200,000	200,000
Interest	380,000	360,000	340,000	320,000	300,000	280,000	260,000	240,000
Mortgage loan								
Principal	75,000	75,000	75,000	75,000	75,000	75,000	75,000	75,000
Interest	92,500	85,000	77,500	70,000	62,500	55,000	47,500	40,000
Total principal	325,000	325,000	375,000	275,000	275,000	275,000	275,000	275,000
Total interest	485,250	453,500	417,500	390,000	362,500	335,000	307,500	280,000
Total cash exp	10,937,376	11,424,534	12,803,831	11,666,796	12,008,663	12,506,045	14,107,495	15,080,121
NET CASH GENERATED	784,445	862,572	79,865	1,503,858	1,263,328	1,318,385	370,067	893,198
Beginning cash in bank	1,000	785,445	1,648,017	1,727,882	3,231,740	4,495,068	5,813,453	6,183,520
Ending cash in bank	785,445	1,648,107	1,727,882	3,231,740	4,495,068	5,813,453	6,183,520	7,076,719

Cash Expenditures

The steps in forecasting cash expenditures follow the sequence of account headings, first in the statement of income and then in the balance sheet. It is assumed that all payables outstanding at the beginning of the period will be paid during the period. The same holds true for material purchases, except for those amounts purchased in the last forty-five days, which are deducted as ending accounts payable. The amounts included as material purchases flow directly from the input section of the inventory forecast.

All direct labor payroll is assumed to have been paid during the period. Like material purchases, direct labor expenditures flow directly from the input section of the inventory forecast.

In the operating expenses category, any accrued expenses at the beginning of the period should be paid off during the period. Current expenditures for manufacturing overhead, selling, and administrative expenses are shown as being paid, except for those incurred toward the end of the period, which are included as accrued expenses and deducted, just like ending payables. Each of the three classes of expenses flows from the statement of income, which used data derived from the operating expense subforecasts. Taxes are shown separately and flow directly from the statement of income.

If any fixed asset purchases are planned, they flow directly from the balance sheet and should be shown as a separate line item.

The final class of expenditures includes all principal and interest payments on both short- and long-term debt. Principal payments flow directly from the balance sheet and interest payments from the statement of income. It usually works best to keep payments for each category of debt segregated, as in Figure 7-10. In this way any prepayment or extended payment against a particular loan can be easily identified.

Net Cash

The final section of the cash flow forecast reconciles all receipts and expenditures for the period with the cash balance shown on the balance sheet. The net cash generated equals the total receipts for the period less total expenditures. Adding net cash generated to the bank account balance from the previous period results in the current cash balance on the balance sheet.

The beauty of this type of cash flow format is that not only can each element of receipts and expenditures be clearly identified, but every line item interacts directly with an account in the statement of income, the balance sheet, or a supporting subforecast.

That finishes the cash forecasting process. Although the MAPAX example represented a typical forecast for a manufacturing company and the numbers used were relatively large, the same format and procedure, with slight modifications, can be used for any type of company of any size. To summarize the three major features of this technique:

Economic and business assumptions. Before beginning a forecast, it is necessary to set out the macroeconomic, industry, competitive, and specific company assumptions that underlie incremental changes in volume, product mix, selling prices, costs, and assets during the forecast period. Such assumptions should incorporate trends in the national economy and the relevant industry business cycle. Published leading and trailing indicators should be acknowledged. Conscious decisions should be made about inflation, interest rates, personnel availability, sources of supply, foreign competition, and the potential for new products or competitors entering the market.

Cost/sales/asset functional relationships. Using historical data, perhaps over several years, functional relationships should be established between each cost element and sales volume, prices, and asset employment. In any business, all income, expense, asset, and liability accounts are interactive. Each has some type of functional relationship to the others. The key to preparing meaningful cash flow forecasts is to thoroughly understand the relationships that are unique to your business.

Interactive financial schedules. Despite the inaccuracies and the variations between companies in applying generally accepted accounting principles, each element of the cash flow forecast must flow from another supporting schedule that has been prepared under the same accounting principles used in preparing your company's financial statements. It is virtually impossible to value any business without starting with historical statements of income and balance sheets. To be believable, the calculation of future cash benefits must be derived from verifiable accounting records as expressed in these statements.

Once a stream of future cash benefits has been established, we can move on to incorporating this data into valuation techniques.

CHAPTER

Putting It All Together

This is probably a good place to pause and summarize the valuation steps covered so far. Although the myriad theories, data, and ratios described in previous chapters may look like a hodgepodge of unrelated approaches and information, there is a method to this whole madness. While it is certainly true that both the various valuation techniques developed over the years and the wide range of opinions expressed by noted authorities and regulatory bodies seem to offer a basket of options, by sorting out those specific matters relevant for a given company, one can make order out of chaos.

The easiest way to pinpoint appropriate methodologies is to break down the valuation process into its basic elements. The following summarizes the points discussed and conclusions reached so far:

- Of the myriad theories to choose from, three command the most respect in today's markets; the capital asset pricing model, the excess earnings method, and the asset value method. Each has merit under certain conditions, although inherent fallacies make all three questionable for valuing small businesses, except to comply with IRS rules. Pragmatically, the value of closely held companies, especially small businesses, is in the eye of the beholder, whether it be a seller, a buyer, a partner, or an investor. This gives credence to valuations based on a straightforward forecasted stream of benefits discounted at a rate based on perceived risk.
- Although the determination of a future stream of benefits should in most cases have its base in pro forma financial statements, the absence of uniform accounting practices makes comparisons of discounted future earnings for investment alternatives difficult, and therefore suspect. Instead, cash flow forecasts derived form historical cost/sales/asset relationships tend to provide a better measure of expected future benefits. Discounting such a stream of future cash flows will in most cases result in a valuation less subject to dispute than those prepared by other methods.

- Gathering company data, assimilating relevant economic and industry indicators, and evaluating a company's accounting reports are important steps that must be performed before proceeding with any form of numerical analysis.
- The analysis process begins by using universally acceptable financial ratios to measure performance. Debt utilization, liquidity, profitability, and asset utilization ratios all contribute insights into a company's overall earnings power. By applying the same ratios to forecasted financial statements, one can determine probable future trends that serve as a basis for judging risk factors. Risk analysis techniques bring additional insights into the uncertainty of achieving expected benefits.
- A cash flow forecast is the major tool for determining future benefits and hence value. It must, however, interact with pro forma financial statements prepared using historical functional relationships.

Probably the clearest way to demonstrate the practical application of these valuation steps is to refer back to the MAPAX Manufacturing Corp. examples used in Chapters 6 and 7. Of course, the same caveats previously stated about the universality of this process for manufacturing and nonmanufacturing companies and for businesses of any size should be recognized. A midsize manufacturing company is used as an example only because (1) manufacturing businesses tend to be the most complex and (2) large numbers demonstrate valuation techniques more clearly than smaller ones.

Figure 8-1 repeats the three-year MAPAX historical financial statements from Chapter 6 and Figures 8-2, 8-3, and 8-4 repeat the pro forma financials and cash flow projections for Year 2 through Year 9 from Chapter 7.

Working from these historical and forecasted financial statements, the following sequence should be used to determine a quantifiable value for MAPAX:

1. Extend the historical financial ratio and risk analyses to the forecasted results, highlighting potential problem areas.
2. Evaluate qualitative factors that could affect future performance.
3. Develop a realistic capitalization rate to reflect your best judgment of future risk.
4. Discount an estimated continuing value.
5. Apply the capitalization rate to discount the future cash flow stream to its present value.

FIGURE 8-1

MAPAX MANUFACTURING CORP.
STATEMENT OF INCOME

	Year 1-2	Year 1-1	Year 1
Sales	$10,914,750	$11,137,500	$11,250,000
Cost of sales:			
Material	5,588,352	5,702,400	5,760,000
Labor	849,430	866,765	875,520
Overhead	703,179	724,927	747,347
Total cost of sales	$7,140,960	$7,294,091	$7,382,867
Gross profit	$3,773,790	$3,843,409	$3,867,133
% of sales	34.6%	34.5%	34.4%
Operating expenses:			
Selling expenses	$584,788	$596,722	$608,900
Administrative expenses	520,297	530,915	541,750
Other expenses	20,000	20,000	20,000
Depreciation	468,000	532,000	585,000
TOTAL	$1,593,084	$1,679,637	$1,755,650
Net income before interest and taxes	$2,180,705	$2,163,772	$2,111,483
% of sales	20.0%	19.4%	18.8%
Interest	$597,500	$548,750	$517,000
Net income before tax	1,583,205	1,615,022	1,594,483
Taxes	601,618	613,708	605,904
Net income	$981,587	$1,001,313	$988,579
% of sales	9.0%	9.0%	8.8%

MAPAX MANUFACTURING CORP.
BALANCE SHEET

	Year 1-2	Year 1-1	Year 1
Cash	$622,852	$121,691	$1,000
Accounts receivable	1,364,344	1,392,187	1,406,250
Inventory	2,721,250	3,125,000	3,636,263
Prepaid expenses	5,000	5,000	5,000
Total current assets	$4,713,446	$4,643,878	$5,048,513
Buildings	2,000,000	2,000,000	2,000,000
Machinery & equipment	6,000,000	7,100,000	8,000,000
Delivery trucks	50,000	50,000	50,000
TOTAL	$8,050,000	$9,150,000	$10,050,000
Less: accumulated depreciation	(2,200,000)	(2,668,000)	(3,200,000)
Net fixed assets	5,850,000	6,482,000	6,850,000
Other assets	100,000	100,000	100,000
Total assets	$10,663,446	$11,225,878	$11,998,513
Bank note payable	$500,000	$250,000	$200,000
Accounts payable	580,440	666,559	775,614
Accrued expenses	200,000	200,000	200,000
Other current liabilities	50,000	50,000	50,000
Total current liabilities	$1,330,440	$1,166,559	$1,225,614
Long-term debt	4,400,000	4,200,000	4,000,000
Mortgage loan	1,150,000	1,075,000	1,000,000
Total liabilities	$6,880,440	$6,441,559	$6,225,614
Common stock	$100,000	$100,000	$100,000
Retained earnings—beginning	2,701,419	3,683,006	4,684,320
Profit (loss)	981,587	1,001,313	988,579
Retained earnings—ending	3,683,006	4,684,320	5,672,899
Total net worth	$3,783,006	$4,784,320	$5,772,899
Total liabilities and net worth	$10,663,446	$11,225,879	$11,998,513

FIGURE 8-2

MAPAX MANUFACTURING CORP.
STATEMENT OF INCOME (in dollars)

	Actual			----Forecasted----					
	Year 1	Year 2	Year 3	Year 4	Year 5	Year 6	Year 7	Year 8	Year 9
Sales	11,250,000	11,789,225	12,358,231	12,958,763	13,200,924	13,282,143	13,901,899	14,559,800	16,175,250
Cost of sales:									
Material	5,760,000	6,051,920	6,360,364	6,686,310	6,798,203	6,845,868	7,170,421	7,514,065	8,422,217
Labor	875,520	919,892	966,775	1,016,319	1,033,327	1,040,572	1,089,904	1,142,138	1,280,177
Overhead	747,347	777,376	808,535	900,391	927,403	991,625	1,021,373	1,136,441	1,267,250
Total standard cost of sales	7,382,867	7,749,188	8,135,674	8,603,020	8,758,932	8,878,065	9,281,699	9,792,644	10,969,645
Gross profit	3,867,133	4,040,037	4,222,556	4,355,743	4,441,992	4,404,078	4,620,200	4,767,156	5,205,606
% of sales	34.4%	34.3%	34.2%	33.6%	33.6%	33.2%	33.2%	32.7%	32.2%
Operating expenses:									
Selling expenses	608,900	632,210	656,560	732,001	812,796	829,310	859,721	891,534	947,746
Administrative expenses	541,750	556,963	571,601	586,679	605,660	621,656	638,132	655,103	672,582
Other expenses	20,000	20,000	20,000	20,000	20,000	20,000	20,000	20,000	20,000
Depreciation	585,000	585,000	585,000	585,000	585,000	585,000	585,000	585,000	585,000
TOTAL	1,755,650	1,794,173	1,833,161	1,923,680	2,023,456	2,055,966	2,102,854	2,151,637	2,225,329
Net income before interest and taxes	2,111,483	2,245,864	2,389,395	2,432,062	2,418,537	2,348,112	2,517,346	2,615,520	2,980,277
% of sales	18.8%	19.1%	19.3%	18.8%	18.3%	17.7%	18.1%	18.0%	18.4%
Interest	517,000	485,250	453,500	417,500	390,000	363,500	335,000	307,500	280,000
Net income before tax	1,594,483	1,760,614	1,935,895	2,014,562	2,028,537	1,985,612	2,182,346	2,308,000	2,700,277
Taxes	605,903	669,033	735,640	765,534	770,844	754,533	928,292	877,047	1,026,105
Net income	988,579	1,091,581	1,200,255	1,249,029	1,257,693	1,231,080	1,353,055	1,430,972	1,674,172
% of sales	8.8%	9.3%	9.7%	9.6%	9.5%	9.3%	9.7%	9.8%	10.4%

FIGURE 8-3

MAPAX MANUFACTURING CORP.
BALANCE SHEET (in dollars)

	Actual	----Forecasted----							
	Year 1	Year 2	Year 3	Year 4	Year 5	Year 6	Year 7	Year 8	Year 9
Cash	1,000	785,445	1,648,017	1,727,882	3,231,740	4,495,068	5,813,453	6,183,520	7,076,719
Accounts receivable	1,406,250	1,473,653	1,544,779	1,619,845	1,650,116	1,660,268	1,737,737	1,819,975	2,021,906
Inventory	3,636,263	4,175,635	4,744,085	5,059,609	5,066,724	5,374,658	5,684,589	7,148,397	8,092,456
Prepaid expenses	5,000	5,000	5,000	5,000	5,000	5,000	5,000	5,000	5,000
Total current assets	5,048,513	6,439,733	7,941,881	8,412,336	9,953,579	11,534,994	13,240,779	15,156,892	17,196,081
Buildings	2,000,000	2,000,000	2,000,000	2,000,000	2,000,000	2,000,000	2,000,000	2,000,000	2,000,000
Machinery & equipment	8,000,000	8,000,000	8,000,000	9,000,000	9,000,000	9,000,000	9,000,000	9,000,000	9,000,000
Delivery trucks	50,000	50,000	50,000	50,000	50,000	50,000	50,000	50,000	50,000
TOTAL	10,050,000	10,050,000	10,050,000	11,050,000	11,050,000	11,050,000	11,050,000	11,050,000	11,050,000
Less: accumulated depreciation	(3,200,000)	(3,785,000)	(4,370,000)	(4,955,000)	(5,540,000)	(6,125,000)	(6,710,000)	(7,295,000)	(7,880,000)
Net fixed assets	6,850,000	6,265,000	5,680,000	6,095,000	5,510,000	4,925,000	4,340,000	3,755,000	3,170,000
Other assets	100,000	100,000	100,000	100,000	100,000	100,000	100,000	100,000	100,000
Total Assets	11,998,513	12,804,733	13,721,881	14,607,336	15,563,579	16,559,994	17,680,779	19,011,892	20,466,081
Bank note payable	200,000	150,000	100,000	0	0	0	0	0	0
New bank note	0	0	0	0	0	0	0	0	0
Accounts payable	775,614	815,255	857,147	868,573	842,124	882,459	925,189	1,100,330	1,155,346
Accrued expenses	200,000	200,000	200,000	200,000	200,000	200,000	200,000	200,000	200,000
Other current liabilities	50,000	50,000	50,000	50,000	50,000	50,000	50,000	50,000	50,000
Total current liabilities	1,225,614	1,215,255	1,207,147	1,118,573	1,092,124	1,132,459	1,175,189	1,350,330	1,405,346
Long-term debt	4,000,000	3,800,000	3,600,000	3,400,000	3,200,000	3,000,000	2,800,000	2,600,000	2,400,000
Mortgage loan	1,000,000	925,000	850,000	775,000	700,000	625,000	550,000	475,000	400,000
Total liabilities	6,225,614	5,940,255	5,657,147	5,293,573	4,992,124	4,757,459	4,525,189	4,425,330	4,205,346
Common stock	100,000	100,000	100,000	100,000	100,000	100,000	100,000	100,000	100,000
Retained earnings—beginning	5,672,898	6,764,479	7,964,734	9,213,763	10,471,456	11,702,535	13,055,590	14,486,562	
Profit/(loss)	1,091,581	1,200,255	1,249,029	1,257,693	1,231,080	1,353,055	1,430,972	1,674,172	
Retained earnings—ending	5,672,898	6,764,479	7,964,734	9,213,763	10,471,456	11,702,535	13,055,590	14,486,562	16,160,734
Total net worth	5,772,898	6,864,479	8,064,734	9,313,763	10,571,456	11,802,535	13,155,590	14,586,562	16,260,734
Total liabilities and net worth	11,998,513	12,804,733	13,721,881	14,607,336	15,563,580	16,559,994	17,680,779	19,011,892	20,466,080

FIGURE 8-4

MAPAX MANUFACTURING CORP.
STATEMENT OF CASH FLOW (in dollars)

	Actual			----Forecasted----				
	Year 1	Year 2	Year 3	Year 4	Year 5	Year 6	Year 7	Year 8
CASH RECEIPTS								
Beginning receivables	1,406,250	1,473,653	1,544,779	1,619,845	1,650,116	1,660,268	1,737,737	1,819,975
Sales	11,789,225	12,358,231	12,958,763	13,200,924	13,282,143	13,901,899	14,559,800	16,175,250
Ending receivables	(1,473,653)	(1,544,779)	(1,619,835)	(1,650,116)	(1,660,268)	(1,737,737)	(1,819,975)	(2,021,906)
Cash receipts from operations	11,721,822	12,287,105	12,883,696	13,170,654	13,271,991	13,824,429	14,477,563	15,973,319
New bank loans	0	0	0	0	0	0	0	0
Other cash receipts	0	0	0	0	0	0	0	0
Total cash receipts	11,721,822	12,287,105	12,883,696	13,170,654	13,271,991	13,824,429	14,477,563	15,973,319
CASH EXPENDITURES								
Beginning payables	775,614	815,255	857,147	868,573	842,124	882,459	925,189	1,100,330
Purchases	6,522,038	6,857,177	6,948,587	6,736,992	7,059,673	7,401,513	8,802,639	9,242,771
Ending payables	(815,255)	(857,147)	(868,573)	(842,124)	(882,459)	(925,189)	(1,100,330)	(1,155,346)
Material cash expenditures	6,482,398	6,815,284	6,937,160	6,763,441	7,019,338	7,358,783	8,627,498	9,187,754
Direct labor	989,146	1,038,413	1,069,566	1,101,653	1,134,702	1,168,743	1,317,372	1,403,683
OPERATING EXPENDITURES								
Beginning accrued expenses	200,000	200,000	200,000	200,000	200,000	200,000	200,000	200,000
Manufacturing expenses	777,376	808,535	900,391	927,403	991,625	1,021,373	1,136,441	1,267,250
Selling expenses	632,210	656,560	732,001	812,796	829,310	859,721	891,534	947,746
Administrative expenses	556,963	571,601	586,679	605,660	621,656	638,132	655,103	672,582
Other expenses	20,000	20,000	20,000	20,000	20,000	20,000	20,000	20,000
Ending accrued expenditures	(200,000)	(200,000)	(200,000)	(200,000)	(200,000)	(200,000)	(200,000)	(200,000)
Total operating expenditures	1,986,549	2,056,696	2,239,071	2,365,858	2,462,590	2,539,227	2,703,078	2,907,579
Taxes	669,033	735,640	765,534	770,844	754,533	829,292	877,047	1,026,105
Machinery purchases	0	0	1,000,000	0	0	0	0	0
FINANCING EXPENDITURES								
Bank note								
Principal	50,000	50,000	100,000	0	0	0	0	0
Interest	12,750	8,500	0	0	0	0	0	0
Long-term loan								
Principal	200,000	200,000	200,000	200,000	200,000	200,000	200,000	200,000
Interest	380,000	360,000	340,000	320,000	300,000	280,000	260,000	240,000
Mortgage loan								
Principal	75,000	75,000	75,000	75,000	75,000	75,000	75,000	75,000
Interest	92,500	85,000	77,500	70,000	62,500	55,000	47,500	40,000
Total principal	325,000	325,000	375,000	275,000	275,000	275,000	275,000	275,000
Total interest	485,250	453,500	417,500	390,000	362,500	335,000	307,500	280,000
Total cash exp	10,937,376	11,424,534	12,803,831	11,666,796	12,008,663	12,506,045	14,107,495	15,080,121
NET CASH GENERATED	784,445	862,572	79,865	1,503,858	1,263,328	1,318,385	370,067	893,198
Beginning cash in bank	1,000	785,445	1,648,017	1,727,882	3,231,740	4,495,068	5,813,453	6,183,520
Ending cash in bank	785,445	1,648,107	1,727,882	3,231,740	4,495,068	5,813,453	6,183,520	7,076,719

Ratio and Risk Analysis

Figure 8-5 summarizes the ratio analysis of MAPAX's three-year historical financial statements and eight-year forecasts. As will be seen in the following discussions, the analysis yields a mixed bag.

FIGURE 8-5 I added .0 to single digets so decimals would align.--Erin

MAPAX MANUFACTURING CORP.
RATIOS AND RISK FACTORS

	Actual			- -Forecasted- -						
	Year 1	Year 2	Year 3	Year 4	Year 5	Year 6	Year 7	Year 8	Year 9	Year 10	Year 11
DEBT UTILIZATION											
Long-term debt/equity	1.5	1.1	0.9	0.7	0.6	0.4	0.4	0.3	0.3	0.2	0.2
Total debt/equity	1.6	1.2	0.9	0.7	0.6	0.4	0.4	0.3	0.3	0.2	0.2
Total debt/total assets	0.6	0.5	0.4	0.4	0.3	0.3	0.3	0.2	0.2	0.2	0.1
LIQUIDITY											
Current ratio	3.5	4.0	4.1	5.3	6.6	7.5	9.1	10.2	11.3	11.2	12.2
Quick ratio	1.5	1.3	1.2	1.9	2.6	3.0	4.5	5.4	6.4	5.9	6.5
PROFITABILITY											
Gross profit/sales	34.6%	34.5%	34.4%	34.3%	34.2%	33.6%	33.6%	33.2%	33.2%	32.7%	32.2%
Net income/sales	9.0%	9.0%	8.8%	9.3%	9.7%	9.6%	9.5%	9.3%	9.7%	9.8%	10.4%
Return on owner's equity	25.9%	20.9%	17.1%	17.3%	16.1%	14.4%	12.6%	11.0%	10.8%	10.3%	10.9%
Return on investment (after taxes)	15.3%	13.9%	12.6%	12.5%	12.3%	11.6%	10.7%	9.7%	9.8%	9.5%	10.1%
Return on assets (after taxes)	13.%	12.3%	11.3%	11.2%	11.2%	10.6%	9.9%	9.1%	9.1%	8.8%	9.4%
ASSET UTILIZATION											
Receivables turnover	7.8	8.1	8.0	8.2	8.2	8.2	8.1	8.0	8.2	8.2	8.4
Receivables days sales	45.6	45.6	45.6	45.6	45.6	45.6	45.6	45.6	45.6	45.6	45.6
Inventory turnover	2.8	2.5	2.2	1.8	1.6	1.6	1.5	1.5	1.5	1.3	1.3
Inventory days sales	156.3	175.9	200	218.6	236.3	239.8	236.1	248.7	251.2	301.4	304.4
Fixed asset turnover	1.9	1.7	1.6	1.9	2.2	2.1	2.4	2.7	3.2	3.9	5.1
Total asset turnover	1.0	1.0	1.0	0.9	0.9	0.9	0.8	0.8	0.8	0.8	0.8

Debt Utilization and Liquidity Ratios

The three-year trend of debt utilization ratios indicates very conservative financial management, perhaps overly cautious about using financial leverage to grow the business. The Year 1-2 ratios of long-term debt to equity and total debt to equity of 1.5 and 1.6, respectively, would be considered ultraconservative in most circles, and the fact that they trend down to 0.9 by Year 1 indicates that MAPAX could be missing out on growth opportunities by ignoring potential expansion to other product lines, international markets, or diversified industries. Conversely, there is certainly nothing wrong with low leverage in terms of the liquidity it brings. Investors should be pleased to see that current ratios are very strong and trending upward while quick ratios remain virtually constant.

The extension of debt utilization and liquidity ratios to the forecasted Year 2 through Year 9 yields even more conservative results, bordering on the absurd. The ratio of total debt to equity decreases to 0.2 over the eight-year forecast and the current ratio skyrockets to more than 12 to 1. Here is a company with a secure market position in a stable, mature industry that does not demand high R&D expenditures. Although it can be considered a cash cow, its cash throwoff is not sufficient to permit it to make major investments, such as business acquisitions. Investors may perceive this as an opportunity to expand through acquisitions by increasing leverage over the next eight years. In terms of financial commitments, future cash flow uncertainty looks very low.

Profitability Ratios

The first two profitability ratios, gross profit to sales and net income to sales, also look very favorable. Although historical ratios of 34 percent and 9 percent, respectively, may not be outstanding for high-tech companies or service businesses, for heavy manufacturing businesses they are very strong. A steady shrinkage in the gross profit percent of just over 2 percent over the eight-year forecast period may be cause for concern, although it can probably be explained by business cycles. In the preceding three years, the cycles for both stoves and furnaces were flat to rising, whereas the long forecast period witnessed a product cycle crossover in the later years, with stove sales falling and furnace sales rising.

Investors might look at this condition as evidence that the addition of more diverse product lines should be considered. Perhaps a less conservative pricing program that incorporates dated invoicing could be employed in order to increase furnace sales. Or it might be possible to tap into foreign markets as an offset to domestic cycles. Any number of alternatives might be feasible with as much leveraging flexibility as MAPAX has. In any event, the gross profit and net income ratios should not be cause for alarm and certainly do not increase investor risk.

The return on equity, return on total investment, and return on total assets ratios present a different story. Historically, MAPAX's returns appear to be on a slippery slope. All three ratios decrease from acceptable levels of approximately 26 percent, 15 percent, and 13 percent in Year 1-2 to 17, 13, and 11 percent, respectively, by Year 1. Although the Year 1 ratios would probably still be acceptable to most investors, the downward trend spells potential trouble.

When these same three ratios are calculated for the forecast years, it can be seen that the deteriorating trends continue for the entire period, with the ratios declining to 11 percent, 10 percent, and 9 percent, respectively, in Year 9. This is not a good sign. It indicates that even though a 9 to 10 percent net income to sales ratio appears satisfactory on the surface, when compared to the capital invested in the business it isn't nearly high enough.

The sliding return on owner's equity and return on investment ratios also indicate that MAPAX is not paying the dividends to equity investors that it should. Some analysts would argue that annual dividend returns to new investors should be forecasted in the pro forma balance sheets. Although this distorts the pure cash flow, adjustments could be made in the future benefits stream to compensate.

For example, assume you plan to pay out dividends of 25 percent of after-tax income each year. If you are the sole recipient, dividends would be added to MAPAX's cash flow to arrive at a cash flow stream. At the same time, the return on owner's equity and return on investment ratios would be improved to approximately 13 percent and 12 percent, respectively, by Year 9, as seen in the following comparison:

| | Without Dividends | | With Dividends | |
Year	% Return on Equity	% Return on Investment	% Return on Equity	% Return on Investment
2	17.3	12.5	17.7	12.6
3	16.1	12.3	17.0	12.7
4	14.4	11.6	15.7	12.3
5	12.6	10.7	14.1	11.6
6	11.0	9.7	12.5	10.7
7	10.8	9.8	12.5	10.9
8	10.4	9.5	12.1	10.8
9	10.9	10.1	12.9	11.6

However, such a calculation doesn't serve much purpose when a valuation is being developed as a base for negotiating a reasonable purchase price or selling price. Since dividend payments will be added back when discounting the cash flow stream to its present value, this exercise serves only to clean up a couple of ratios by juggling numbers. Actually, prospective investors in any company with MAPAX's cash balances shouldn't be too concerned about these two return ratios. The deterioration does, however, point to increased risk.

The return on assets ratio doesn't lend itself to this type of manipulation, and therefore many consider it a better indicator of true profitability, especially for companies with a substantial hard-asset base, such as MAPAX. The relative similarity of the results from the return on assets ratio and the return on equity ratio confirms that MAPAX finances most of its assets with internally generated cash, not long-term debt. If in fact there was a large disparity between the two ratios, with return on equity substantially higher than return on assets, the reverse would be true: that is, the company would be financing a high proportion of its assets with leveraged debt.

A satisfactory return on assets may be achieved through high profit margins or rapid turnover of assets, or both. High-tech companies, distribution companies, service businesses, retail stores, and other companies that have a low asset base normally rely primarily on improved profit margins to increase earnings. MAPAX, on the other hand, enjoys the benefit of relatively high asset turns, as well as respectable margins. The only major deterrent is its inventory policy.

One major drawback in placing too much reliance on return on assets involves the age of the fixed assets included in the base. Generally accepted accounting principles dictate that hard assets must be recorded at original cost. To the extent that companies have old assets and high reserves for depreciation, the asset base will probably reflect amounts that are substantially less than the current market value of the assets. In that case, asset turnover and the return on assets ratio will both be understated. Analysts should guard against this and make financial statement adjustments as warranted.

Asset Utilization Ratios

Analysis of MAPAX's current assets indicates contrary trends. At a constant forty-five days sales or 8 percent turnover, receivables are clearly under control and offer no risk to an investor. Inventory ratios, on the other hand, present a dilemma. From Year 1-2 through Year 1, MAPAX's inventory turns decreased from 2.8 times to 2.2, not a big shift. However, days sales increased from an already high 156 days to 200 days during the same period.

When these ratios are calculated for the pro forma forecasts, conditions deteriorate further. Inventory turnover slips from 2.2 times in Year 1 to 1.3 times in Year 9—a significant drop. Days sales show an even worse picture, jumping from 200 days to more than 300 days during the same period.

This should be a red flag for potential investors. Something unfavorable is happening. It could be one or a combination of the following events:

- Inadvertent changes in purchasing procedures that bring materials into the company much earlier than in the past, indicating a lack of management attention
- Increasing scarcities of critical materials, forcing advance buying to ensure supplies
- A deterioration in the company's internal control procedures, allowing unwarranted inventory buildups
- Production problems, creating increased scrap rates and/or quality rejects
- Material theft

Although further investigation should be attempted when a ratio analysis yields such an anomaly, the likelihood that an outsider can uncover the real reason is probably remote. That being the case, the only alternative is to weight this risk very high when calculating the capitalization rate.

Risk Analysis

After completing the ratio analysis and highlighting those ratios that indicate serious uncertainty, the final analytic step, risk analysis, can be performed. To briefly review, Chapter 6 described four risk analysis methods commonly used to quantify the uncertainty of future benefits:

1. Business risk ratio, comparing the operating income standard deviation to its mean
2. Operating leverage ratio, comparing the percent change in operating income to the percent change in sales
3. Financial leverage ratio, comparing the percent change in net income to the percent change in operating income
4. Professor Altman's Z score, weighting a series of five ratios to yield an overall index of performance

Using the MAPAX ratios in Figure 8-5, we can slot numbers into these formulas. Since the business risk formula that uses the standard deviation of operating income can be meaningful only when comparing alternative investment options and MAPAX is the only option being considered, this measurement will be ignored in favor of the operating leverage ratio, which also measures business risk. This ratio, along with the standard deviation, reflects the impact on earnings of sales and fixed operating costs and is appropriate for a company like MAPAX, which has a high percentage of its nonmaterial costs as fixed costs.

The formula to measure operating leverage is:

$$\text{Operating leverage} = \frac{\text{Percent change in operating income}}{\text{Percent change in sales}}$$

The percent change in both categories should be measured over the forecast period. For MAPAX, this calculation results in a factor of 0.94. This means that for every 1 percent change in sales during the period, operating income will vary 0.94 percent. Since returns to both debtholders and equity investors are derived from earnings, such a small fluctuation relative to sales makes MAPAX a fairly secure investment.

The financial leverage ratio reflects the risk to equity shareholders from a company's financing costs, specifically interest expense. Any company that uses debt financing incurs financial risk as well as business risk, and such is the case with MAPAX. Since payments to debtholders come before those to shareholders, in a business downturn—or if sales are less than forecasted—a double-barreled effect occurs: Less earnings means lower returns to all investors, and a higher percentage of these reduced earnings will go to debtholders, with a corresponding lesser percentage to equity investors.

The formula to calculate financial risk is:

$$\text{Financial risk} = \frac{\text{Percent change in net income}}{\text{Percent change in operating income}}$$

As with business risk, the percent change should be measured over the forecast period. For MAPAX, this calculation results in a factor of 1.69, which means that for every 1 percent change in operating income, net income fluctuates approximately 1.69 percent. Factors for companies with high debt-to-equity ratios will be much higher than this, approaching 4 to 5 percent in some cases. Obviously, the higher the factor, the greater the volatility of income available for common shareholders. The MAPAX ratio of 1.69 is very respectable, however, and does not warrant further concern.

The final risk analysis uses Professor Altman's overall index, called the Z score, as described in Chapter 6. The Z score is primarily a measure of the potential for failure, so it isn't very relevant to a strong company like MAPAX. To confirm this, MAPAX shows a Z score of 3.16, well above Professor Altman's upper limit of 2.99 that might signify trouble on the horizon.

Evaluation of Qualitative Factors

Qualitative data gathered during the due diligence process should include, among other things, sufficient nonfinancial data to permit ferreting out information that might increase the uncertainty of receiving future returns. Such data may or may not be quantifiable and in most cases will add little to an independent appraisal of the value of a business. It can, however, detract from a company's value or confirm suspicions of potential problems developed through more formal ratio analyses.

For instance, qualitative information may substantiate or disprove suspicions about MAPAX relative to inventory buildups, deteriorating returns on assets, or slipping returns on investment. For manufacturing companies, the following relationships are important:

- Sales per employee
- Percentage of total material cost accounted for as scrap
- Percentage of total labor hours spent on rework
- Percentage of units shipped returned by customers

For both manufacturing and nonmanufacturing companies, important qualitative data includes:

- Trends showing an increase in sales allowances or discounts
- Employee turnover

- Average accounts payable balances as a percentage of average receivables
- Accounts payable turnover
- Aging of accounts receivable
- Aging of accounts payable

In addition to these data, the level of management capability has a great deal to do with business value. Unfortunately, no one has yet come up with a way to measure the ability of managers to manage or with a universal measure of management technical capability. However, the fact that universal measures do not exist does not in any way detract from the importance of forming subjective judgments about management competence; it only makes conclusions more susceptible to disagreement.

For purposes of the MAPAX example, we can assume that management is capable and that other qualitative factors do not add to or subtract from the risks already established through quantitative ratio and risk analyses.

Choosing a Capitalization Rate

The next step in the valuation process is the selection of an appropriate capitalization rate to apply against future cash flows. To review what has been covered in previous chapters, the capitalization rate, or discount rate, is made up of a risk-free rate and a premium to be added for perceived uncertainty risk. The risk-free rate is easy to determine. In most cases, a current U.S. Treasury interest rate for obligations with maturities comparable to the forecast period is about as risk-free as one can get.

However, determining the premium for perceived risk is a different matter entirely. To a great extent, regardless of whether you use one of the many cost of capital theories, risk analyses, or ratio analyses, in the end, the assignment of a capitalization rate becomes either a personal judgment or a negotiated factor.

Nevertheless, we can establish a justifiable base from which to negotiate. One method is to isolate and then weight the various levels of risk that evolve through ratio and risk analyses. Another method is to rely on one of the traditional valuation models constructed by Badger, Dewing, Schilt, or by a current valuation appraiser such as Shannon Pratt, among others, as described in Chapter 3. The following discussion compares the weighted risk factor method with that advanced by James H. Schilt.

Weighted Risk Factor Method

Earlier in this chapter, MAPAX ratio and risk analyses highlighted three conditions that could conceivably detract from future returns. They were:

1. The absence of leverage for major expansions
2. A severe slippage in returns on equity and total investment
3. An unusual inventory buildup

Management's decision to ignore leverage financing for major expansions could conceivably cause MAPAX to stagnate over the next eight years. It is certainly possible that the modest $1 million purchase of machinery in Year 4 will not be sufficient to allow the company to resist competitive pressures. The long business cycle for furnaces coupled with projected worldwide economic recovery toward the end of the decade could mean that new foreign competition will enter the market or even that new products will be developed from synthetic materials, forcing MAPAX into major expansions or product development efforts.

The hesitancy on the part of MAPAX management to utilize reasonable leverage might be a serious enough error to increase the capitalization factor. However, it seems unlikely that if such pressures arose, management would not bend to the forces and borrow sufficiently to keep up. Therefore, although conservative financial policies add to risk, they don't increase it materially. On a scale of one to ten, a factor of two will probably suffice.

The slippage in returns on equity and total investment presents a slightly different risk problem. In this case it's difficult to tell how much of the slippage is caused by conservative financial policies that build unreasonable levels of cash reserves and how much is a result of a low net income to sales ratio. While MAPAX falls within the industry average of 8 to 10 percent return on sales, this may not be sufficient to support the company's cost structure.

If, in fact, the forecasted deterioration in returns is accurate, this could mean that major cost structure and management adjustments would have to be made by a new investor. Such restructuring could add costs initially; however, it's impossible at this time to determine the type or level of short-term cost increases, or the effect such actions would have on the company's performance in later years. With such a high degree of uncertainty and the potential for serious degradation of future earnings power, a factor of six would probably be warranted.

The last serious flaw in MAPAX's forecasted performance results from what appears to be an exorbitant inventory buildup. Such high inventory levels could be one reason for the declining return on assets. They could also have a detrimental effect on the company's gross profit margins if, in fact, part of the buildup can be attributed to increased scrap, rework, or customer returns. Of course, out-of-control inventory or purchasing systems could have an even greater negative effect. Since we cannot determine the reasons behind the inventory increase with any accuracy, the only solution is to compensate with a factor of eight in our capitalization rate.

To summarize:

	Weighting Factor
Conservative financial planning	2
Slippage of returns on equity and investment	5
Inventory buildup	8

The MAPAX weighting calculation then becomes:

	Percent Decrease/ Increase	Weighting Factor	Percent Risk
Long-term debt to equity	0.81	2	1.62
Return on equity and return on investment	0.30	5	1.50
Inventory days sales	0.52	8	4.16
TOTAL			7.28

Schilt Method

Chapter 3 described a set of simplistic guidelines for determining risk premium developed by James H. Schilt in 1982. He grouped closely held companies into five categories. The most stable and secure fell into Category 1, "Established businesses with a good trade position, good management, stable past earnings, and a predictable future." The least stable and secure fell into Category 5, "Small personal service businesses with a single owner/manager."

Of the five categories, MAPAX seems to fit the first one best. This category is assigned a risk premium ranging from 6 to 10 percent. The weighted risk factor method results in a factor of 7.28 percent for MAPAX, easily within the Schilt range. Since the two methods complement each other, one can reasonably argue that a risk premium of 7 to 8 percent is probably reasonable for this company. The following discussion uses a rate of 7.5 percent.

With a justifiable risk premium of 7.5 percent plus a risk-free rate of 7.5 percent based on the U.S. Treasury ten-year note rate, a total capitalization factor of 15 percent can be used to arrive at the present value of MAPAX's future cash flow available to equity investors. (Please note that we are using a U.S. Treasury ten-year note carrying a 7.5 percent rate for demonstration purposes only. In actual practice, you would use the rate for the then current U.S. Treasury ten-year note.)

Before making the calculation, however, two additional steps are necessary. First, determine an appropriate method for treating the cash stream allocated to debtholders. Second, estimate the cash flow associated with continuing operations beyond the forecast period.

Discounting Cash Flow to Debtholders

There are four ways to treat the cash stream going to debtholders. The simplest method is to forecast interest payments in the same manner as any other expense, and principal payments in the same manner as payments on long-term leases (i.e., as a reduction in long-term liabilities). Looking at net cash flow from the perspective of a potential equity investor, payments made against long-term debt are no different from those made for other operating needs.

This is the approach most commonly used for valuing minority interests and partnership interests in small businesses whose long-term debt comprises nonmarketable bank loans and mortgages. It is also a very popular method for valuing the entire business in buy/sell transactions.

A second method eliminates long-term debt and corresponding interest payments from the pro forma financial statements. The assumption here is that the purchase price will provide sufficient cash for the seller to liquidate present long-term debt before transferring ownership of the business. The buyer then has the freedom to finance the acquisition with new debt that may carry different payment terms and interest rates.

This method works for buy/sell transactions affecting the entire business, but not for valuing minority or partnership interests. Although it can be used in a stock sale, it is used primarily when selling assets.

A third method treats long-term debtholders as investors, the same as common shareholders. The assumption here is that operating capital can be derived from either debt or equity. Common shareholders earn a return from dividends and the potential appreciation of their investment. Debtholders earn a return from interest payments only. Principal payments to debtholders are merely a return of capital.

Theoretically, both the uncertainty of receiving interest payments and the uncertainty of receiving a full return of capital are recognized when setting the initial interest rate. This eliminates the need to calculate a new present value by discounting future principal payments. The forecast of net cash flow to equity holders treats principal payments like any other operating expenditure. The present value of interest payments is then deducted from the present value of total cash flow to arrive at a present value for future equity benefits.

This method has merit when valuing minority or partnership interests because new stockholders will share in the same capital benefits derived from existing debt as present owners. It also serves as a handy method for valuing the entire business in a buy/sell common stock transaction, assuming the buyer retains the same capital structure.

A fourth method strives to value debt obligations separately from equity holdings. This becomes necessary, for example, when (1) debt is exchanged for equity, (2) a merger involves the assumption of previous liabilities, (3) debt obligations are sold to third parties, or (4) a company solicits new loans from banks, other lenders, or investors.

Valuation theory holds that the fair market value of a future stream of cash flows is equal to the present value of the future cash flows. The higher the uncertainty associated with the cash flows, the higher the appropriate interest rate will be. This theory applies as well to valuing debt as to equity.

The information needed for determining the value of closely held debt securities is:

- The amount of future cash flows generated by the debt security
- The timing of the future cash flows generated by the security
- The appropriate rate of interest or yield to maturity to apply to future cash flows for determining present value

Data for the first two requirements is readily obtained from the security itself. The discount rate, or yield to maturity, requires analyses and judgments similar to those applied to equity interests. Ideally, the security could be compared to similar publicly traded securities to arrive at yields. In most cases, however, small business debt securities do not have enough of the same characteristics as public issues to make such comparisons practical. For a full discussion of the yield-to-maturity calculation for the valuation of various types of debt securities, see Chapter 11.

In the MAPAX example, the first method will be used; that is, interest payments and principal payments will be treated the same as any other operating expenditure. Future cash streams net of these payments will be considered as the future benefits to investors and discounted accordingly.

Calculation of Continuing Value

MAPAX's stream of earnings will certainly continue for many years beyond the forecast period. This is a profitable company, in a mature but slowly growing industry, selling products with only a very slight chance of technological obsolescence. An investor would have every reason to expect the company to continue along its current growth pattern for an indefinite number of years.

Because MAPAX's expected life as a going concern is indeterminable, some estimate must be used. It may be one hundred years, seventy-five years, fifty years, or some other period. The longer the period, the greater the stream of cash flow—and the greater the uncertainty of achieving it. To quantify MAPAX's continuing value, we will arbitrarily assume a period of fifty years.

The capitalization rate applied to continuing value may be the same as that used for the forecast period. Or it may be the discount rate applied in the final year of the forecast. Or it may be an entirely different rate, determined independently to reflect changing conditions.

In the MAPAX case, the latter choice is probably the most sensible. Even though new product development is not currently a major concern and the industry appears to be immune to radical technological change, it seems prudent to assume that future discoveries in materials technology, energy sources, or flow mechanics will have a strong bearing on MAPAX's performance in the distant future. Therefore, a discount rate of 50 percent, or approximately six times the forecast period risk factor of 7.5 percent, will be used to quantify risk for continuing value calculations.

The Final Calculation

The only step remaining to reach a valuation for the MAPAX example is to apply the appropriate capitalization rate to the forecasted cash flow stream. The following cash flow stream from Figure 8-4 is the starting point:

Year	Cash Flow
2	$784,445
3	862,572
4	79,865
5	1,503,858
6	1,263,328
7	1,318,385
8	370,067
9	893,198
TOTAL	$7,075,718

Using this cash flow stream, the following sequence of steps should be followed to arrive at a present value:

1. Estimate continuing cash flow for fifty years beyond the forecast period. Rather than extrapolating the cash flow from the Year 1-2 for fifty additional years, it would be more accurate to strike a mean of the cash flows for the forecast period, which turns out to be $884,465. Then multiply this mean by fifty to arrive at $44,223,241, the total cash flow from Year 9 to Year 2059.
2. Apply the forecast capitalization rate of 15 percent to the forecast period stream of cash flows, which yields a present value of $3,875,884.
3. Apply the estimated capitalization rate of 50 percent to the continuing cash flow stream, resulting in a present value of $1,768,930.
4. Add the two present values to get a total value for the business of $5,644,814.

In this calculation, the present value of cash flow generated during the period beyond Year 9 amounts to 31 percent of the total company present value. Although this is still a high percentage, it appears reasonable based on the maturity of MAPAX and the stability of the stove and furnace industry.

If the purpose of this business valuation is to arrive at a selling price for the company, it should be noted that the present value calculation should be used as the starting point. In closely held businesses, as opposed to public companies, calculated selling prices are nearly always subject to further negotiation between the two parties. However, using the present value as a base point, the parties can negotiate pluses and minuses to reflect qualitative factors that defy numerical analysis. It goes without saying that the desire of each of the parties to reach an accord will have a strong bearing on the final negotiated value.

In many cases, especially for small service businesses, the present value calculation may play a minor role in determining the final price. Competitive bidders, continued participation in the business by the seller, guarantees, noncompete covenants, outstanding contracts, the composition of customer bases, and a variety of other nonquantifiable matters enter into the final decision. But to be meaningful, any negotiation should begin with numerical analyses. The primary purposes of the entire present value exercise is to lay a foundation upon which such analyses can be based.

Depending on the circumstances, one additional step may enter the determination of business value: an analysis that compares the calculated value to a verifiable value for similar businesses. The next chapter briefly looks at the major ways to compare the value of closely held companies with values of other companies or standards.

CHAPTER

Conducting Research on the Internet

The Internet makes it relatively easy to do the comparative analyses so necessary for rounding out business valuations. As the premier business research tool, the Internet offers a convenient, efficient, and fast way to get not only street addresses, phone numbers, and e-mail addresses of providers of financial, market, and industry data, but also to uncover previously unreachable economic and business statistics for small, closely held companies.

Founded in 1998, Google Inc. has become the industry standard for Internet search engines. Its popularity has grown to the point where, for example, we now use the name Google as a verb, as in "Google the State Department" when we want the address, telephone number, or information about the U.S. Department of State.

Google, along with Yahoo, MSN, and other search engines, is only one part of the Internet that helps in business valuations. In fact, so much data is available that it's easy to become overwhelmed. Moreover, the Internet is still growing. New sites arise daily, many from new companies and publications, others replacing original sites because of mergers or dissolutions. Financial ratios; trend lines; leading, co-incident, and lagging indexes; share prices and bond yields; industry barometers; and a variety of other financial, industry, and government data can easily be extracted from the Internet. Some of the most usable data for business valuations are the buy/sell prices of companies of similar size and in the same or similar industries. These prices are then used as an integral part of a comparative analysis.

Using the Internet for Comparative Analysis

Previous chapters offered a variety of methods for establishing a company's value when purchasing, selling, or merging all or part of the business. These calculations result in an absolute numerical value that, theoretically, serves as a base for negotiations between a willing buyer and a willing seller. They are also used by the IRS for assessing estate and gift taxes. And, for internal purposes, these absolute values become the foundation of a company's strategic planning process and are used for establishing growth objectives, incentive compensation measures, and management stock option prices.

But calculating an absolute value doesn't fully answer the question: How much is the business worth? What is its fair market value? To complete the puzzle, absolute values must be compared with actual buy/sell prices of similar businesses.

For instance, the MAPAX eight-year cash flow forecast in Chapter 7 was prepared using historical financial relationships plus a series of future economic and business assumptions. Ratio and risk analyses were then used to estimate a capitalization rate, also referred to as the *cost of capital*. The last step was to determine the present value of the forecasted stream of future cash benefits, including continuing benefits beyond the forecast period. These calculations resulted in an absolute value for the entire business of $5,644,814.

But what adjustments should be made to this value if a competitor of comparable size was sold recently for a price that was 50 percent higher or 50 percent less? Should that affect the MAPAX value? If so, how should it be incorporated into an expanded valuation?

Another pragmatic reason for doing a comparative analysis is that the Internal Revenue Service's Revenue Ruling 59-60 states that "the market price of stocks of corporations engaged in the same or a similar line of business having their stocks actively traded on a free and open market, either on an exchange or over-the-counter" must be considered as one of the fundamental factors affecting gift and estate tax valuations. It's interesting to note that the IRS specifically refers to comparison with stock values of publicly traded companies. Such a comparison may not be possible for small, privately held businesses. For example, it would be ludicrous to compare the value of a corner grocer with the common stock prices of a national chain of supermarkets, or to relate the value of a one-person engineering consulting practice to stock prices of an international contractor such as Halliburton, or to match the value of a small machine shop with the prices of the Boeing Corporation's common shares.

Nevertheless, there are methods by which small, privately held businesses can be compared either with other closely held companies or, in some cases, with public companies. The process of finding appropriate comparisons involves four steps:

1. Put together a list of companies in your industry.
2. Cull this list down to companies that compete in your niche markets (e.g., product/service niches, location niches, or marketing niches).
3. Cull this list down further to segregate publicly traded companies from those that are closely held.
4. Dig out as many financial ratios and as much raw data as possible about those companies that seem to be the closest match.

North American Industry Classification System

In 1997 the North American Industry Classification System (NAICS), developed jointly by the United States, Canada, and Mexico, replaced the U.S. Standard Industrial Classification (SIC) codes. Several iterations of the NAICS have occurred since 1997 so be sure to use the most recent one. Also, it's a good idea to order a copy of the original 1997 Manual which shows the correlation between the 1997 NAICS codes and the 1987 SIC codes. Order from the Census bureau at: U.S. Census Bureau, 4600 Silver Hill Road, Washington, DC 20233 or the Census Bureau call center at 800-923-8282. Also see: *www.census.gov.*

The first approach to finding similar businesses should come from sources that supply data on publicly traded companies in your industry. This is relatively simple once appropriate NAICS codes have been established. However, since virtually all publicly traded companies sell to more than one class of customer or handle more than one product line or service, it's necessary to determine the appropriate NAICS code for products that represent the bulk of a company's business.

As a general rule, it pays to keep the number of NAICS codes to a minimum by making the industry definition as broad as possible. It's hard enough to locate comparative data for one NAICS code; it may be impossible to do so for several codes in multiproduct companies. Also, the NAICS numbering scheme is structured with several subindustry headings and therefore subcodes. The further down the hierarchy one goes, the fewer companies will be found and the more difficult the selection task will become. For example, MAPAX sells products in at least two top-level industrial codes, stoves and furnaces, and conceivably in as many as eight subcodes:

Residential stoves
Commercial stoves
Residential furnaces
Commercial furnaces
Residential stove accessories
Commercial stove accessories
Residential furnace accessories
Commercial furnace accessories

It seems unlikely that comparative data can be found for each of the eight subcodes. And even if it is available, to value a small business at this level serves no purpose, unless, of course, the company plans to spin off one or more of its product lines.

All NAICS codes are listed and defined down to the lowest subheadings in the latest official NAICS Manual, *North American Industry Classification System.*

These codes are structured to permit the collection of data for all business-oriented statistics published by the government and therefore must be kept up-to-date and complete.

Sources of Government Data

Once appropriate NAICS codes have been determined, you can quickly tap into a vast number of government databases. The U.S. Department of Commerce and the U.S. Department of Labor collect reams of monthly, quarterly, and annual data from practically every company, both public and private, doing business in the United States. This data is sorted by various levels of NAICS codes. It can be especially valuable when private-sector organizations either do not publish compilation reports or are hesitant to release data to nonsubscribers and nonmembers.

The categories of government-compiled statistics are similar to those used by larger, more active private-sector organizations. However, in addition to traditional financial information, the U.S. Department of Commerce compiles a virtually unlimited number of statistics in special areas. Here is a sampling:

- Sales volume compared to inventory purchases
- Number of new employees hired compared to employees terminated
- Square feet of floor space used in production
- Building permits and building starts
- Various employee benefit statistics
- Employee accident statistics
- Bad debt ratios

Organizationally, the U.S. Department of Commerce is segregated into bureaus. Each of these bureaus has its own database of information. The hierarchy of bureaus is as follows:

1. Bureau of Industry and Security: *www.bis.doc.gov*
2. Economics and Statistics Administration: *www.esa.doc.gov*
   a. Bureau of the Census: *www.census.gov*
   b. Bureau of Economic Analysis: *www.bea.gov*
3. Economic Development Administration: *www.eda.gov*
4. International Trade Administration: *www.trade.gov*
5. Minority Business Development Agency: *www.mbda.gov*
6. National Oceanic and Atmospheric Administration: *www.noaa.gov*
7. National Telecommunications and Information Administration: *www.ntia.doc.gov*
8. Patent and Trademark Office: *www.uspto.gov*
9. Technology Administration: *www.technology.gov*

Many of these bureaus staff offices in cities across the country where you can peruse vast files and computer databases related to the current year and many prior years.

Sources of Publicly Traded Company Data

Government databases may be all you need. However, the following private-sector sources are easier to use and include data not available through government channels:

• *Standard & Poor's Register of Corporations, Directors, and Executives* and *Standard & Poor's Netadvantage*: *www.netadvantage.standardandpoors.com*. Standard and Poor's Netadvantage is the Internet equivalent of a catalog of S&P directories and reports. It will take you to sources of information for both listed and unlisted companies. The only problem is that it does not distinguish between publicly traded and privately held firms. To make such a separation, use the National Quotation Bureau's *pink sheet* reports (*www.pinksheets.com*) in conjunction with the S&P directories. Pink sheets list the bid and ask prices of stocks of unlisted companies that have appeared within the past month. Only about 3,200 of the myriad publicly owned small companies find their way into NASDAQ markets. Traded shares of the rest remain relatively unnoticed, with most trades conducted between brokers using pink-sheet advertisements. The pink sheets can be invaluable for determining whether a small, unknown company is public or private. If it isn't listed on the pink sheets, it's probably privately held.

From the S&P directories and the National Quotation Bureau's pink sheets you can get information about company history, listings of subsidiaries, location of principal plants and other properties, business and products, officers and directors, comparative income statements, balance sheet statistics, financial ratios, and a description of outstanding securities.

• *Mergent's* (formerly Moody's) *Manuals.* In many respects, the eight Mergent manuals, *Mergent's Industrial Manual and News, Mergent's Bank & Finance Manual and News, Mergent's OTC Manual and News, Mergent's OTC Unlisted Manual and News, Mergent's Public Utilities Manual and News, Mergent's Transportation Manual and News, Mergent's International Manual and News,* and *Mergent's Municipal and Government Manual and News,* are more comprehensive than the S&P directories. These manuals list both large and small companies whose shares are traded in public markets. Of the eight, *Mergent's Industrial Manual and News,* which covers companies listed in the NASDAQ market, and *Mergent's OTC Unlisted Manual and News,* which covers pink-sheet companies are the most helpful. Both provide an array of information about publicly traded companies of all sizes. The range of data includes company history and background, mergers and acquisitions, subsidiaries, business and products, location of principal plants and other properties, names and titles of officers and directors, financial statements, financial and operating ratios, and a description of total capitalization. You can subscribe to any of the Mergent manuals at *www.mergent.com*.

• *DIALOG Information Services.* Although this service was sold to the Thomson Company in 2000, it continues to be one of the most popular online database services and is reachable at *www.dialog. com*. Subscribers to DIALOG can download public company annual reports and SEC 10-K filings. The major drawback in using DIA-LOG and other online database services is that they are expensive.

• *Value Line Investment Survey.* This reference service is one the most widely used resources by both individual investors and securities advisers. Value Line tracks the financial and business performance of 8,000 stocks, 13,000 mutual funds, and 80,000 options and other securities. The *Investment Survey* presents a one-page summary for each company that includes historical trends, historical and current stock prices, description of the business and product lines, beta, and a wealth of profit, sales, and asset information. It also uses a unique evaluation system to rate the timeliness and safety of investing in each company's stock, based on historical trends and regression analysis. Updated periodically, Value Line volumes can be found in the reference section of libraries or you can subscribe to the service online at: *www.ec-server.valueline.com*.

• *D&B's Key Business Ratios.* This Dun & Bradstreet publication contains fourteen significant financial ratios for more than 800 different lines of business listed by NAICS code. Current ratios, quick ratios, debt-to-equity ratios, and net income-to-sales ratios are representative of those included. Although this service doesn't pinpoint specific companies, ratios by NAICS code can help establish comparative standards. The major drawback is that the ratios are drawn from publicly traded companies. Subscribe to *D&B's Key Business Ratios* at: *www.dnb.com*.

Once you start digging into these reference works, it helps to narrow your prospects early in the game. Otherwise your research can go on and on with the cost mounting. With a workable list in hand, you won't find the next steps too time consuming, unless, of course, you happen to be searching in an obscure or highly specialized market.

Begin by phoning each of the companies on your list and asking for information. The amount of data companies will send you is truly amazing. Obtaining sales literature, product descriptions, published quarterly and annual reports, statistical compilations, names of directors and officers, and facility locations is seldom a problem.

Financial data can also be obtained from more than fifteen thousand filed SEC reports. These reports are open to the public and can be accessed through the previously mentioned subscription-based services. With all this data, you can then sort out which companies are relevant for your analysis.

None of the government or private-sector sources described so far will yield specific sell price data for closely held companies or for publicly traded companies whose shares are not actively traded. The best that can be hoped for is financial ratios, sales and earnings trends, and management backgrounds. However, such information can be helpful when compared to similar ratios, trends, and management credentials in your company. Indirectly, this adds credence to the reasonableness of a calculated business value. With financial ratios and sales and earnings trends you can calculate historic cash flows, even for publicly traded companies. Value Line's trends and predictions can then be used to extrapolate these cash flows to the future. The application of a risk-free capitalization factor or a risk-free plus premium capitalization factor produces the present value of the cash stream. This can then be compared to recent traded share prices. A final comparison can be made to the calculated value of your company. The result won't validate your calculated value, but at least it gives you one more test.

Sources of Data for Privately Held Companies

Although it's relatively easy to gather data about publicly traded companies, getting similar information for closely held companies is a bit trickier. Much of the comparative analysis must be derived from scratchy, incomplete data that has to be massaged and analyzed to make any sense. You can, however, tap the Internet. An increasing number of Internet companies collect very valuable data on many industries and sell it to subscribers. The following discussion touches on a few of the more popular ones.

Pratt's Stats

As mentioned in this book, one of the world's most authoritative publications on business valuations is *Valuing a Business*, by Shannon P. Pratt. Mr. Pratt has also developed a private transaction database, Pratt's Stats, offered for subscription by Business Valuation Resources, LLC, *www.bvmarketdata.com*. This database "compiles and reports information on up to 81 data points highlighting the financial and transactional details of the sales of nonpublic, closely held companies." Pratt's Stats is hard to beat as a definitive source of comparable data on large and small closely held companies.

BizStats.com

BizStats.com (*www.bizstats.com*), a comprehensive Internet site, was acquired by BizMiner in October 2007. It is arguably the most complete source of closely held company data available anywhere. BizStats.com offers profitability and operating ratios for small business companies in a raft of industries, ranging from computer services to dentists to advertising agencies to motels to general building and construction companies. It also covers a plethora of closely held company business statistics—such as the safest and riskiest businesses, debt/equity ratios, the most popular small businesses, current ratios and balance sheet ratios by industry, S-corporation operating ratios, and employee productivity data. BizStats.com offers a vast array of ratios, industry data, buy/sell prices, and many other types of business and economic data that will enable you to benchmark your company against companies of similar size and in similar industries.

Trade Associations

Most active trade associations solicit data from member firms to compile quarterly and annual statistics, which are then merged into industry averages. A few associations release a modest amount of qualitative information on specific member companies. Be sure to check out the following if you can get company specific qualitative data:

- Credit status, which is easily obtained from Dun & Bradstreet or other credit agencies if trade associations won't provide it
- Depth and experience of management, which reveals technical certification and tenure with the company
- Competitive position and intensity of competition, which is derived from market size and number of member firms
- Tenure of the business

Some trade associations compile industry average statistics, such as:

- Employee turnover
- Number of employees
- Average sales
- Gross profit and operating profit as a percent of sales
- Annual capital expenditures
- Annual R&D expenditures
- Inventory turns
- Receivables days sales

Although such data will probably be incomplete, it should help you make at least gross comparisons.

Buy/Sell Data

So far we have dealt with data sources related to securities of publicly traded companies and industry financial ratios of privately held companies. More definitive data that pinpoint exact business values can be derived from the actual selling prices of companies, subsidiaries, divisions, or product lines. This is the ultimate comparison for buy/sell valuations.

The selling prices of privately held companies of a size comparable to your company and in the same industry and market would be of significant help in valuing your business. Selling prices of subsidiaries and divisions of public companies that meet comparable size and industry criteria might also be informative, although additional adjustments would have to be made to reflect overhead expenses borne by the parent organization. Other than that, values should be comparable. The question then becomes: Where can you find data about recent sales of similar businesses? The answer lies in the wealth of buy/sell data accumulated primarily by database companies, merger and acquisition (M&A) consultants, and the Conference Board.

- The Conference Board, Inc. (*www.conference-board.org*). Among many other services, the Conference Board offers members several publications that include a surprisingly thorough analysis of completed buy/ sell deals. The Board's main criterion is that the deal must have involved the transfer of at least 50 percent of the entity's ownership, thereby excluding the sale of minority interests and stock market trades. The report includes transactions involving publicly traded and privately held companies, corporate and noncorporate entities, subsidiaries, divisions, and affiliates in a wide range of industrial classifications, such as manufacturing, mining, retail, services, forestry and fisheries, wholesale trade, and construction. It discloses total assets, business description, and location. Beyond that, however, it contains a minimum of financial data.

- *Mergerstat Review* by FactSet Mergerstat, LLC. FactSet Mergerstat is a " . . . leading provider of global M&A information." Its *Mergerstat Review* (*www.mergerstat.com*) is an annually updated book that has financial data on completed and pending transactions. It contains statistics on such diverse topics as merger announcements, buy/sell prices paid, names of foreign buyers, methods of payment, and corporate tender offers. It also provides historical data in each category. The publication's main weakness is that by being published in book format, some transactions have occurred too far in the past to be useful for current comparisons.

- *The Merger and Acquisition Sourcebook* by NVST, Inc. At *www.nvst.com* this is one of the premier sites for private investment opportunities. The Sourcebook includes M&A facts on more than 3,900 companies. Among these facts are buy/sell prices paid by industry, takeover law updates, tax matters, and industry surveys on acquisitions. NVST also offers the *Data Retriever-Online Database*, which includes information about buy/sell transactions, offers to buy/sell, and buy/sell deals that fell through. Its coverage of financial data can be very useful in conjunction with the annual Sourcebook.

- *Valuation Resources.com.* This is a free guide to business valuation resources, including information on industries and companies as well as many other business and economic facts. It is well worth a look at *www.valuationresources.com.*

- Bizcomps Studies. This company collects a variety of business and economic data and publishes a micro-business sales transactions database. This database has over nine thousand small business buy/sell transactions by NAICS code. All transactions are priced at less than $1 million. Check it out at *www.bizcomps.com.*

- BizMiner. At *www.bizminer.com* this database provides a huge number of small business financial ratios by industry.

One of the biggest problems you'll encounter when digging out buy/sell information is that the parties to these transactions are not required by law to divulge any information about the deal—unless, of course, at least one party is a public company, in which case, it must file a disclosure with the SEC on Form 8-K. Privately held company buy/sell transactions are included in the above publications only if buyers or sellers choose to disclose them.

One seldom advertised source of data on closely held companies that have recently been sold is the M&A consulting business itself. Although ethical M&A consultants won't divulge specific company or transaction financial details, most keep track of the pertinent facts of their own deals. Up-to-date, larger consulting firms maintain databases of transactions they have handled and for a fee, might be willing to give you access. Even those who do not compile their own databases often release financial ratios and buy/sell prices in specific industries that they have researched.

The only way to authoritatively justify a calculation of the market worth of a business is to test it against the buy/sell price of similar companies. But this can be a trying, frustrating exercise and more than one buy/sell transaction has fallen through because neither party was willing to take the time to match valuation calculations with market and industry pricing data.

Internet Addresses

Here are several Internet addresses that should be helpful in digging out comparative analysis data as well as other information related to business valuations:

Trade Organizations
* American Society of Appraisers: *www.bvappraisers.org*
* American Hotel and Motel Association: *www.hftp.org*
* American Business Appraisers Network: *www.businessval.com*
* International Business Brokers Association: *www.ibba.org*

Private Companies/Organizations
* Bank for International Settlements: *www.bis.org*
* BizMiner: *www.bizminer.com*
* BizStats.com: *www.bizstats.com*
* BondsOnLine: *www.bondsonline.com*
* Business Valuations Resources, Inc.: *www.bvmarketdata.com*
* Conference Board, The: *www.conference-board.org*
* Dialog Information Services (a division of the Thomson Corporation): *www.dialog.com*
* Dislosure, Inc.: *www.oclc.org*
* Dun & Bradstreet: *www.dnb.com*
* FactSet Mergerstat, LLC: *www.mergerstat.com*
* Hay Group, The: *www.haygroup.com*
* Houlihan, Lokey, Howard & Zukin, Inc.: *www.hlhz.com*
* Mergent, Inc. (acquired the Financial Information Services division of Moody's Investors Services in 1998): *www.mergent.com*
* NASDAQ (National Association of Securities Dealers Automated Quotation System): *www.nasdaq.com*
* National Bureau of Economic Research, Inc.: *www.nber.org*
* National Quotation Bureau: *www.pinksheets.com*
* NoLo: *www.nolo.com*
* NVST, Inc.: *www.nvst.com*
* Standard & Poor's: *www.standardandpoors.com*
* Valuation Resources: *www.valuationresources.com*
* Value Line Survey: *www.valueline.com*
* Value Line Investment Survey: *www.ec-server.valueline.com*
* Willamette Management Associates, Inc.: *www.willamette.com*

Publications and Databases
- Barrons: *www.barrons.com*
- Biz Comp Studies: *www.bizcomp.com*
- CPA Journal, The: *www.nysscpa.org/cpajournal/*
- Federal Reserve Bulletin: *www.federalreserve.gov/pubs/bulletin*
- Journal of Finance: *www.afajof.org*
- Kelley Blue Book: *www.kbb.com*
- North American Industry Classification System (NAICS): *www.census.gov/naics*
- Simplified Employee Plan: *www.dol.gov/edsa/publications*
- Standard & Poor's Netadvantage: *www.netadvantage.standardandpoors.com*
- Standard & Poor's Credit Week: *www.creditweek.com*
- Valu Adder: *www.valuadder.com*
- Wall Street Journal: *www.wsj.com*

U.S. Government
- U.S. Department of Commerce: *www.commerce.gov*
- U.S. Department of Labor: *www.dol.gov*
- U.S. Census Bureau: *www.census.gov*

PART II

VALUATIONS
FOR SPECIAL
SITUATIONS

CHAPTER

Minority Interests

Experience has shown that more disputes arise over the value of small business minority interests than over practically any other matter. The value of an entire business for IRS purposes is based on the tax code, revenue rulings, and tax court precedents. The value of an entire business in a merger, acquisition, or disposition begins with the calculated present value of a future stream of benefits and ends with a negotiated price. Determining the value of a minority interest is a different matter entirely. The reason is simple: A minority shareholder has no control over the board of directors, operating policies, or the distribution of earnings. A shareholder with a 49 percent interest in a company is in as weak a position as one with 1 percent.

This tends to be a hard pill for small business owners to swallow, especially when strategic plans call for bringing in one or more partners. The common assumption is that a 49 percent interest is worth 49 percent of the total company's value. But this is totally at variance with the benefits arising from minority versus majority control.

For example, small business owner Smith decides to plan for retirement in ten years by selling 49 percent of the outstanding shares to a partner, who will eventually buy the entire business. Smith goes through a traditional business valuation, multiplies the total company value by 49 percent, and offers that as a price to the new partner. Smith argues that if the new partner, Jones, is to receive 49 percent of the earnings of the business, the purchase price should be 49 percent of the company's value. Jones flatly refuses on the basis that Smith retains absolute control and could back out of the promised distribution, leaving Jones with nothing.

Smith sweetens the pot, agreeing to write a partnership contract stipulating that Jones will receive a distribution of 49 percent of the cash earnings each year and Smith 51 percent. Still not good enough, argues Jones. What will prevent Smith from taking an outrageous salary or bonus or charging personal expenses to the company, thereby diminishing the cash available for distribution? And on and on it goes. It is virtually impossible to write a contract guaranteeing Jones a 49 percent cash distribution when Jones has no authority to determine the total available cash.

Or take another example that is equally problematical in partnership arrangements. Assume that Smith and Jones agree to equal ownership, but that Smith's wife wants 2 percent. In this case, a 2 percent owner has more control than either of the two 49 percent shares, because when disputes arise, Smith's wife can cast her vote one way or the other and therefore control the decision.

Or assume that Smith and Jones each own a 50 percent interest, thereby sharing control. With neither partner holding a controlling interest, who will arbitrate disagreements over policy decisions? Such disputes bring inaction, and inaction can ruin the business. If value is based on control, and it should be, then a 50-50 split severely diminishes the value of both parties' ownership interests.

Similar situations can arise with different minority interest percentages in virtually any conceivable business with more than one owner. And in all cases, the value of an interest is either enhanced by control over a company's policies or diminished by the lack thereof.

To further complicate the problem, laws relating to minority shareholder rights vary from state to state. In states with laws that give minority shareholders substantial power under certain circumstances, minority interests have a greater value than in those states that do not. Take, for example, three situations.

Some states require a simple majority vote of shareholders to approve major policies, such as the sale or merger of the company or the acquisition of another company. Other states require a two-thirds or greater majority. If a two-thirds majority vote is required, a minority shareholder with just over a one-third interest can block decisions, and this increases the value of that interest.

In a second situation, minority interests are enhanced in those states that permit an aggregate number of minority shares, up to a defined percentage of the total, to petition the courts to force a dissolution of the corporation under certain circumstances. Usually, controlling interests can prevent dissolution by buying the minority shares for their fair value; however, as in the first example, such laws increase the value of minority interests beyond what they would be in states without such statutes.

In a third case, many states now have dissenting shareholder laws that give minority shareholders the right to dissent from major corporate decisions, such as the disposal of a major part of the business, a merger, the acquisition of another business, or the sale of the entire company. So long as dissenting shareholders follow the state statutes for *perfecting their dissent*, courts will normally decree the remedy to be a purchase of the dissenter's shares in cash at a stipulated value. Once again, minority interests are worth more than in those states without such laws.

Clearly, the problem of valuing minority interests when selling part of the business, when raising equity capital, or when determining the amount that must be paid to satisfy disgruntled minority shareholders is a major one confronting any business with more than one owner.

How then should minority interests be valued? Leaving the question of value enhancement by state statute to the lawyers and courts to grapple with, there are only two practical ways to quantify the value of minority interests: (1) as a percentage of the total business value, plus or minus negotiated premiums or discounts; or (2) by calculating a stream of future benefits to the specific minority interest, discounted to its present value.

Although many other approaches have been tried, they are all offshoots of one or the other of these two methods.

Despite the desire of most parties to have a clean, mathematically precise value to hang onto, the fact remains that pragmatically, the price determined for the purchase or sale of a small business or majority interest only begins with a calculated amount. Forthright negotiation between the parties is necessary to reach agreement on a price the market will bear. Nevertheless, the starting point should be a calculated value.

Pro Rata Share of Total Business Value

Although the determinations of total company value for buying or selling an entire company and for buying or selling minority interests are very similar, two distinct differences stand out. The following discussion will use the buyer as a focal point, although it should be understood that the same conceptual differences apply to valuations for both buying and selling.

The first difference relates to expectations of changes in the company's performance after the purchase. When buying an entire company or a controlling interest, an investor has the authority to make any desired changes in its operations. Therefore, when analyzing the company's historical financial statements or when preparing pro forma statements, adjustments can be made that reflect planned changes subsequent to the takeover. Such adjustments might include changing the inventory valuation method or depreciation schedules, implementing new purchasing practices or employee benefit programs, arranging short- or long-term financing, and a raft of other matters. Naturally, such adjustments could have a major bearing on the stream of forecasted cash flows and its present value.

The buyer of a minority interest clearly doesn't have that kind of authority. The absence of control brings with it an acceptance of the decisions of controlling shareholders. For this reason, financial statement adjustments may be significantly different when performing a total company valuation.

A second major difference may also arise. In most cases the purchaser of a minority interest does so with the intention of (1) paying additional funds at a later date for a controlling interest, as with a successor partnership; (2) cashing out the investment through a public stock offering; or (3) reaping returns by selling the shares back to the company or to controlling shareholders. In any event, the holding period for a minority interest is finite.

Therefore, the inclusion of a continuing value calculation over fifty, seventy-five, or 100 years would be meaningless.

Referring back to the MAPAX example used in previous chapters, it was assumed that no significant adjustments to either historical or fore-casted financial results were necessary. However, a continuing value period of fifty years was assumed, and this resulted in an increase in the company's value. The total stream of future cash flows, including those for the fifty years beyond the forecast period, totaled $51,298,960, although the stream of cash flows for the forecast period was only $7,075,719.

In the previous MAPAX example, which assumed a purchase of the entire company, the continuing cash flow was discounted by a risk factor of 50 percent, while the risk factor for the forecast period was only 7.5 percent. Finally, the discounted present value of the entire company was calculated as $5,644,814; the present value without the continuing period was $3,875,884. It is the latter value from which a pro rata minority interest should be calculated.

To carry forward with the MAPAX example, assume that instead of selling the entire company, MAPAX's owners chose to sell a 25 percent minority interest. The first step of the calculation would be to multiply the previously calculated total company value of $3,875,884 by 25 percent, resulting in a base for the minority interest value of $968,971. The next step involves the determination of a minority discount.

Minority Interest Discount

More than one investor, seller, or even professional appraiser has become confused about the intent of calculating a minority interest discount. Confusion arises because the parties misdefine the reason for making the calculation. Aside from the uncertainty associated with receiving a forecasted stream of earnings, which is reflected in the capitalization rate, two conditions arise that could devalue a business interest: (1) the inability of shareholders to sell their interests, and (2) a lack of shareholder control over company policies. The two concepts are entirely different and result in substantially different valuation results.

Take the question of marketability first. The uncertainty of a shareholder's ability to cash in an investment is related to investment liquidity. To measure this liquidity, the value of the minority interest must be subtracted from a total company base that has the same liquidity profile. In other words, if the probability of finding a buyer for an entire business is very low, as in a personal services business, the total business value should reflect this, and the minority interest value can then be calculated as a pro rata share of that base. Marketability, or liquidity, has nothing to do with determining a minority interest discount factor.

Now take the second condition, minority shareholders' lack of control over company policies. In addition to the fact that controlling shareholders in a closely held company can do what they please with the business while minority shareholders cannot, minority shareholders do not have the ability to liquidate their interests without approval from controlling shareholders. The latter not only have the right to determine the timing and selling price of minority shareholders' interests; they also decide when, if ever, the company will go public, thereby creating a liquid market for all shareholders. When valuing a minority interest, it is this lack of control that causes a discount, not the lack of marketability.

In the parlance of the Business Valuation committee of the American Society of Appraisers:

- *Minority discount* means "the reduction from the pro rata share of the value of the entire business to reflect the absence of the power of control."
- *Marketability discount* means "an amount or percentage deducted from an equity interest to reflect the lack of marketability."

Having put to bed the matter of marketability, at least temporarily, the question then arises: How does one calculate a minority discount?

Over the last twenty years several studies have been undertaken in order to develop standards that would reflect appropriate discounts for minority interests in public companies. Of course, millions of shares are traded on exchanges every day, nearly all representing minority interests. However, in most cases, the stock of public companies is so widely dispersed that no one holds a controlling interest. Therefore, market prices per se, or market averages, were useless for determining minority interest discounts.

In many cases, however, corporate takeovers created controlling interests, not necessarily majority interests, but certainly controlling interests. Several studies conducted by W. T. Grimm & Company (acquired by Merrill Lynch in 1988), Willamette Management Associates, Inc., Houlihan, Lokey, Howard & Zukin, Inc. (an international investment bank), and other professional appraisal and financial advisory services firms analyzed market prices for shares immediately before the acquisition of controlling blocks of shares at premium prices and market prices immediately after. On average, nearly all studies concluded that prices dropped on average between 30 and 40 percent from the pre-takeover norms. The conclusion was that the absence of control caused this discount.

Studies of closely held companies indicated that discounts of 33 to 40 percent from book value were the norm. Some, in fact, found that discounts were as high as 50 to 75 percent when calculated against a discounted present value of future benefits for the entire company rather than book value.

From such authoritative studies, it seems safe to conclude that in most closely held companies, minority discounts ranging from 30 percent to 50 percent would not be unreasonable. In addition, minority interests in businesses with virtually no marketability should include a reduction in total company value to reflect illiquidity.

Returning to the MAPAX example, the value of a pro rata 25 percent minority interest was $968,971. As shown in the following calculation, the application of a 40 percent minority discount to reflect the absence of control yields a value of $387,588 for minority shareholders:

Discounted present value of future benefits for entire company (excluding continuing value)	$3,875,884
Minority interest percent	25%
Minority interest pro rata share of present value	$968,971
Minority discount	40%
Minority interest value	$387,588

Separate Calculation for the Present Value of Minority Benefits

The second method for calculating the value of a minority interest takes a completely different approach. This method makes no attempt to value the entire company. Instead, it calls for the development of a future stream of cash benefits specifically applicable to minority interests. It then discounts this stream to its present value, using an appropriate capitalization rate to reflect the degree of uncertainty in receiving these benefits.

In other words, this *base zero* method goes through the same forecast mechanics developed in previous chapters for entire companies, but this time only the future benefits for minority shareholders are discounted. Typically, such a forecast recognizes two distinct types of future cash benefits: (1) a stream of dividends and (2) a gain on selling the interest.

Once again using the MAPAX example, Figure 10-1 shows the cash flow forecast assuming that an annual dividend of 25 percent of net income is paid to all shareholders, controlling and minority.

From the forecast, we can extract dividend payments and calculate the minority shareholders' portion, as follows:

Year	Total Dividends Paid	Minority Interest @ 25%
2	$272,895	$68,224
3	300,064	75,016
4	312,257	78,064
5	314,423	78,606
6	307,770	76,942
7	338,264	84,566
8	357,743	89,436
9	418,543	104,636
TOTAL	$2,621,959	$655,490

FIGURE 10-1

MAPAX MANUFACTURING CORP.
STATEMENT OF CASH FLOW (in dollars)

| | Actual | | | ----Forecasted---- | | | | |
	Year 1	Year 2	Year 3	Year 4	Year 5	Year 6	Year 7	Year 8
CASH RECEIPTS								
Beginning receivables	1,406,250	1,473,653	1,544,779	1,619,845	1,650,116	1,660,268	1,737,737	1,819,975
Sales	11,789,225	12,358,231	12,958,763	13,200,924	13,282,143	13,901,899	14,559,800	16,175,250
Ending receivables	(1,473,653)	(1,544,779)	(1,619,835)	(1,650,116)	(1,660,268)	(1,737,737)	(1,819,975)	(2,021,906)
Cash receipts from operations	11,721,822	12,287,105	12,883,696	13,170,654	13,271,991	13,824,429	14,477,563	15,973,319
CASH EXPENDITURES								
Beginning payables	775,614	815,255	857,147	868,573	842,124	882,459	925,189	1,100,330
Purchases	6,522,038	6,857,177	6,948,587	6,736,992	7,059,673	7,401,513	8,802,639	9,242,771
Ending payables	(815,255)	(857,147)	(868,573)	(842,124)	(882,459)	(925,189)	(1,100,330)	(1,155,346)
Material cash expenditures	6,482,398	6,815,284	6,937,160	6,763,441	7,019,338	7,358,783	8,627,498	9,187,754
Direct labor	989,146	1,038,413	1,069,566	1,101,653	1,134,702	1,168,743	1,317,372	1,403,683
OPERATING EXPENDITURES								
Beginning accrued expenses	200,000	200,000	200,000	200,000	200,000	200,000	200,000	200,000
Manufacturing expenses	777,376	808,535	900,391	927,403	991,625	1,021,373	1,136,441	1,267,250
Selling expenses	632,210	656,560	732,001	812,796	829,310	859,721	891,534	947,746
Administrative expenses	556,963	571,601	586,679	605,660	621,656	638,132	655,103	672,582
Other expenses	20,000	20,000	20,000	20,000	20,000	20,000	20,000	20,000
Ending accrued expenditures	(200,000)	(200,000)	(200,000)	(200,000)	(200,000)	(200,000)	(200,000)	(200,000)
Total operating expenditures	1,986,549	2,056,696	2,239,071	2,365,858	2,462,590	2,539,227	2,703,078	2,907,579
Taxes	669,033	735,640	765,534	770,844	754,533	829,292	877,047	1,026,105
Machinery purchases	0	0	1,000,000	0	0	0	0	0
FINANCING EXPENDITURES								
Bank note								
Principal	50,000	50,000	100,000	0	0	0	0	0
Interest	12,750	8,500	0	0	0	0	0	0
Long-term loan								
Principal	200,000	200,000	200,000	200,000	200,000	200,000	200,000	200,000
Interest	380,000	360,000	340,000	320,000	300,000	280,000	260,000	240,000
Mortgage loan								
Principal	75,000	75,000	75,000	75,000	75,000	75,000	75,000	75,000
Interest	92,500	85,000	77,500	70,000	62,500	55,000	47,500	40,000
Total principal	325,000	325,000	375,000	275,000	275,000	275,000	275,000	275,000
Total interest	485,250	453,500	417,500	390,000	362,500	335,000	307,500	280,000
Dividends paid	272,895	300,064	312,257	314,423	307,770	338,264	357,743	418,543
Total cash expenditures	11,210,272	11,724,597	13,116,088	11,981,219	12,316,433	12,844,308	14,465,238	15,498,664
NET CASH GENERATED	511,550	562,508	(232,392)	1,189,435	955,558	980,121	12,324	474,655
Beginning cash in bank	1,000	512,550	1,075,058	842,666	2,032,101	2,987,659	3,967,780	3,980,104
Ending cash in bank	512,550	1,0705,058	842,666	2,032,101	2,987,659	3,967,780	3,980,104	4,454,760

The next step is to determine a capitalization rate. The original MAPAX calculation from Chapter 7 assumed a capitalization rate comprising a risk-free rate of 7.5 percent (this rate used for demonstration purposes only) plus a perceived risk discount of another 7.5 percent, for a total of 15 percent. The risk-free rate should be applicable to the minority interest as well.

However, based on previous analyses, a risk discount of 7.5 is much too low. In fact, when MAPAX was compared with the few public companies in this industry, it was determined that a minority discount of 30 percent was more reasonable to account for the absence of control.

But minority shareholders also face the same uncertainty related to future company performance as controlling interests. Therefore, the minority discount should be added to the original 7.5 discount, providing a total of 37.5 percent. Adding in the risk-free portion, the total capitalization rate comes out to be 45 percent. Applying this to the dividend stream of $655,490, the discounted present value comes out to $159,213.

That isn't the end, however. The second future cash benefit must also be reckoned with, that is, the gain that can be expected upon the sale of minority shares. Assume that a potential minority investor discovers that a MAPAX competitor issued an IPO this year that sold for a per share price of six times earnings. MAPAX's net income for Year 9 is forecasted to be $1,674,000 (see Chapter 7), and six times this amount totals $10,044,000.

Now assume that the controlling shareholders have told the minority investor that they plan to go public with 30 percent of the company. Six times earnings times 30 percent equals $3,013,200 of the total expected IPO. The minority investor gets 25 percent, or $753,300. This amount should be included as future cash benefits along with expected dividends.

So far so good, except that the uncertainty attached to receiving $753,000 from a public offering in eight years is certainly higher than that of receiving dividends over the same period. There isn't any scientific way to calculate this risk, so the best that can be done is to estimate. If the uncertainty of receiving dividends rates a 30 percent minority discount, the uncertainty of cashing in for the projected amount in eight years is probably two or three times as great. For the sake of argument, we will split the difference and assume a 75 percent discount rate. The present value of $753,000 in eight years at a 75 percent discount equates to $8,560.

We can now arrive at the total value of a 25 percent minority interest in MAPAX by adding the present value of the dividend stream, $159,213, and the present value of the expected capital gain, $8,560, for a total value of $167,773.

Comparing the present value calculated under this method with that calculated under the pro rata share method ($387,588), it's easy to see the wide difference. In fact, the zero base method yields a value only 43 percent as great as the total company pro rata share method. Which one is correct? Probably neither, although for negotiating purposes, an average of the two might be a good starting point.

Minority Interests in Micro Businesses

Valuation of minority interests in micro businesses, defined as companies with less than $1 million annual sales, is much less precise than the previous calculations. Owners of or investors in a pharmacy that turns $600,000 in sales, a machine shop that does $800,000, a computer software development business doing $400,000, or a construction company grossing $200,000 will normally be unable to use either the pro rata share method or the base zero method, for several reasons:

- It doesn't make sense to compare such micro businesses with traded stock prices to determine discount rates. That's like comparing apples to oranges.
- The resale marketability of a minority interest in a business this small is usually nil. Typically, the only buyers are relatives or the controlling shareholder.
- Most micro businesses do not maintain the type of accounting records necessary to reasonably forecast future cash flows for any length of time. In fact, more often than not, local market and general economic conditions affect sales fluctuations far more than management efforts do.
- Most owners of companies this size wouldn't dream of paying dividends.

Yet sales of partial interests in micro businesses do occur. Employees buy in, relatives contribute equity, occasionally banks might exchange debt for a small equity position, customers purchase small interests in suppliers, and suppliers buy small interests in customers. Although occasionally such minority interest may be purchased as investments, the great majority are defensive measures.

Businesses that have no other source of capital may turn to relatives of the owner for a fresh injection. Companies that have missed debt service payments may be able to convince lenders to take a minority interest in exchange for part of the debt obligation. Major corporations that buy critical parts or materials from small suppliers frequently take a small equity interest as a means of exerting control over shipment schedules or product quality. Conversely, large suppliers have been known to buy minority interests to safeguard the financial viability of key customers.

Since dividends will not be forthcoming, such defensive investments are normally made without reference to the risk of receiving a stream of future dividend benefits. For benefits other than those derived from the defensive action, investors must look to the eventual sale of their interests.

However, unless the micro business grows significantly, the marketability of minority interests is very slight.

To compensate for this lack of marketability, a contract is frequently executed, stipulating that the company will repurchase the interest for a specified buyout price at a given date in the future or upon the occurrence of a future event. The buyout price is usually tied to one of several company performance indicators, such as book value, sales growth, excess profits, or the sale of significant business assets.

Seldom do micro business owners or investors go through a formal valuation process to arrive at either a buyout price or the initial interest given up in exchange for the equity contribution. In both cases, arbitrary amounts are agreed upon, or negotiated, without reference to financial statements or pro forma forecasts, unless the buyout price is based on book value.

A complete discussion of valuations used in buyout agreements can be found in Chapter 12. Valuations for buy/sell transactions for professional practices and personal service businesses are covered in detail in Chapter 15.

CHAPTER

11

Debt Securities

Most discussions about the valuation of debt securities center on various types of publicly issued corporate and government bonds; however, the topic is equally relevant for closely held businesses. Although invested capital may be either debt or equity, the risks of holding each are entirely different. On the one hand, the stream of future cash benefits to equity investors is the sum of dividend payments and appreciation gains in the value of common shares. Since the amount and timing of dividends is at the discretion of the company, and the amount and timing of future appreciation gains is indeterminable, the risk of receiving future benefits plays a major role in equity valuations.

On the other hand, debt securities carry specific settlement dates and fixed-income provisions in the form of interest rates. The amount and timing of interest payments is established at the date of issue. The amount and specific due dates of principal payments are set out contractually in the body of the instrument. Since both the periodic stream of income and the amount and timing of the eventual return of capital are contractually determined, the risk of holding debt securities should be substantially less than that of holding equity investments.

Except for differences in the degree of risk, similar valuation methods are employed for both debt and equity securities. In both cases the general valuation theory holds: The fair market value of a future stream of cash flows is equal to the present value of future cash flows. And in both cases, perceived risk is recognized in the capitalization rate.

Before proceeding, it might be helpful to clarify two points. First, the debt securities referred to in the following sections are only those issued by closely held businesses. Debt instruments issued by financial institutions (e.g., certificates of deposit), government agencies (e.g., U.S. Treasuries), and public corporations are specifically excluded. By definition, then, the debt securities under discussion are not traded in public markets and therefore cannot be directly tracked through capital market quotes, prices, or indexes.

Second, debt securities issued by closely held businesses include promissory notes, mortgage notes, and contractual agreements. Small businesses occasionally issue derivatives of these basic securities, such as convertible debentures or preferential preferred stock, which is really a debt instrument. However, the use of these derivatives is so minimal that they are excluded from the following discussions.

This chapter reviews acceptable methods for valuing debt securities from three perspectives:

1. Companies issuing new securities
2. Investors buying those securities
3. Investors buying securities from third parties

Reasons for Valuing Debt Securities

There seems to be a common misconception among small business owners that we have little or no choice in setting terms or interest rates when applying for loans. Thankful to get a loan, we willingly agree to interest rates and repayment terms dictated by intimidating bankers. But this doesn't have to be the case. Armed with the knowledge of how banks calculate risk, we should be able to determine our maximum rate and terms before submitting an application. If a bank insists on more onerous conditions, remember that at last count there were about ten thousand banks in the United States, many of them hungry for loan business.

Three conditions determine interest rates and repayment terms:

1. Current market risk-free rates reflected by the prime rate in banking circles and by the rate paid on U.S. Treasury ten-year notes nearly everywhere else
2. Perceived risk of receiving interest and principal payments on schedule
3. Collateral backing the loan (the quality of this collateral detracts from or adds to the risk factor)

Collateral quality is the key to reducing the risk premium: the higher the quality of the assets securing the loan, the less uncertainty an investor should have about being repaid on schedule. Collateral quality relates directly to the ease with which an investor could convert the collateral to cash in an amount at least equal to the outstanding loan balance.

Collateral comprising cash or cash equivalents in the amount of the loan placed in escrow obviously has the highest quality and should eliminate any loan premium. A promise to repay from a business owner who has defaulted previously and does not own any convertible assets to attach represents the lowest-quality collateral, encouraging investors to assess a maximum premium.

In addition to determining the value of a debt instrument that will ensure the lowest rate with the best terms, there may be other reasons for small businesses to value debt. The most common are the following:

- Excess cash may be invested in corporate or government bonds. A valuation of the debt security will ensure the right choice to maximize returns.
- A buy/sell transaction may involve the exchange of debt for equity. To ensure the negotiation of a fair exchange, it's necessary to know the value of the debt security. This is particularly important when buying/selling small businesses because frequently part or all of the purchase price is paid out over a period of time and secured by a promissory note. This creates a debt obligation, and a determination of the obligation's fair market value, which in many cases is below its face value, is required.
- Estate and gift tax laws require that debt obligations be valued at fair market value. Again, this value may be significantly below the debt instrument's face value.
- In a leveraged buyout, new classes of debt are created that must be valued along with the entire enterprise in order to allocate the purchase price among the classes of participants.
- Not infrequently, companies need to recapitalize their balance sheets to increase the amount of leverage they have to work with. This involves issuing debt obligations in exchange for equity shares, requiring a valuation of both securities.
- Reorganization in bankruptcy cases involves the rearrangement of debt securities, both before the reorganization plan is adopted and as an integral part of the reorganization plan itself. Such a recapitalization frequently requires the creation of new classes of debt securities or the exchange of debt for equity shares. In both cases, a debt valuation is required.

The valuation of debt securities is also an important part of the risk evaluation process for private investors. Investors should employ the same risk analysis techniques for valuing debt securities that they use for determining the advisability of purchasing all or a controlling equity interest in a small business.

Several interesting avenues for investing in debt securities are available, including the acquisition of defaulted bank loans, foreclosed mortgages, junk bonds, asset-backed debt obligations, senior/subordinated notes and bonds, and a variety of other financial innovations. Debt valuation is also an extremely important part of the evaluation process when investigating the purchase of common shares in bankrupt companies.

Fundamentals of Debt Valuation

Except for the risk factor, virtually the same process is used to value debt securities as to value equity interests. It comprises:

- Due diligence investigations
- Analysis of historical financial statements
- Preparation of pro forma financial statements and cash flow forecasts
- Ratio analysis
- Financial and business risk analysis
- Comparative analysis
- Calculation of the present value of the stream of future cash flows

In addition to these steps, debt valuations require an analysis of the underlying collateral backing the security. As previously stated, the quality of the underlying collateral is the main ingredient in determining the capitalization rate. All valuation steps leading to the calculation of the present value of future cash flows should be directed toward uncovering the quality of the collateral being pledged. With an evaluation of collateral quality in hand, one can proceed with the valuation calculation.

To demonstrate this calculation, we will use another fictitious company, this time called OMORE, Inc. OMORE sells imported fabric, women's and men's designer wear, and cruise clothing and accessories. All products are sold to Caribbean and South Florida resorts. The company does not perform any modifications on the merchandise, opting instead to act as a pure distributor to retail outlets. Its business has been growing recently, and sole-source contracts with Danish and French manufacturers eliminate direct competition. Its major sales deterrent is the national economic cycle. When recessions hit, OMORE loses business; during boom times, it cannot fill market demand fast enough.

Such a cyclical business means that OMORE must borrow working capital during boom periods and liquidate it as the economy turns down. To date, it has been successful in meeting this schedule. The company is now entering a new boom cycle and needs to float five-year notes totaling $2 million to expand its distribution network and to purchase inventory. Figure 11-1 shows OMORE's actual Year 1 financial statements and pro forma projections for six years. Figure 11-2 shows cash flows for the same forecast period.

This profitable company is growing at a sustained rate of 4 percent per year over the six-year forecast period, showing an overall 27 percent growth in sales from Year 1 to Year 7. Although 45 percent gross profit and 17 percent net income before interest and taxes are acceptable ratios for this type of business, they are not extraordinary. To sustain a 4 percent compound growth rate with average profit margins, OMORE's inventory buildup and receivables of sixty days sales will eat up $500,000 of the new term loan, plus a good portion of the cash surplus resulting from extended terms negotiated for trade payables in Year 2. Unless the company can be sold or taken public at a substantial price/earnings ratio, a straight equity investment in OMORE is not very attractive, as seen by the annual cash flows:

Year	Cash Flow
2	$989,092
3	(211,170)
4	(177,479)
5	(143,033)
6	(107,795)
7	(71,730)
TOTAL	277,885

To determine the attractiveness of a $2 million debt investment requires a more convoluted analysis. For a debt security traded in open markets, the market-determined present value of its future cash flows is observable from the market price of the security at any given time. The application of a security's rate of interest to its future cash flows produces a present value equal to the security's observed market price. This is called the security's *yield to maturity*.

However, for privately held companies whose debt securities are not traded in open markets, security value must be calculated using the present value formula. To make the calculation, one needs to determine:

- The amount of future cash flows generated by the security
- The timing of these cash flows
- An appropriate rate of interest or yield to maturity

The phrase *yield to maturity* is used interchangeably with the phrase *market rate of interest*. When one reads or hears that the market rate of interest is 10 percent, it means the same as saying that the yield to maturity is 10 percent.

FIGURE 11-1

OMORE, INC.
STATEMENT OF INCOME (in dollars)

| | Actual | | | ---- Forecasted---- | | | |
	Year 1	Year 2	Year 3	Year 4	Year 5	Year 6	Year 7
Sales	3,525,000	3,666,000	3,812,640	3,965,146	4,123,751	4,288,701	4,460,250
Cost of sales	1,935,750	2,016,300	2,096,952	2,180,830	2,268,063	2,358,786	2,453,137
Gross profit	1,586,250	1,649,700	1,715,688	1,784,316	1,855,688	1,929,916	2,007,112
% of sales	45%	45%	45%	45%	45%	45%	45%
Selling expenses	410,000	422,300	434,969	448,018	461,459	475,302	489,561
Commissions	176,250	183,300	190,632	198,257	206,188	214,435	223,012
Administrative expenses	364,000	374,920	986,168	397,753	409,685	421,976	434,635
Other expenses	5,000	5,000	5,000	5,000	5,000	5,000	5,000
Depreciation	17,500	17,500	67,500	67,500	67,500	67,500	67,500
Total expenses	972,750	1,003,020	1,084,269	1,116,528	1,149,831	1,184,213	1,219,709
Net income before interest and taxes	613,500	646,680	631,419	667,788	705,857	745,702	787,403
% of sales	17%	18%	17%	17%	17%	17%	18%
Interest expense	0	150,000	150,000	150,000	150,000	150,000	150,000
Net income before taxes	613,500	496,680	481,419	517,788	555,857	595,702	637,403
Taxes	233,130	188,738	182,939	196,759	211,226	226,367	242,213
Net income	380,370	307,942	298,480	321,028	344,631	369,336	395,190
% of sales	11%	8%	8%	8%	8%	9%	9%

OMORE, INC.
BALANCE SHEET (in dollars)

| | Actual | | | ---- Forecasted---- | | | |
	Year 1	Year 2	Year 3	Year 4	Year 5	Year 6	Year 7
Cash	525,000	1,467,592	1,647,122	1,841,743	2,052,210	2,279,315	523,885
Receivables	587,500	611,000	635,440	660,858	687,292	714,784	743,375
Inventory	1,185,716	1,601,126	2,033,152	2,482,458	2,949,738	3,435,708	3,941,117
Total current assets	2,298,216	3,679,718	4,315,714	4,985,059	5,689,240	6,429,807	5,208,377
Building	100,000	1,600,000	1,600,000	1,600,000	1,600,000	1,600,000	1,600,000
Equipment & vehicles	120,000	120,000	120,000	120,000	120,000	120,000	120,000
TOTAL	220,000	1,720,000	1,720,000	1,720,000	1,720,000	1,720,000	1,720,000
Less: Accumulated depreciation	(85,000)	(102,500)	(170,000)	(237,500)	(305,000)	(372,500)	(440,000)
Net	135,000	1,617,500	1,550,000	1,482,500	1,415,000	1,347,500	1,280,000
Other assets	5,000	5,000	5,000	5,000	5,000	5,000	5,000
Total assets	2,438,216	5,302,218	5,870,714	6,472,559	7,109,240	7,782,307	6,493,377
Accounts payable	355,715	800,563	1,016,576	1,241,229	1,474,869	1,717,854	1,970,559
Accrued expenses	88,929	200,141	254,144	310,307	368,717	429,463	492,640
Total current liabilities	444,644	1,000,704	1,270,720	1,551,537	1,843,586	2,147,317	2,463,198
Long-term note	0	2,000,000	2,000,000	2,000,000	2,000,000	2,000,000	0
Total liabilities	444,644	3,000,704	3,270,720	3,551,537	3,843,586	4,147,317	2,463,198
Common stock	100,000	100,000	100,000	100,000	100,000	100,000	100,000
Retained earnings—beginning	1,513,204	1,893,573	2,201,514	2,499,994	2,821,022	3,165,654	3,534,989
Profit	380,370	307,942	298,480	321,028	344,631	369,336	395,190
Retained earnings—ending	1,893,573	2,201,514	2,499,994	2,821,022	3,165,654	3,534,989	3,930,179
Total equity	1,993,573	2,301,514	2,599,994	2,921,022	3,265,654	3,634,989	4,030,179
Total liabilities and Equity	2,438,216	5,302,218	5,870,714	6,472,559	7,109,240	7,782,307	6,493,377

FIGURE 11-2

OMORE, INC.
STATEMENT OF CASH FLOW (in dollars)

	Actual			----Forecasted----		
	Year 1	Year 2	Year 3	Year 4	Year 5	Year 6
CASH RECEIPTS						
Receivables—beginning	587,500	611,000	635,440	660,858	687,292	714,784
Sales	3,666,000	3,812,640	3,965,146	4,123,751	4,288,701	4,460,250
Receivables—ending	(611,000)	(635,440)	(660,858)	(687,292)	(714,784)	(743,375)
Receipts from operations	3,642,500	3,788,2000	3,939,728	4,097,317	4,261,210	4,431,658
Long-term note	2,000,000	0	0	0	0	0
Total receipts	5,642,500	3,788,200	3,939,728	4,097,317	4,261,210	4,431,658
CASH EXPENDITURES						
Accounts payable—beginning	355,715	800,563	1,016,576	1,241,229	1,474,869	1,717,854
Purchases	2,431,710	2,528,978	2,630,137	2,735,342	2,844,756	2,958,546
Accounts payable—ending	(800,563)	(1,016,576)	(1,241,229)	(1,474,869)	(1,717,854)	(1,970,559)
Material expenditures	1,986,862	2,312,965	2,405,484	2,501,703	2,601,771	2,705,842
Accrued expenses—beginning	88,929	200,141	254,144	310,307	368,717	429,463
Selling expense	422,300	434,969	448,018	461,459	475,302	489,561
Commissions	183,300	190,632	198,257	206,188	214,435	223,012
Administrative expense	374,920	386,168	397,753	409,685	421,976	434,635
Other expenses	5,000	5,000	5,000	5,000	5,000	5,000
Accrued expenses—ending	(200,141)	(254,144)	(310,307)	(368,717)	(429,463)	(492,640)
Total operating expenditures	874,308	962,765	992,865	1,023,921	1,055,967	1,089,033
Purchase of new building	1,500,000	0	0	0	0	0
Financing costs:						
Interest	150,000	150,000	150,000	150,000	150,000	150,000
Principal	0	0	0	0	0	2,000,000
Total financing costs	150,000	150,000	150,000	150,000	150,000	2,150,000
Taxes	188,738	182,939	196,759	211,226	226,367	242,213
Total expenditures	4,699,908	3,608,670	3,745,107	3,886,850	4,034,105	6,187,088
NET CASH GENERATED	942,592	179,530	194,621	210,467	227,105	(1,755,430)
Cash in bank—beginning		525,000	1,467,592	1,647,122	1,841,743	2,052,210
Cash in bank—ending	1,467,592	1,647,122	1,841,743	2,052,210	2,279,315	523,885

Since the amount and timing of future cash flows can be derived from the contractual documents supporting the debt issue, the only judgment to be made is the appropriate interest rate or yield to maturity, commonly referred to as *the internal rate of return*. Three conditions are possible:

- The market-determined yield to maturity is equal to the security's interest rate, in which case the security's fair market value equals its face amount
- The yield to maturity is less than the interest rate, as indicated by the market yields of similar issues, in which case the security's fair market value is greater than its face value
- The yield to maturity is greater than the interest rate, in which case the security's fair market value is less than its face value

Although the interest rate determines the amount of cash flow from the security, the yield to maturity indicates the fair market value of those cash flows at any point in time.

In each of these cases, the debt issue's yield to maturity must be established by market prices. For privately held companies this involves the comparison of the company's financial characteristics with those of similar public companies whose debt yields to maturity are set by the market. As seen in Chapter 9, such a comparative analysis for the purpose of valuing equity interests can be a very tedious and difficult, if not impossible, task. Comparative ratio analysis for debt investments doesn't have to be as precise and therefore can be accomplished without undue complications.

One of the best sources of comparative data is *Standard & Poor's Credit Week*, which lists key financial ratios of industrial long-term debt issuers for which the service provides credit ratings. Figure 11-3 shows average ratios compiled by S&P for the last thirty years and their classification by credit rating. Periodically S&P publishes these ratios as broad three-year averages. The numerical values shown in Figure 11-3 are for demonstration purposes only; they were intentionally taken from an out-of-date report to ensure that they will not be used for current comparative analyses. For that, get a current S&P report direct from Standard & Poor's.

The S&P credit ratings represent a current assessment of the creditworthiness of a debtor company with respect to a specific obligation and may take into consideration such corollary obligators as guarantors, insurers, or lessees. The ratings are based in varying degrees on three factors:

1. The likelihood of default and the capacity and willingness on the part of the company to make timely payment of interest and repayment of principal in accordance with the terms of the contractual documents supporting the security
2. The nature and provisions of the security
3. The protection afforded by and the relative position of the obligation in the event of bankruptcy reorganization, or other arrangement under the laws of bankruptcy and other laws affecting creditors' rights

FIGURE 11-3

STANDARD & POOR'S CORPORATION
KEY FINANCIAL RATIOS AND DEFINITIONS
Industrial Long-Term Debt

	AAA	AA	A	BBB	BB	B
Pretax interest coverage	12.63	9.06	5.24	3.19	2.49	1.83
Pretax interest coverage excluding rents	7.39	4.62	3.02	2.32	1.83	1.54
Percent of working capital to long-term debt	226.67	124.00	67.51	46.05	28.94	19.43
Percent of working capital to total debt	135.22	90.32	54.63	40.45	24.64	16.43
Percent of net income from operations to capital employed (A)	24.80	21.38	18.16	13.30	12.75	11.40
Percent of operating income to sales	20.63	14.85	12.21	10.91	11.44	10.55
Percent of long-term debt to capitalization (B)	11.31	17.67	26.85	31.61	43.10	53.15
Percent of total debt to capitalization including short-term debt	18.59	24.11	31.52	34.81	45.77	55.00
Percent of total debt plus 8 times rents to capitalization including short-term debt and 8 times rents	30.39	35.40	46.14	48.18	58.24	65.78
Percent of total liabilities to tangible net worth (C)	78.89	107.29	118.28	146.11	188.22	224.97

Notes:

(A) Capital employed = the sum of (1) and (2). (1) the beginning and end of year averages of current debt, long-term debt, noncurrent deferred taxes, minority interests, and stockholders' equity

AND

(2) average short-term borrowings during the year

(B) Capitalization = long-term debt + equity

(C) Tangible net worth = equity less goodwill, patents, deferred assets, and other assets

S&P defines its ratings as follows:

AAA: The highest rating issued by S&P. Capacity to pay interest and repay principal is extremely high.

AA: Very strong capacity to pay interest and repay principal, only slightly below the AAA rating

A: Strong capacity to meet interest and principal payments, although more susceptible to the adverse effect of changes in circumstances and economic conditions

BBB: Adequate capacity to meet payment obligations, but even more susceptible to changing business and economic conditions

BB, B, CCC, CC, C: Regarded as speculative with regard to meeting payment obligations. BB is least speculative; C is most speculative. Large uncertainty and high risk of being affected by adverse conditions and economic swings

D: In default

The first step in determining a yield to maturity is to decide in which credit rating category the company belongs. Then select a specific publicly traded bond or other debt instrument that carries the same rating and has approximately the same interest rate and maturity date. It's easy to get a listing of all currently traded debt securities and their associated credit ratings from either *Mergent* (formerly Moody's) *Bond Record* or *Standard & Poor's Bond Guide*, both of which can be found on the Internet (see Chapter 9) or by subscription.

As a cross-check, compare the privately held company's financial ratios with those of the public company whose debt is being used for comparison purposes. If the ratios are way off, try a different comparison. Once the right company and the right debt issue have been selected, you can check current yields in any quote sheet from the *Wall Street Journal*, *Barron's*, or other publications that list current market trades. Current yield has a different meaning than yield to maturity, however. Current yield is annual interest payments divided by the price of the security. On the OMORE $2,000,000 par value security that carries a 7.5 percent interest rate, the annual interest payment is $150,000. If the security is trading at, for instance, its present value of $1,295,923, the current yield can be calculated as $150,000 divided by $1,295,923, or 11.57 percent.

This means that the annual cash rate of return for annual interest payments of $150,000 on a $1,295,923 investment is 11.57 percent. The current yield method, however, does not take into account the maturity date or any capital gains or losses that may result if the security is held to maturity.

The yield to maturity calculation is more complicated. It recognizes (1) the annual interest received, (2) the difference between the current price of the security and its maturity value, and (3) the number of years to maturity. If the present value of OMORE's $2,000,000 debt security equals $1,295,923 (assume that this approximates market value) and the maturity is six years, investors would receive the annual interest payments plus the differential of $704,077 ($2,000,000 minus $1,295,923) spread over six years, or $117,346 per year. This would give a total annual return of $150,000 interest plus the $117,346 differential or $267,346. Comparing this return to the average investment over the six-year period (the sum of the beginning investment of $1,295,923 and the maturity face value of $2,000,000 divided by two, we can see that the return is 16.22 percent.

For those who enjoy working formulas, the following represents the approximate calculation of yield to maturity:

$$Y/M = \frac{\text{Interest} + \dfrac{\text{Par} - \text{market}}{\text{Period}}}{\dfrac{(0.6)\,\text{market} + (0.4)\,\text{par}}{\text{Period}}}$$

Where:

Y/M = approximate yield to maturity
Interest = annual interest payment
Par = par value of security
Market = market value
Period = number of periods

The 60 percent and 40 percent factors in the denominator adjust for the slight differences caused by mathematical averaging over time.

Using the OMORE example, the following quantities can be slotted into the equation:

- The coupon interest payment is $150,000.
- The par value of the security is $2,000,000.
- The market value can be estimated as the present value of principal payments, or $1,295,923.
- The number of periods is six.

The solution then becomes:

$$
\begin{aligned}
Y/M &= \frac{\$150,000 + \dfrac{\$2,000,000 - \$1,295,923}{6}}{(0.6 \times \$1,295,923) + (0.4 \times \$2,000,000)} \\[2mm]
&= \frac{\$150,000 + \$117,346}{\$777,553 + \$800,000} \\[2mm]
&= \frac{\$267,346}{\$1,577,553} \\[2mm]
&= 16.95\%
\end{aligned}
$$

Using formulas may be interesting, but it's much easier to use amortization tables. PC software as well as the Internet contain a variety of reference works that provide such tables, including the present value of an annuity or coupon interest payments, the present value of a single amount at maturity, bond values with yields to maturity, and so on.

So far so good. These calculations give us a check against market yields to maturity of comparable traded securities. But what of the issuing companies themselves? The same types of quantitative and qualitative comparisons suggested in Chapters 8 and 9 for equity investments should be used for debt issues, with one proviso. The risk of investing in a company's debt obligation should be much lower than that of investing in an equity interest.

To review the previously stated reasons for this low risk:

1. Growth companies with profitability and market characteristics similar to OMORE's generally provide negative or very low net cash flows after debt service during the growth period. They need cash to build inventory, expand marketing efforts, and perhaps develop new distribution channels. These are all relatively low-risk efforts for this type of company. If they have decent credit histories, they have little trouble attracting sufficient short-term debt to carry them through the building process, allowing them to conserve internal cash flows to meet long-term debt payments. In other words, a company may not show a terrific net cash flow but may still have the capacity to meet debt service payments.

2. Debt obligations always carry a higher legal priority than equity instruments. If the company does get into trouble, secured creditors will get paid long before common shareholders. This is the key reason investors insist on quality collateral to back the debt.

Risk judgments derived from quantitative and qualitative analyses of an issuing company's financial performance may alter yield calculations and hence the required interest rate. As the uncertainty of achieving forecasted cash flows increases, so should the required yield. Higher risk can be reflected by increasing the present value capitalization rate applied to principal payments, by discounting interest payments, or both. When banks evaluate long-term loan applications, such a judgmental interpretation of risk has a direct bearing on how much interest they charge. They merely reverse the yield to maturity calculations, solving for interest payments based on required yields.

So far we have concentrated on debt valuations that are typically used for:

- Determining a reasonable interest rate for borrowed money
- Valuing buy/sell transactions
- Valuing leveraged buyouts (LBOs)
- Planning for estate and gift taxes
- Establishing values for recapitalizations and reorganizations

Debt valuations are also useful for determining prices and returns from more unusual investments. The balance of this chapter looks at the following capital-raising innovations requiring the application of debt valuation techniques:

- Defaulted debt obligations
- Sale/leaseback of hard assets
- Securitized debt

A brief review of how credit-poor companies can attract debt investors by using new credit-enhancement techniques is also included.

Defaulted Debt Obligations

As operating companies suffer hangovers from excess credit, so do the banks that made the loans. Many of the balance sheet problems banks face are of their own making. But tightened capital-ratio guidelines from the Bank of International Settlements, Basel, Switzerland (sort of a global central bank for national central banks such as the Federal Reserve Bank) and affirmed by the U.S. Comptroller of the Currency haven't helped.

To meet these guidelines, money center, regional, and small local banks have had to resolve or dispose of defaulted (or near-default) loans, typically referred to as *problem loans* or *work-out loans*.

Pressures to dispose of problem loans have created a unique opportunity for issuing companies to substantially reduce their debt service requirements and for investors to acquire debt obligations at a significant discount from par value. Although few banks are willing to unilaterally write off loan balances, if they sell the obligations at a discount they can at least show a partial recovery. The question to be resolved is: How much should the loans be discounted to produce a fair market value that will attract buyers?

Naturally, defaulted or near-default debt obligations carry significantly higher risks than debt securities from profitable, going businesses. As with other investments, it is the risk factor that determines the amount of discount necessary to arrive at fair market value. Comparison with publicly traded securities won't work: In most cases there isn't an active trading market for defaulted obligations, other than a few junk bond issues. Projecting a stream of future cash benefits through normal cash flow forecasting won't work: Most defaulted companies don't throw off excess cash. Other, more creative means must be found to determine fair market value.

The most influential factor in valuing defaulted loans is the quality of collateral backing the loan. When banks foreclose, they must have a means of disposing of the collateral or nothing has been gained. They have merely substituted worthless collateral assets for worthless receivables, which doesn't solve their capital-ratio dilemma. Some collateral may have been valuable at the time the loan was placed, but subsequent market conditions have reduced its value excessively, as in the used machinery market. Other collateral, such as personal guarantees, may never have been sufficient to cover the loan but in their exuberance to make loans, banks closed their eyes to potential recovery difficulties.

On the other hand, certain types of collateral can usually be disposed of at some price regardless of how badly market conditions deteriorate. Land and/or buildings normally fall into this class. And some collateral never loses its value, such as third-party guarantees from Eximbank or the SBA. The higher the quality of collateral, the less discount banks need to take to sell their problem loans.

Although many variations enter the equation, collateral assets may be ranked in descending order of quality as follows:

- Eximbank-guaranteed export receivables
- Export receivables backed by irrevocable letters of credit confirmed by a U.S. bank
- Guarantees from the Small Business Administration or other federal agency
- Current open accounts receivable from major corporations
- Current open accounts receivable from less well known but reputable customers
- Finished inventory ready for shipment or resale
- Commercial/industrial buildings and land
- Generic raw materials and parts inventory
- Operating equipment, vehicles, and fixtures
- Third-party guarantees backed by liens against disposable hard assets
- Personal guarantees backed by liens against personal assets

In addition to the quality of loan collateral, two other factors enter into a valuation calculation: (1) a debtor company's payment history against the loan and (2) the likelihood of a debtor filing for bankruptcy. Companies that boast a record of timely payments over several years are more likely to resume payments once their immediate financial difficulties are resolved. Such companies have already proven their creditworthiness, and creditors who put up with deferred debt service payments during difficult times should benefit from full repayment once the company's market conditions improve. If other factors remain constant, debt obligations from these companies should be valued at or near the fair market value of the underlying collateral.

Conversely, experience has shown that companies with a record of slow or missed debt service payments in the past will continue that practice even after economic conditions improve. Debt instruments from these deadbeats should be valued at a significant discount from the marketability of the underlying collateral assets.

Debt from companies facing inevitable bankruptcy requires a different perspective. It is usually impossible to predict the eventual outcome of a bankruptcy reorganization and the settlement percentages that will be applied to debt obligations. Without an inside track that permits an investor to work with company management in arriving at a prepackaged bankruptcy, thereby safeguarding an initial debt investment, it's difficult to place the value of any debt obligation much above zero.

The only other condition that might warrant a higher value would be if an investor wishes to take a *superpriority* position after the filing. In that case, the value of the debt obligation approaches the marketability of its underlying collateral.

A good rule of thumb is that with a bankruptcy filing near, the security's discount from par should be close to 95 percent. In cases other than those with a high potential for bankruptcy filing, discounts from face value should range from 30 percent for the highest-rated loans to 90 percent for those carrying the lowest-grade security.

The approach to valuing mortgage obligations should focus on the salability of the underlying property. Many investors have grabbed up defaulted or near-default mortgages with the specific intention of seizing the underlying asset—assuming, of course, that the mortgagor holds a first position against the collateral asset. Since even in a depressed real estate market, good property can be sold if priced properly, valuation discounts should be established that bring the loan balance down to the fair market value of the underlying property.

When valuing debt obligations at or near the marketability value of underlying assets, it's important to recognize the possibility that the company may not recover sufficiently to repay the obligations, thereby requiring foreclosure and subsequent collateral liquidation. This, in turn, requires a judgment as to asset marketability in a forced liquidation.

To review the general guidelines for liquidation values:

- Machinery, equipment, furniture, fixtures, and vehicles bring 20 to 30 percent of fair market appraised value. If the asset is unique, one of a kind, or of such a special nature that buyers are difficult or impossible to locate readily, then the liquidation value is zero.
- Material and standard parts inventories in good condition can be liquidated at auction for about thirty cents on the dollar; finished goods for about fifty cents, except for very high-demand items.
- Real property that houses operating businesses and/or current leases can generally be liquidated for 50 to 70 percent of market value, depending on the condition of the business, the property, and its location.

Although liquidation values move up or down from time to time as demand for particular assets varies, these guidelines are fairly reliable and are used by most reputable auction houses.

By definition, valuations must begin with liquidation values and then be discounted downward to arrive at an investment return. For example, if the liquidation value of a piece of equipment is $100,000 and an investor wants a 10 percent return, the value of the obligation cannot be higher than $90,000, assuming, of course, that the asset can be liquidated in less than one year. To the extent that the liquidation occurs beyond one year, the value must be further discounted to present value. The following factors discount $1 at a 10 percent return for each of five years:

Year	Present Value
1	0.909
2	0.826
3	0.751
4	0.683
5	0.621

Sale/Leaseback of Hard Assets

Debt valuations are also useful for arriving at the periodic rent for sale/leaseback transactions. A whole series of accounting and tax matters affect a lease's form and terms, all of them requiring expert counsel. Here we are concerned only with the valuation of the debt obligation.

Sale/leaseback arrangements can be beneficial whether or not the leased assets currently secure a bank loan. If they are pledged, a sale/leaseback can provide cash to pay down the debt. If not, a sale/leaseback gives a company an immediate capital infusion.

Although unusual, it is possible for companies to be cash-poor and still have assets that are not pledged against loans. Hotels are a good example. The building itself might secure a mortgage loan, while the equipment used in the kitchen, bar, air conditioning system, telephone system, computer system, and so on, remains free and clear. These assets could be sold to a leasing company for a cash infusion and then leased back.

In many companies, however, all hard assets are pledged as loan collateral. Although approval for a sale/leaseback arrangement must be obtained from secured creditors, this normally isn't a problem as long as proceeds of the sale are used to reduce the outstanding loan.

Typically, a sale/leaseback agreement lists several pages of assets. Each asset may have a different useful life. Some may be old, some new. Some may have a normal useful life of ten years, some perhaps only three. Because of the variations in ages, lives, and replacement costs of various assets, a variable-term lease could be executed, with each item returnable to the lessor as its useful life expires.

A more common arrangement, however, stipulates a fixed monthly, quarterly, or annual lease payment against the total list of items. As one item wears out, the lessor replaces it with a new one and the monthly lease payments are adjusted for the incremental cost. These leases are normally written for five years with automatic renewal options granted the lessee.

Valuing a lease for purposes of effecting a sale/leaseback arrangement uses a discounted cash flow approach similar to that previously discussed for bonds and other debt instruments, but with slight variations. Lessors must calculate the rent based on:

- *Cost of the asset.* Cost is defined as the asset's appraised fair market value. When necessary, appraised fair market value may be reduced for estimated disposal costs.
- *Leveraging costs*, if any. If lessors borrow money to purchase the assets, the interest paid is a leveraging cost. Theoretically, even though this is added to rental payments, when the purchase is leveraged, lessors have less equity in the transaction, and this should be reflected in a decreased return on investment amount.
- *Residual value.* Residual value is the market price that the asset could be sold for at the end of the lease period. Theoretically, this amount reduces the cash flow needed from rents to realize the desired return on investment.
- *Cost of capital* (capitalization rate). As with other present value calculations, the capitalization rate reflects the perceived uncertainty of collection rents over the lease period and of realizing the estimated residual value.

As an example of the calculation, assume that CORP sells LESS its manufacturing machinery with an appraised value of $110,000. LESS estimates it will cost $10,000 to dispose of the machinery if CORP defaults. LESS purchases the machinery with its own money (no leveraging involved). LESS estimates that after usage depreciation and a decline in the used equipment market, the machinery can be sold for its residual value of $15,000 at the end of the lease period.

CORP has a mediocre credit history, and after analyzing CORP's financial statements, LESS perceives a midrange risk of collecting the rents. LESS also calculates that the used equipment market could be softer than anticipated, thereby creating an additional risk. LESS places the sum of the two risk factors at 15 percent. This is added to the current U.S. Treasury ten-year note rate to reach the total capitalization rate. The following steps determine the amount of annual rental payments that CORP must pay, the total value of the lease, and the yield to LESS:

1. *Yield to maturity.* Calculate the market price of a risk-free U.S. Treasury ten-year note, assuming a 7 percent coupon rate:
   a. The present value of annual interest payments of 7 percent on a $100,000 note for five years equals $28,665.
   b. The present value of the $100,000 note at maturity equals $71,000.
   c. The sum of the two present values equals $99,665, which is the market value of the U.S. Treasury note.
   d. The application of the yield-to-maturity formula previously described with a 22 percent capitalization rate results in a return of 22.11 percent.
2. *Annual rental payments*
   a. Calculate the present value of a stream of equal cash payments over five years to amortize $85,000 ($100,000 less residual value of $15,000), using a capitalization rate equal to the yield to maturity (22.11 percent). This gives annual payments of $29,753.27.
   b. Calculate the present value of the residual value of $15,000, which equals $4,549.17.
   c. Add the five annual payments to the residual value to get a total lease value of $153,315.

As a comparison, if LESS estimated that the total capitalization rate should be 10 percent rather than 22 percent, annual payments would be $22,472.80 and the value of the lease $120,831. In other words, CORP's deteriorated financial condition costs the company a premium of $32,484 to enter into this sale/leaseback transaction.

Securitization

The attempt by banks and other financial institutions to limit their lending to profitable, financially strong businesses leaves a vacuum for closely held companies with overleveraged balance sheets or low credit ratings. Taking a page from international trade finance, several nonbank organizations—some privately owned, some subsidiaries of industrial and commercial parents, some pseudo government agencies formed by states and municipalities—will lend against off-balance sheet collateral. One of the most interesting innovations is referred to as *securitization.*

Companies that have borrowed from secured lenders will recognize a similarity between securitization and the practice of securing long-term loans with hard assets. Securitization goes one step further, however. Instead of collateralizing loans with balance sheet assets, securitized debt uses future cash flow contracts.

For public companies, securitized debt instruments include bonds, commercial paper, and short-term or medium-term notes. Privately held companies normally evidence securitized debt obligations with short-term promissory notes.

Such transaction financing is ideally suited to financially weak companies that need to finance specific transactions independent of other balance sheet debt or credit history. Future cash flow contracts that qualify as collateral include construction contracts, credit card receivables, mortgage obligations, export orders, and any other contract for future cash flows that has embedded collateral. *Embedded collateral* means that, independent of the debtor company, the financial instrument itself is secured by third-party assets such as good credit ratings, letters of credit, bank or government agency guarantees, or real property.

The mechanics of securitization are simple: Companies sell debt obligations that represent rights to the future cash receipts from legally binding contracts. In most cases, but certainly not all, the selling company guarantees the collection of the contract, making it a contingent liability and not recorded on the company's balance sheet. Since specific cash flow contracts collateralize the securities, overly high leverage ratios that preclude borrowing from banks do not come into the picture.

Of course, securitized issues are normally sold at a discount, making it necessary to determine their fair market value. Calculations identical to those previously described for valuing traditional debt securities are used to value securitized notes. The longer the cash flow contract extends, the greater the applicable capitalization rate. Short-term notes secured by credit card or expert receivables carry very little risk. Long-term notes secured by mortgage obligations carry a much greater discount.

There is one major difference from valuing traditional debt obligations, however. The perceived risk attached to receiving the stream of future cash benefits must be weighed against both the quality of the paying company and the guarantee of the selling company. To the extent that the embedded collateral is risk-free—as in an Eximbank guarantee—or nearly risk-free—as in a confirmed, irrevocable letter of credit—or to the extent that the selling company has free assets to back its guarantee, the uncertainty of receiving future benefits is very low. This makes the capitalization rate low and increases the value of the security.

One way financially weak companies can increase the value of securitized cash flow contracts is to enhance their guarantees with additional collateral. Financial markets refer to this as *credit enhancement*. Although credit enhancements have become a popular way for financially weak public companies to attract investors to new bond issues, the principle applies as well to small, closely held businesses.

Surety bonds are probably the best credit enhancement, eliminating virtually all risk from cash flow contracts. A surety (usually an insurance company), issues a surety bond guaranteeing that it will pay the principal and interest on the security if the cash flow from the company's debt collateral fails to cover payments. In the common vernacular, such a guarantee is referred to as *bond insurance*.

Another popular credit enhancement is what the financial markets call *overcollateralization*. This mouthful means exactly what it says. Companies with deteriorating balance sheets are the main users. One variation increases the assets backing a loan over and above contractual cash flows. For example, if the debt obligation calls for a pledge of $1 million in qualified receivables, an extra 10 percent or $100,000 thrown into the collateral pool to reduce risk and increase value should be an attractive enhancement. The extra 10 percent could be in the form of cash or cash equivalents, inventory, noncollaterialized receivables, or any other company asset.

Two types of cash accounts are used for credit enhancement. The first is an escrow cash reserve that the issuing company funds from internal operations. The amount required depends on the present value of the collateral cash flows.

A second type of reserve utilizes a cash collateral account. In this case the issuing company borrows money to put into escrow as collateral to the issue. It then reinvests escrow funds in secure certificates of deposit or Treasuries and uses the interest earned to partially offset the interest expense incurred in borrowing the cash.

CHAPTER

Buyout Agreements

Upon the withdrawal, disability, or death of one or more owners of a privately held business, a buyout agreement should be in place to provide for the disposal of their interests. Ownership interests may be sold back to the operating entity, to a specified partner or partners, or to all remaining partners. In this context, and throughout this chapter, the term *partners* refers to both holders of partnership interests and shareholders in closely held corporations, either C corporations or S corporations.

The main reasons for executing a formal buyout agreement are (1) to clearly delineate the rights of all partners and (2) to specify a mutually agreed upon method for valuing the interest to be disposed of. Properly drawn, such an agreement:

- Ensures an equitable price
- Provides a mechanism for liquidating ownership interests
- Prevents an ownership interest from being sold to outsiders
- Determines a binding price for estate tax assessment
- Establishes a price and liquidation mechanism for use in divorce proceedings

Several provisions in both federal and state tax codes affect the structuring of buyout agreements, making it necessary to consult competent counsel before deciding on form and content. Setting aside tax considerations, three general types of buyout arrangements are in common use:

1. Repurchase agreements, whereby the partnership or corporation buys back a partner's interest
2. Multiple purchase agreements, whereby the partnership or corporation buys back part of a partner's interest and one or more partners buy the remainder
3. Cross-purchase agreements, whereby one or more partners buy all of the withdrawing partner's interest.

Some buyout agreements specify that the method of sale is binding on all parties. Others make the transaction voluntary on the part of the purchaser. Agreements may also be written to leave the door open for a voluntary purchase during a partner's lifetime but make the transaction mandatory upon the partner's death. Virtually all buyout agreements provide for a *right of first refusal* by other partners before an ownership interest can be offered for sale to third parties not associated with the business.

Furthermore, the same agreement does not have to cover all partners. Separate contracts may be executed to stipulate a repurchase agreement for some partners and a cross-purchase or multiple-purchase arrangement for others. This is an especially popular arrangement in limited partnerships, where the general partner is subject to one set of buyout provisions and limited partners to another.

The agreement's structure depends to a large extent on the number of parties involved. Two equal partners may agree to a straightforward cross-purchase plan in which one buys the shares of the other and both interests are valued equally. In majority-minority ownership structures, the agreement might stipulate a proportionate or disproportionate split of the total company's value, with one party buying out the other. Many two-partner businesses write repurchase buyout agreements stipulating that company-owned life insurance policies will be put in place to provide buyout funds in the event of a partner's death. Agreements that provide for deferred payments upon voluntary withdrawals are also popular.

Multiparty ownership structures are far more difficult to deal with. Cross-purchase agreements generally become too complex to either execute or fund, as partners' interests are too varied to value uniformly. Most multiparty businesses use repurchase agreements, with clauses that provide for the entity to buy back partners' interests when they withdraw or die. In the end, the type of agreement must be governed by (1) the relationships of the respective partners to one another, (2) their objectives with respect to beneficiaries and heirs, and (3) their mutual agreement to provide either for the continuity of the business or for its liquidation.

When valuations involve both controlling and minority interests, a proportionate allocation of the total entity value deprives controlling parties of the premium that goes with a controlling interest and avoids the discount that typically accompanies minority interests. As discussed in Chapter 10, controlling owners have the option of making distributions, spending company funds, executing contracts, and hiring or firing employees, any one of which may enhance or impair the total value of the business. Minority owners, however, do not enjoy these prerogatives and therefore have little control over investment value.

Theoretically, controlling interests should be valued at a greater than proportionate share to reflect the authority of the holder to influence the total company's value. Minority interests are then valued at less than a proportionate share of the total company's value. In small businesses, however, such a differentiation is seldom made.

Regardless of the form buyout agreements take, a predetermined valuation for each partner's interest is the cornerstone on which they all rest. In far too many cases, however, inexperienced attorneys acquiesce to overly exuberant clients and draft binding contracts without paying sufficient attention to the method by which interests will be equitably valued. Over time, attitudes and personal life styles change. Partners who were once completely trusted and cooperative become obstinate and, in far too many cases, disloyal to the business. Disputes over buyout agreement language are hard enough to resolve; disputes over the sale price of a partner's interest may be virtually impossible to settle outside of a courtroom. And hardly anyone wants that to happen.

Valuation Theory

The book value method and the fair market value method are the two most common techniques for valuing an entire business. *Book value* is derived from the company's financial statements, *fair market value* from either an independent appraisal or a negotiation between the parties. Furthermore, nine times out of ten, proportionate shares of the total company value are allocated to partners, without regard to the distinction between minority and controlling interests.

Book Value Method

Because of its simplicity, the book value method has the biggest following. Anyone who can read financial statements can immediately determine a company's book value. As explained in earlier chapters, book value is represented by that section of the balance sheet called stockholders' equity, net worth, or partners' capital accounts.

Rarely, however, should book value be taken directly from the financial statements without adjustments. Many accounting transactions are, by definition, vague and misleading. LIFO versus FIFO inventory valuations, various depreciation methods, bad debt reserves, and the amortization of capitalized leases are four examples of procedures that can cause radical year-to-year changes in book value even when sales volume and cost structures remain relatively constant.

Financial statements for small businesses that record transactions on the cash basis will always require adjustments to bring them into line with accrual accounting practices. The fair market value of company investments in real estate, marketable securities, or other businesses changes from year to year and must be reconciled to recorded amounts. Disproportionate cash distributions to one or more partners may distort book value in any given year. And small businesses that keep their books on a tax basis will never show a book value that represents the actual worth of the business.

The biggest problem with the book value method occurs when the business shows a zero or negative net worth. A negative net worth results from bookkeeping losses. Bookkeeping losses are a very common way for small businesses to reduce income taxes. However, such losses and the consequent negative net worth they create do not necessarily indicate failing businesses. A case in point happened when a small business client engaged me to help structure a succession partnership. The company kept its books as an S corporation. Cash distributions to the owner in excess of net worth were recorded as loans-to-stockholders. The company's book value was zero.

When it came time to draft the buyout agreement for the new equal partner, both parties felt that book value would increase over the years, making it a viable base for a buyout price. Their will prevailed. Seven years later, when my original client decided to retire, his partner quickly pointed out that the company's book value had descended into a negative position, and therefore the purchase price was zero. In fact, he tried in vain to get the selling partner to pay him a proportionate share of the negative book value for the privilege of getting out.

If you decide to use the book value method, the agreement should stipulate the type of financial statement adjustments to be made; whether book value is on a tax basis, cash basis, or accrual basis; and the date at which book value will be computed, whether it's the last year-end, the prior month or quarter, the date of withdrawal or death, or another date. In addition, provision should be made in the agreement for dealing with a zero or negative book value as of the valuation date.

Be aware, however, that book value seldom reflects fair market value, even for companies with a high percentage of current assets that can be liquidated at or near recorded amounts. Also, both the IRS and the courts have denied the use of book value as a basis for assessing income or estate taxes.

A further complication arises when life insurance policies are used to provide funding under a repurchase agreement. Since book value may change radically between the date of inception and the date of a partner's withdrawal, insurance policies may not provide the sums needed for the buyout without periodic increases in coverage.

Capitalization of Future Benefits Method

Although the capitalization of a future stream of either earnings or cash flows is certainly a viable method for valuing a total entity, it creates several problems when valuing partial interests. As with the book value method, wide variations in accounting practices over a period of years invalidate many of the financial ratios and functional relationships needed to arrive at a meaningful forecast.

In addition, other factors affect both the forecast of future benefits and the perceived risk of attaining them:

- Adjustments to prior years financial statements for the same types of accounting peculiarities as described for the book value method must be made.
- Adjustments must be made for cash or property distributions to owners in excess of normal salaries.
- Adjustments must be made to reflect future tax liabilities resulting from the buyout, such as the tax on built-in gains for S corporations, recapture provisions, or buyouts of negative capital account interests.
- Yearly revisions to the capitalization rate must be recognized as the uncertainty of future benefits changes.

If you can cope with these adjustments, the capitalization of future benefits works well for two-partner or three-partner businesses provided shares are equally held. As with any method based on a valuation of the total entity, allocations should, theoretically, be proportionate only when all interests have the same authority to exercise control over company activities.

The capitalization of future benefits method seldom proves satisfactory for valuing partial interests. Aside from the question of control, determining the amount of future earnings or cash flows generated by a single partner is, in most cases, impossible, other than in certain types of professional practices. Although less true today than in the past, physicians and dentists—and to a lesser extent CPAs and lawyers—retain continuing relationships with and generate fees from their own patients/clients, independent of fees generated by other partners in the practice. To the extent that such patients/clients shift their allegiance to other partners when one withdraws, cash flow forecasts can be realistic. However, even in this case, the capitalization rate must be continuously updated for changes in future uncertainties.

Another variation on the theme of capitalization of future benefits bases cash flow forecasts on the amount of cash or property withdrawn by each partner, usually in the year immediately preceding the date of the valuation. The theory is that the departing partner's distributions will, in the future, be shared by the other partners. The annual withdrawal is merely extrapolated to future years and a capitalization multiplier applied to calculate present value.

Of course, this method ignores any contributions from the departing partner to the success of the business. If, in fact, the departure precipitates a loss of sales or revenues, then prior distributions mean nothing in the determination of future benefits. To compensate, this method frequently commands a sizable discount rate, usually between 20 and 50 percent.

Independent Appraisals

Many times an independent business appraisal is the only way parties can agree on a buyout value. In other cases, independent appraisals are mandated by the court, as in a divorce proceeding. Professional appraisers, quite naturally, advocate this as the only sensible method. Lawyers, management consultants, CPAs, financial planners, and other professional advisers also frequently push for an independent appraisal as the only viable way to establish fair market value. Despite the fact that each of these professionals earns fees from independent appraisals, their outlook does have merit.

It seems to be a truism that as owners, we tend to overvalue our businesses. The intrinsic value we assign to our companies is akin to the incalculable value we attach to treasured personal property: a car, boat, work of art, or personal library. Seldom, if ever, does an outsider view such a treasure with the practiced eye of the owner. When we decide to sell one of our prized possessions, we find it hard to believe that it isn't worth as much to anyone else.

Just as a competent real estate agent is better qualified than a homeowner to establish the selling price for a house, a thoroughly qualified independent appraiser can usually come up with a fairer business valuation than a business owner. Unfortunately, the amounts of such valuations are usually less than we prefer if we're trying to sell our share of the business or more than we like for tax purposes or divorce proceedings.

Basing a buyout agreement on an independent appraisal has other negatives as well. In the first place, all partners must agree on the specific appraiser or appraisal firm. This in itself can preclude using this method. A second problem is cost. Independent business appraisals do not come cheap. It takes a great deal of time and effort to do the job right, and hourly rates can quickly increase the cost beyond a reasonable level.

A third problem is that businesses change over time, either grow or decline, making old appraisals worthless. To keep the buyout agreement current, updated appraisals must be conducted on a regular basis. And finally, small businesses have a way of changing their customer base, product lines, and market penetration over a period of years. A qualified appraisal firm, well versed in a given market or industry, may be acceptable now, but in ten years conditions may change so radically that a new firm must be recruited, and that could take a lot of time and effort.

Despite these disadvantages, valuations performed by independent business appraisers do carry more weight in the courts and with the IRS than do values arrived at by internal calculations. Courts invariably rely on expert testimony to settle valuation disputes, and expert testimony means a qualified independent appraiser. Independent appraisals could also bring other benefits, including:

- Acceptance by the IRS for estate and gift tax assessment
- Avoidance of personal value judgments by partners that could lead to disputes
- Assistance in negotiating buy/sell prices in the event of a merger, acquisition, or sale of the entire business

Negotiating a Value

For smaller companies with few partners, the most satisfactory method of determining business value usually comes down to negotiations between the parties. Even with an independent appraisal or an internally calculated valuation in hand, the parties to a buyout agreement must eventually arrive at mutually acceptable buyout prices through give-and-take negotiations. Of all the small business clients I have worked with, I have never seen a buyout valuation performed by appraisers or calculated internally that was totally acceptable to all parties. Negotiation among the parties was always the final leg in reaching mutual agreement.

That being the case, here are a few general rules about negotiating tactics:

- Don't let personal dreams about the future of the business cloud your reason.
- Negotiate a new business value each year.
- Incorporate a penalty clause in the buyout agreement, stipulating that the last valuation will govern if a new one isn't negotiated within twelve months, eighteen months, or some other time period.
- Provide for an independent arbitrator, a management consultant, lawyer, CPA, appraiser, or anyone thoroughly familiar with valuation techniques applicable to your type of business, with the authority to establish values in the event that partners reach a negotiating stalemate.
- If the parties cannot reach agreement on an arbitrator, provide in the buyout agreement for each side to choose one arbitrator and for the group of arbitrators to choose the final one.

Buyout agreements specify more than valuation methods. Corollary matters such as provision for funding the buyout, agreements on payment terms, and acceptable restrictions on the transfer of ownership interests to outsiders must be spelled out in the agreement and updated periodically.

Repurchase Agreement Funding and Terms

Under the best of circumstances, raising cash to buy out a partner can be a difficult undertaking. In most cases, neither individuals nor small businesses have sufficient idle cash to fund a partnership buyout. Yet, when the time arrives for a partner to retire, or when serious disputes signal a parting of the ways, or when a partner dies or becomes incapacitated, buyout terms need to be implemented. For a buyout agreement to work effectively, funding provisions and terms of payment must be clearly spelled out.

Funding repurchase buyouts when the company itself buys back a partner's share following the death of that partner can be made relatively straightforward by using key manager life insurance. Policies should be updated periodically to reflect currently negotiated buyout values, but when this is done, life insurance is usually a satisfactory way to fund buyouts from estates. To mitigate tax consequences, it's important that the company own the policy, pay the premiums, and be the sole beneficiary.

Figure 12-1 contains a sample repurchase agreement between a small corporation and its shareholders. Although this agreement applies to two partners with equal equity shares, it is just as applicable to companies with more than two owners.

FIGURE 12-1: Sample Repurchase Agreement Between Corporation and Shareholders

THIS AGREEMENT, entered into this _____ day of _____, 19XX, between SMALL Corp. ("the Corporation") and (name of shareholder) ("Jones");

WITNESSETH:

WHEREAS, Jones is the owner of 100 shares of Common Stock of the Corporation ("Stock"); and,

WHEREAS, the parties hereto mutually desire to make provisions in the event of the death of Jones for the sale and purchase of his/her Stock on a fair and equitable basis; and,

WHEREAS, the Corporation is currently the owner and beneficiary of a policy of insurance on the life of Jones in the face amount of $1,000,000, the purpose of such insurance being to fund the purchase of the Stock in the event of Jones' death;

NOW THEREFORE, the Corporation and Jones hereby agree:

ARTICLE I
STOCK SUBJECT TO AGREEMENT

1.1 *Stock Subject to Agreement.* The terms of this Agreement shall apply to all Stock presently owned by Jones. In the event that the Corporation shall declare any dividend or other distribution on its outstanding capital stock payable in shares of stock (a *stock dividend*), or so subdivide its outstanding shares of capital stock into a greater number of shares (a *stock split*), or shall combine the outstanding shares of its capital stock into a smaller number of shares (a *reverse stock split*), then this Agreement shall apply to any Stock acquired by Jones during his lifetime as a result of such stock dividend, stock split, or reverse stock split. However, this Agreement shall not apply to any Stock acquired by Jones after the date of this Agreement as a result of a purchase of other stock of the corporation by Jones from the Corporation or any other shareholder.

1.2 *Endorsement of Stock Certificates.* Each stock certificate representing shares of Stock held or hereafter acquired by Jones shall be endorsed substantially as follows:

"The shares represented by this certificate are subject to the provisions of the Agreement to Purchase Corporate Stock, dated _____, which Agreement is available for inspection at the principal office of the Corporation."

Provided, however, that failure so to endorse any of the Stock certificates shall not invalidate this Agreement. The Corporation shall keep a copy of this Agreement available for inspection by all properly interested parties at the principal office.

1.3 *Use of Stock as Collateral.* Jones shall have the right to pledge Stock owned by him as Collateral security for personal indebtedness, even though the certificate of such Stock is endorsed as provided in Section 1.2, but any Stock so pledged shall remain subject to the terms of this Agreement.

1.4 *Transfer of Stock.* This Agreement shall without further mention and despite reference to "Stock owned by Jones" be applicable to all Stock as defined in Section 1.2 hereof which is at any time transferred by Jones to any other person or entity.

1.5 *Voting and Dividend Rights.* The Stock owned by Jones subject to this Agreement shall be voted by him/her, and, after his death, by the personal representatives of his estate, until purchased pursuant to this Agreement. Any dividends payable on the Stock shall be paid to Jones or the personal representatives of his estate, as the case may be.

ARTICLE II
DEATH OF Jones

2.1 *Death of Jones.* In the event of the death of Jones, the Corporation shall purchase and the legal representatives of his estate shall sell, at a price determined by Article III, all but not part of the shares of Stock owned by Jones on the date of his death.

ARTICLE III
PURCHASE PRICE AND PAYMENT

3.1 *Determination of Purchase Price.* The purchase price for all of the Stock subject to this Agreement shall be determined as follows:

a. *Stipulated Value.* The purchase price for the Stock owned by Jones shall be equal to $1,000,000 or such other value as may from time to time be established by resolution adopted by a vote of at least a majority of the entire Board of Directors of the Corporation and agreed to in writing by Jones (such $1,000,000 value or the value later established is herein referred to as the *stipulated value*); provided, however, that if Jones' death occurs more than eighteen months from the date of this Agreement, and if no such resolution has been adopted by the Board of Directors and agreed to in writing by Jones within the eighteen-month period preceding the death of Jones, then the purchase price for such Stock shall be determined in accordance with the following paragraph (b).

b. *Alternative Value.* Given the conditions of (1) above, then the purchase price of Jones' Stock shall be equal to the stipulated value last established pursuant to paragraph (a) of this Section 3.1 plus or minus, as the case may be, the increase or decrease in the book value per share of the Stock from the last day of the fiscal year immediately preceding the date on which the stipulated value was last determined to the last day of the fiscal year immediately preceding the date of Jones's death, multiplied by the number of shares of Stock owned by Jones which are subject to this Agreement.

The book value per share shall be computed by the CPAs regularly retained by the Corporation and in accordance with generally accepted accounting principles on a consistent basis and shall include all adjustments which in the opinion of the CPAs are necessary for a fair statement of the results of operations of the Corporation for the interim period. In determining such book value, there shall be excluded the amount by which the proceeds of any life insurance on the life of Jones which are payable to the Corporation exceed the value of any such insurance policy as carried on the books of the Corporation prior to Jones' death.

3.2 *Payment of Purchase Price.* The payment of the purchase price for any stock purchased under this Agreement shall be made as follows:

a. *Initial Payment.* In the event of the death of Jones, the Corporation shall pay to the legal representatives of Jones's estate for application on the purchase price of stock owned by Jones the total net proceeds, if any, of life insurance on the life of Jones payable to the Corporation up to but not to exceed the total purchase price therefore as determined in accordance with this Article III.

Such initial payment shall be made on or before the later of (1) the date on which the Corporation receives such insurance proceeds as the designated beneficiary and (2) the thirtieth day following the date on which the accountants determine the value of the Stock (if a stipulated value is not then in effect). If no such insurance on the life of Jones is paid to the Corporation, then there shall be no initial payment, and the entire purchase price shall be paid in the manner provided in the following paragraph (b).

b. *Balance.* (i) The Corporation shall pay to the legal representatives of Jones's estate that balance of the purchase price (herein called the Balance) represented by the amount (if any) by which the aggregate price of the Stock exceeds the amount of the initial payment under paragraph (a) above, in not more than forty consecutive equal quarterly installments of principal, plus accrued interest thereon, commencing on the first day of January next following:

1. the date of Jones's death if a stipulated value is then in effect, or,

2. the date on which the valuation of the Stock is determined pursuant to Section 3.1 hereof if no stipulated value is in effect at the time of Jones's death.

The amount of the unpaid balance outstanding from time to time shall bear interest at the rate of 9 percent per annum, which shall be payable semiannually with installments of principal, and such interest shall accrue from (1) the date which is thirty days from the date of Jones's death if a stipulated value is then in effect or (2) the date on which the value of the Stock is determined pursuant to Section 3.1 hereof if no stipulated value is in effect at the time of Jones's death, and,

(ii) The obligation to pay the balance and interest due thereon shall be evidenced by a duly executed promissory note payable to the order of the party or parties from whom the Stock is purchased, containing the aforesaid terms and such other terms as are customary for such instruments, including the right of prepayment, in whole or in part, without penalty, from time to time.

c. *Allocation of Purchase Price.* If the Stock purchased under this Agreement includes Stock owned by anyone other than Jones as a result of transfer made by Jones during his lifetime, a pro rata share of the initial payment and installments of the balance shall be made to such person in the same proportion as the purchase price for the Stock held by them bears to the total purchase price of all Stock so transferred.

3.3 *Transfer of Stock.* At such time as the first payment is made for the purchase of Stock pursuant to Section 3.2 hereof, the seller of the Stock so purchased shall deliver the stock certificates representing such Stock, properly endorsed for transfer in blank, to the Corporation for cancellation.

ARTICLE IV
AMENDMENT AND TERMINATION

4.1 *Amendment.* This Agreement may be amended at any time by written instrument executed by the Corporation and Jones.

4.2 *Termination.* Notwithstanding any other terms or provisions of this Agreement, this Agreement shall terminate:

    a. Upon the written agreement of the Corporation and Jones,

    b. Upon the bankruptcy, insolvency, or dissolution of the Corporation occurring during the lifetime of Jones, or,

    c. Upon the disposition of all of his Stock to persons other than his wife, children, or other issue.

ARTICLE V
MISCELLANEOUS PROVISIONS

5.1 *Scope of Agreement.* This Agreement shall be binding on and be enforceable by the parties hereto and their respective heirs, legal representatives, successors, and assigns, who are obligated to take any action which may be necessary or proper to carry out the purpose and intent hereof.

5.2 *Effective Date.* This Agreement is effective as of the day and year first above written.

5.3 *Life Insurance Policies.* The Corporation shall not at any time without the express written consent of Jones, cancel, transfer or fail to pay the premium on the policy or policies it owns on the life of Jones as of the date of this Agreement.

5.4 *Governing Law.* This Agreement shall be governed by and construed and enforced in accordance with the laws of the State of Delaware.

IN WITNESS WHEREOF, the Corporation and Jones have executed this Agreement in the manner appropriate to each, the day and year first written above.

_____   _____

the Corporation SMALL Corp.   Shareholder Jones

By_____

Its_____

Note in the preamble that the company already owns a $1 million life insurance policy on each of the partners. Article III spells out several additional features:

- The stipulated value of each partner's interest
- The method to be used to revalue each interest up to the date of death
- Payment terms in case the life insurance policies do not cover the full funding requirements
- The specific debt obligation to evidence the company's liability for deferred payments

The use of a stipulated value in lieu of the present value of future cash flows was agreed to by the partners specifically because they intended to renegotiate the amount every year, based on current company performance and market cycles. Since they recognized the fallacy of using book value as a base, the partners hedged by agreeing to let the company's CPA firm determine book value adjustments to reflect current conditions. They believed that it was too costly to use appraisers and that their CPA firm knew more about their business than an outside appraiser anyway.

They also agreed that qualifying for annual increases in life insurance coverage was too uncertain, since neither could predict the condition of the other's health. However, they did not want the company to face the problem of having to raise cash to cover increases in value beyond the $1 million, so they agreed to a deferred payment plan. An arrangement whereby any balance in excess of life insurance proceeds would be paid out over forty consecutive quarters seemed to give the corporation enough latitude to make the payments out of operating cash without incurring additional debt. With a promissory note as collateral, the estate would have concrete evidence of the value of the partner's interest for tax purposes. The note also provided a funding mechanism to settle legal claims in the event of default. In a side agreement, it was agreed that the company would pledge the common shares of the deceased partner as security for the promissory note.

Stipulating a 9 percent interest rate in the promissory note meant that no attempt was made to adjust the rate to market conditions. However, since market rates will inevitably vary over a ten-year period, stipulating a fixed rate is generally not a good policy for either the deceased partner or those remaining with the company. A much better approach would be to tie the interest rate to some index that reflects market rates over the duration of the note. In this case, the parties could have used the index of U.S. Treasury notes appearing in the *Federal Reserve Bulletin*. The *Bulletin* lists indexes of various tenures of Treasury notes and bonds. Another approach might be to tie the interest rate to the yield on *Barron's* intermediate-grade bond index.

It is generally not a good idea to index the rate to the prime rate, particularly for a payout period as long as ten years. The prime rate fluctuates over too wide a range and frequently over short time intervals. This causes the company extra work when calculating interest payments. Furthermore, the prime rate does not reflect the market rate of interest on intermediate- or long-term debt obligations, which include most deferred payment plans.

A second problem, more difficult than providing funding for the repurchase of a deceased partner's interest, also needs to be addressed: funding the repurchase of a physically or mentally incapacitated partner's interest. One way to fund such a buyout is for the company to carry a life insurance policy for each partner that builds cash surrender value. Cash surrender values could then be liquidated to pay for the incapacitated partner's interest.

This gets very expensive, however, especially with multiple partners. Also, family members of a mentally or physically disabled partner could very well need a monthly flow of income rather than a lump sum settlement. An annuity might be the answer, but here again, the cost is prohibitive for many small businesses.

The most common and probably best solution is to include in the buyout agreement provisions to continue the salary of disabled partners for life. The amount should be based on the partner's salary at the time of withdrawal, with annual adjustments to cover inflation. Over the long term, this type of funding may cost the company more than an annuity, but it does conserve short-term cash, which could be a good tradeoff.

Life insurance, annuities, and extended salary arrangements work well for buying out the interests of deceased or disabled partners, but what about funding buyouts of partners who leave the company of their own volition?

Except in very unusual cases, the company should not be expected to borrow money to buy out a shareholder who withdraws voluntarily, for three reasons:

1. Incurring additional debt decreases the value of the entire company. If such borrowings were provided for in the buyout agreement, the departing partner would receive proportionately less. If they were not provided for in the buyout agreement, the departing partner would receive payment based on an unleveraged valuation, decreasing ownership values for the remaining partners even further.
2. Many small companies have the ability to borrow small amounts of working capital but are fully leveraged with long-term debt. This could make it impossible to borrow sufficient funds to pay off the departing partner in full.
3. The company may be fully leveraged with both short- and long-term debt and unable to borrow any additional funds.

A more equitable arrangement might be to provide for a deferred payment plan with sufficient flexibility to allow the company to meet the obligation out of earnings. The same circumstances concerning collateral and interest rates previously described for an involuntary withdrawal apply here.

Cross-Purchase Agreements

So far we have looked only at funding alternatives for repurchase agreements. Although the same insurance and deferred payment provisions could be written for a cross-purchase agreement, the administrative effort can get very cumbersome for individual buyers, especially when there are more than two partners.

Although the options for valuing cross-purchase interests are identical to those for repurchase agreements, both the form of the buyout agreement and the funding arrangements differ. Figure 12-2 shows a sample of a two-partner cross-purchase agreement.

FIGURE 12-2: Sample Cross-Purchase Agreement Between Shareholders

THIS AGREEMENT, entered into this ___ day of _____, 19XX, between (name of shareholder) ("Jones") and (name of second shareholder) ("Smith"), hereinafter referred to as Shareholder or collectively as Shareholders;

WITNESSETH:

WHEREAS, MIGHTY-MITE CORP., a Delaware corporation ("the Corporation"), has authorized and outstanding shares of no par value Common Stock ("Stock"); and,

WHEREAS, the Shareholders are interested in the management of the business of the Corporation and are respectively the owners of the Stock set forth below in Section 1.1; and,

WHEREAS, the parties hereto mutually desire to make provision for the purchase and sale of the Stock upon the occurrence of certain significant events; and to make provision for other significant events involving the transfer and ownership of the Stock;

NOW THEREFORE, the Shareholders mutually hereby agree:

ARTICLE I

STOCK SUBJECT TO AGREEMENT

1.1 *Stock Subject to Agreement.* The following number of shares of Stock are presently held by the Shareholders:

Shareholder	Shares
Jones	100
Smith	100

The terms of this agreement shall apply to all Stock presently held by the Shareholders and any additional Stock acquired by a Shareholder during his lifetime in his own behalf, or by his estate after his death, whether by purchase, Stock dividend, or otherwise. It is contemplated that any such additional Stock will be endorsed in accordance with Section 1.2 hereof and identified by a written memorandum executed by the parties and attached hereto, but failure so to endorse and include the additional Stock in a memorandum shall not remove such Stock from the terms of this Agreement.

1.2 *Endorsement of Stock Certificates.* Each Stock certificate representing shares of Stock now held or hereafter acquired by the Shareholders shall be endorsed substantially as follows:

"The shares represented by this certificate are subject to the provisions of the Agreement to Purchase Corporate Stock, dated _____, which Agreement is available for inspection at the principal office of the Corporation."

Provided, however, that failure so to endorse any of the Shareholders' Stock certificates shall not invalidate this Agreement. The Corporation shall keep a copy of this Agreement available for inspection by all properly interested parties at the principal office.

1.3 *Use of Stock as Collateral.* The Shareholders have the right to pledge Stock owned by them as Collateral security for personal indebtedness, even though the certificate of such Stock is endorsed as provided in Section 1.2, but any Stock so pledged shall remain subject to the terms of this Agreement. The mere pledge of Stock shall not be an event which provides the Shareholders the option to purchase or sell Stock pursuant to Article II of this Agreement.

1.4 *Rights of the Shareholders.* The Stock owned by the respective Shareholders subject to this Agreement shall be voted by them, and upon the death of a Shareholder by the legal representative of his/her estate, until purchase of his/her Stock pursuant to this

Agreement or other permitted transfer or disposition, as the case may be. Any dividends payable on the Stock shall be paid to the respective Shareholders or their respective legal representatives, as the case may be.

ARTICLE II
PURCHASE AND SALE OF STOCK

2.1 *Restrictions of Lifetime Transfer of Stock:* A Shareholder shall not, during his lifetime, sell, assign, give, or otherwise transfer or dispose of any shares of Stock without first giving written notice to the nontransferring Shareholder of such intention to sell or make disposition thereof, which notice shall state the Stock proposed to be disposed of, the amount of the consideration offered, if any, and the name of the prospective purchaser or assignee. The date the nontransferring Shareholder receives such notice shall be the Transfer Notice Date. The nontransferring Shareholder may, at his option, purchase all, but not part, of the shares of Stock offered in such notice for a purchase price which is the lower of (i) the price offered as contained in such notice, or (ii) $500,000, which amount shall be payable within ninety days of the Transfer Notice Date.

ARTICLE III
INDEMNIFICATION

3.1 *Indemnity.* In the event the Stock of a Shareholder is purchased and the Shareholder no longer owns the Stock, the Purchasing Shareholder agrees to assume all obligations of the Selling Shareholder relating to the Selling Shareholder's personal guarantee of certain debt of the Corporation ("Guarantee") and to indemnify and save the Selling Shareholder harmless from any liability on account of the Guarantee. This Section 3.1 is not intended, however, to require the Purchasing Shareholder to cause the release of the Selling Shareholder from his commitment under the Guarantee.

ARTICLE IV
AMENDMENT AND TERMINATION

4.1 *Amendment:* This Agreement may be amended at any time by written instrument executed by the Shareholders.

4.2 *Termination:* Notwithstanding any other terms or provisions of this Agreement, this Agreement shall terminate:

a. Upon the written agreement of the Shareholders.

b. With respect to any particular Shareholder, upon the disposition by the Shareholder, in accordance with this Agreement of all of his Stock.

c. With respect to any Stock transferred as permitted pursuant to Section 2.1, but only with respect to the Stock so transferred.

Provided, however, that regardless of the termination f this Agreement, the rights and obligations of the parties and their successors and assigns shall continue beyond the termination.

ARTICLE V
MISCELLANEOUS PROVISIONS

5.1 *Scope of Agreement:* This Agreement shall be binding on and be enforceable by the parties hereto and their respective heirs, legal representatives, successors, and assigns, who are obligated to take any action which may be necessary or proper to carry out the purpose and intent hereof; provided, however, that the rights of the Shareholders hereunder are personal to them, their families and representatives and, without the written consent of the parties hereto, or as specifically provided herein, may not be assigned to or be enforceable by any assignee, transferee, or other present or future Shareholder of the Corporation.

5.2 *Severability:* Any provision of this Agreement which is prohibited or held unenforceable by final order of any court of competent jurisdiction shall, within such jurisdiction, be ineffective to the extent of such order without invalidating the remaining provisions of this Agreement or affecting the validity or enforceability of such provision in any other jurisdiction.

5.3 *Effective Date:* This Agreement is effective as of the day and year first above written.

5.4 *Articles and Bylaws of the Corporation:* All provisions of the Articles of Incorporation and Bylaws of the Corporation shall remain in full force and effect as to the Shareholders' Stock except to the extent inconsistent with the express provisions of this Agreement, in which event the provisions of this Agreement shall control. The Shareholders agree to cause the Corporation to waive its rights relating to its "first refusal" option under the Eighth Article of the Corporation's Certificate of Incorporation in the event of an event giving rise to the conditions under Section 2.1 hereof.

5.5 *Arbitration:* Any dispute arising out of or relating to this Agreement or the breach thereof shall be discussed between the parties hereto in good faith effort to arrive at a mutual settlement of any such controversy. If, notwithstanding, such dispute cannot be thus resolved within a period of thirty days, any party may submit the same for arbitration in the City of Wilmington, State of Delaware, to an arbitrator selected from the panel of the American Arbitration Association in accordance with its rules and regulations. The award shall be made by the decision of the arbitrator, and judgment upon the award rendered by the arbitrator may be entered in any court having jurisdiction thereof.

5.6 *Notice:* All notices herein provided for, if mailed rather than delivered, shall be mailed by certified or registered mail with return receipt requested, addressed to the addressee at his or its last known address.

5.7 *Governing Law:* This Agreement shall be governed by and construed and enforced in accordance with the laws of the State of Delaware.

IN WITNESS WHEREOF, the Shareholders have executed this Agreement in the manner appropriate to each, the day and year first written above.

_____
Shareholder Jones

_____
Shareholder Smith

Three important points should be noted in this sample agreement:

- It includes a *right of first refusal* section and a maximum price.
- It is between two equal partners.
- It does *not* include any reference to funding the buyout.

Cross-purchase agreements are used extensively in professional practices, and for good reason. In a personal service business, the last thing the remaining partners want is to suddenly be faced with a new partner not of their choosing. When clauses giving the remaining partners the first right to acquire the departing partner's interest are included, this cannot happen. It is also important to establish a maximum price that all partners commit to.

This type of buyout agreement works perfectly well for a two-partner company. It is especially well suited to voluntary withdrawals, in that cross-purchase agreements keep the company completely out of the transaction. Such matters as potential breach of contract by either party or default on deferred payments remain where they belong, between individuals. The remaining partner can then be free to make major policy decisions affecting the company, such as business acquisitions or disposal of product lines, without concern for repercussions from the departed partner.

Normally, cross-purchase agreements are not a satisfactory arrangement for companies owned by a group of partners or for several partners with varying percentages of ownership. Cross-purchase buyouts can be used in these cases, but they get extremely complicated and nine times out of ten result in major disputes.

Providing for the funding of a cross-purchase buyout within the buyout agreement is very difficult. Occasionally agreements are written that allow the company to lend partners sufficient funds to make the buyout, but this puts companies in the same type of capital-raising quandary as a repurchase buyout. Since everyone has a different personal financial status and different objectives, it isn't practical to specify how or where funds will be raised. In fact, nearly all cross-purchase buyouts stipulate deferred payment terms so that partners can use normal draws from the company to buy the interest over a reasonable time period.

In closing, it should be pointed out that the age-old axiom "buyer's price, seller's terms" holds in buyout agreements as well as in any form of purchase contract. In effect, this means that if deferred payment terms are a requirement of the remaining partners, then the departing partner's interest increases in value. This premium can be calculated relatively easily by comparing the present value of the payment stream with the cost of a cash-out purchase. The longer the deferred payment term, the lower the present value and the higher the price should be.

CHAPTER

Multibusinesses

Large corporations don't have a monopoly on multibusiness organizations. Thousands of small companies also enjoy the fruits of diversification, although their books of account often do not reflect it. Take, for example, restaurants. Many have at least two distinct businesses, food and beverages. Each requires different sales strategies, personnel, pricing, and probably advertising. Some restaurants also offer take-out service, which requires yet another type of personnel, advertising, and pricing. Diversification is as much the name of the game in small businesses as in corporate boardrooms. And diversification leads to multibusiness companies.

If a multibusiness company is valued as a single entity, large distortions in fair market value inevitably occur. Some business segments may operate at losses, others at very high margins, and still others at low margins or breakeven. Some segments require an inordinate amount of working capital, others virtually none. Long-term debt may have to be incurred to support one business segment, while other segments can get along with short-term credit lines. Market demand for products in one business unit may be growing at 20 percent a year; that for products in a second could be in a down cycle; and the market for a third may be stagnant.

If total company sales, costs, assets, and debt are combined into one pool, ratio analyses, risk analyses, and comparative analyses become very distorted. Pro forma financial statements and cash flow forecasts that reflect a wide array of businesses are practically impossible to relate to business cycles. Functional relationships blur. The probability of achieving projected earnings and cash flows tends to follow the poorest performing segment. And in most cases, the worth of the total company will be much less than if each business segment were valued individually. This is one of those rare cases where the whole may not be equal to the sum of its parts.

Since the future growth of a multibusiness company depends on the successful management of the entire portfolio of businesses, the most valuable asset of the company as a whole is the managerial talent of the top echelon of personnel. Yet, the future benefits derived from specific business segments tend to be more a function of the talents and skills of lower-level managers, efficient marketing organizations, tailored customer service, and quality product design and production. Such a distinction can be vitally important in buy/sell analyses. The investment value of a business that is dependent on basic marketing, product design, and production skills is normally higher than that of one that relies primarily on management talent.

Multibusiness valuation allows investors to assess the investment quality of each business segment as if it were a stand-alone company. It also permits the weighting of specific benefits created by a headquarters or top management activity. The focal question is what benefits these extra overhead layers contribute to the company and whether greater benefits could be achieved by trimming the fat, as it were.

Multibusiness valuation is not just an important analytic tool for potential investors. Business segment analysis also gives business owners the means for a critical examination of company activities that can help them determine future growth and profit-improvement strategies. Perhaps the greatest contribution of a multibusiness valuation comes from its role in determining specific actions that may be taken to reorganize product line responsibilities, implement cost-reduction programs, acquire complementary business segments, or dispose of nonperforming segments. All of these actions aim at strengthening the company's operating base and improving its long-term profit potential.

The multibusiness valuation process follows a sequence similar to that used for the valuation of single-business companies:

1. Due diligence investigation
2. Ratio and risk analysis of historical financial performance
3. Preparation of pro forma financial statements and cash flow forecasts based on functional relationships
4. Ratio and risk analyses of projected future financial results
5. Comparative analysis against similar companies
6. Calculation of the present value of a stream of future cash benefits

In the case of multibusiness companies, however, these steps must be performed for each business segment, and also for the unallocated headquarters costs and assets. When all business unit valuations have been completed, their sum should be compared to a single valuation of the company as a whole. This enables both business owners and potential investors to make a final determination for buy/sell strategies and/or other enhancements. The starting point in this process is to define and collect data for each business segment.

Defining and Collecting Data by Business Segment

Most small business owners tend to think of their company as a single unit, not a group of separate businesses. They organize personnel, arrange financing, and develop plans along a single track. To reverse the field and view the company as a composite of separate, stand-alone businesses is a radical departure. This job can best be done by professional advisers familiar with business segment accounting.

A case in point arose not long ago when a small business client ran into trouble with a bank. The business consisted of two distinctly different activities and markets: (1) a distribution center that supplied disposable and nondisposable products to hospitals and other health care facilities, and (2) a home care segment that rented physical therapy equipment to homebound patients. The company's borrowing base composed of receivables and inventory was fully extended, but the company still needed additional loans. The bank said no.

As an outsider, I saw clearly that we had two businesses to deal with, not one, and that one, the home care segment, was highly profitable while the distribution center was dying on the vine. My client couldn't see this, arguing vociferously that despite separate personnel, floor space, pricing, advertising, delivery, and credit and collection activities, home care and distribution had to be looked at as one company.

Undaunted, I prepared a business segment analysis of the prior year's financial statements, cash flow forecasts for each segment, and business valuations for two stand-alone businesses. Proceeds from the eventual sale of the distribution center paid off all short-term bank debt, and the client's home care business became even more profitable than forecasted.

Some authors consider business segments separable entities that have no significant relationship with each other. This may be an adequate description for large corporations, but it does not do the trick for small businesses, which, by definition, may have facilities, office personnel, and other tangible and intangible assets that are common to several or all segments.

A more reasonable definition of a business segment for small businesses is a product line or group of product lines, a division, a subsidiary, or a market such as exporting that could operate efficiently as a stand-alone business with minor additions of support personnel or hard assets. Business segments may or may not have synergistic characteristics, and transfers of products, services, or support activities between segments may or may not be desirable.

Once separate business segments have been defined, relevant data for each segment needs to be gathered and assimilated. Since business segment accounting records have probably not been kept, data gathering may be difficult. Some data is easily identifiable by segment, such as sales, cost of sales, customer orders and backlog, inventory, and probably receivables and payables. It may even be possible to identify specific machinery and vehicles and related costs that are dedicated to each segment.

Most companies code payroll records by job function and department. In that case, labor hours, payroll, and numbers of employees for each business segment can be accumulated. Costs of supervisory personnel should be related directly to the employees supervised.

If each business segment has dedicated sales personnel, selling costs related to these employees (e.g., payroll, commissions, fringe benefits, travel and entertainment, samples, sales literature, and probably advertising expense) can be segregated. The cost of automobiles could also be related to specific sales personnel.

In the administrative expense category, such costs as payroll and fringe benefits of credit and collections employees and payroll clerks, auto insurance, product liability insurance, and the salary and benefits of business segment managers should be identified and segregated.

Gathering all this data can be a time-consuming, frustrating task if accounting records are not divided into business segments. Companies that rely on tax returns, canceled checks, and deposit receipts for their accounting information will probably not be able to segregate costs and assets sufficiently to make the effort worthwhile. In most cases, however, even micro businesses keep track of product-identifiable expenditures in some manner. Although general-use assets, liabilities, and debt obligations appear to be unassignable, every attempt should be made to allocate as many items as possible out of headquarters pools.

Once as much data as possible has been accumulated, business segment financial statements can be prepared. Missing information needed to perform a reasonably intelligent ratio analysis, such as total debt or capital employed, can be estimated using asset turnover and other ratios from industry or government statistics and possibly from reasonably comparable public companies. However, the same caveat about comparing apples to oranges discussed in previous chapters applies even more for valuations of business segments.

Business Segment Pro Forma Forecasts

Except for start-up businesses, the preparation of business segment pro forma forecasts must begin with the actual financial statements for at least the preceding year. In addition to using actual operating results as a forecast base, analysts must make certain that each segment's financial statements constructed from raw data can be reconciled with the total company's balance sheet and income statement. The easiest way to demonstrate this is with another fictitious company, this time called MULTICORP. Figure 13-1 shows MULTICORP's actual financial statements from the previous year broken down into business segments and reconciled with total company accounts.

By analyzing these statements, one can see that the retail store business segment earned a net income after taxes of 9 percent of sales, whereas MULTICORP as a whole earned only 3 percent. The retail store also accounted for 55 percent of the company's sales; the catalog unit was 31 percent, and the made-to-order segment accounted for 14 percent. Comparing net income, however, we see that, excluding corporate office expenses, the retail store contributed $197,000, or nearly 80 percent of the total, while the catalog unit produced a net loss.

FIGURE 13-1

MULTICORP
STATEMENT OF INCOME ($000)

	Catalog Resale	Made-to-Order	Retail Store	Corporate Office	Total Company
Sales	1,235	575	2,190		4,000
Cost of sales	1,100	240	1,260		2,600
Gross profit	135	335	930		1,400
% of sales	11%	58%	42%		35%
Manufacturing expenses	0	120	0		120
Selling expenses	70	40	420	75	605
Commissions	0	0	44		44
Administrative expenses	75	60	70	100	305
Other expenses	5	0	20	25	50
Depreciation	0	10	4	3	17
Total expenses	150	230	558	203	1,141
Net income before interest and taxes	(15)	105	372	(203)	259
% of sales	-1%	18%	17%	((blank))	6%
Interest expense	0	4	54	11	69
Net income before taxes	(15)	101	318	(214)	191
Taxes	(6)	38	121	(81)	72
Net income	(9)	63	197	(132)	118
% of sales	-1%	11%	9%		3%

MULTICORP
BALANCE SHEET ($000)

	Catalog Resale	Made-to-Order	Retail Store	Corporate Office	Total Company
Cash	0	0	0	1,887	1,887
Receivables	0	144	91	0	235
Inventory	131	70	1,026	0	1,226
Total current assets	131	213	1,117	1,887	3,348
Building	0	0	0	100	100
Equipment & vehicles	0	100	24	10	134
TOTAL	0	100	24	110	234
Accumulated depreciation	0	(50)	(10)	(20)	(80)
Net	0	50	14	90	154
Other assets	12	0	0	25	37
Due from corporate/business units	16	251	891	0	1,159
Total assets	159	514	2,022	2,002	4,698
Bank loan	0	0	600	70	670
Accounts payable	139	104	223	20	485
Accrued expenses	14	52	111	10	187
Total current liabilities	153	156	934	100	1,342
Due to corporate/business units	0	0	0	1,159	1,159
Long-term note	0	45	0	47	92
Total liabilities	153	201	934	1,306	2,593
Common stock	0	0	0	100	100
Retained earnings—beginning	16	251	891	729	1,887
Profit	(9)	63	197	(132)	118
Retained earnings—ending	7	314	1,088	597	2,005
Total equity	7	324	1,088	697	2,105
Total liabilities and equity	159	514	2,022	2,002	4,698

MULTICORP
Statement of Cash Flow ($000)

	Catalog Resale	Made-to-Order	Retail Store	Corporate Office	Total Company
CASH RECEIPTS					
Receivables—beginning	-14-	05		235	
Sales	1,235	575	2,190		4,000
Receivables—ending	0	(144)	(91)		(235)
Receipts from operations	1,235	571	2,194		4,000
New bank loan	0	0	600		600
Total receipts	1,235	571	2,794		4,600
CASH EXPENDITURES					
Accounts payable—beginning	116	45	142	25	328
Purchases	1,111	250	1,336	0	2,696
Accounts payable—ending	(139)	(104)	(223)	(20)	(485)
Material expenditures	1,088	191	1,255	5	2,539
Accrued expenses—beginning	0	30	30		60
Selling expenses	70	40	420	75	605
Commissions	0	0	44		44
Administrative expenses	75	60	70	100	305
Other expenses	5	0	20	25	50
Accrued expenses—ending	(14)	(52)	(111)	(10)	(187)
Total operating expenditures	136	78	472	190	877
Financing costs:					
Interest	0	4	54	11	69
Principal	0	9	0	5	14
Total financing costs	0	13	54	16	83
Taxes	(6)	38	121	(81)	72
Total expenditures	1,219	320	1,902	129	3,571
NET CASH GENERATED	16	251	891	(129)	1,029
Due to/(from) corp/business units	(16)	(251)	(891)	1,159	0
Cash in bank—beginning	0	0	0	858	858
Cash in bank—ending	0	0	0	1,887	1,887

Without looking at the balance sheet or cash flows, if the catalog segment could be sold as a going business, MULTICORP's sales would be substantially reduced. At the same time, however, its profit would be increased by at least the amount of the catalog loss. Furthermore, with a lower sales volume, it seems likely that corporate office expenses could be cut, thereby increasing total company profits even more.

A slightly different picture evolves from analyzing the balance sheet. Of the three operating units, the catalog employs only $159,000, or 6 percent of operating assets; made-to-order uses 15 percent, and the retail store 79 percent. The building that houses all three business units cannot be allocated and shows up in corporate office accounts. The following tabulation summarizes the actual and forecasted operating ratios for each of the three operating units.

MULTICORP BUSINESS SEGMENTS
OPERATING RATIOS

	ACTUAL		----FORECASTED----			
	Year 1	Year 2	Year 3	Year 4	Year 5	Year 6
CATALOG						
Current ratio	0.9	0.9	1.0	1.0	1.1	1.1
Quick ratio	N/A	N/A	N/A	N/A	N/A	N/A
Asset turnover	7.8	8.2	8.8	9.4	10.3	11.4
Receivables turnover	N/A	N/A	N/A	N/A	N/A	N/A
Inventory turnover	8.4	8.0	7.5	7.1	6.8	6.5
Total debt to equity	N/A	N/A	N/A	N/A	N/A	N/A
Return on equity	N/A	N/A	N/A	N/A	N/A	N/A
Return on assets	N/A	N/A	N/A	N/A	N/A	N/A
MADE-TO-ORDER						
Current ratio	1.4	1.4	1.5	1.6	1.6	1.6
Quick ratio	0.9	0.9	0.9	1.0	1.0	1.0
Asset turnover	1.5	1.3	1.2	1.1	1.0	0.9
Receivables turnover	4.0	4.0	4.0	4.0	4.0	4.0
Inventory turnover	3.4	3.1	2.8	2.5	2.4	2.3
Total debt to equity	0.2	0.1	0.1	0.0	0.0	0.0
Return on equity	32%	24%	21%	19%	17%	16%
Return on assets	16%	14%	13%	13%	12%	12%
RETAIL STORE						
Current ratio	1.2	1.2	1.3	1.3	1.4	1.4
Quick ratio	0.1	0.1	0.1	0.1	0.1	0.1
Asset turnover	1.1	1.0	1.0	0.9	0.9	0.8
Receivables turnover	24.0	24.0	24.0	24.0	24.0	24.0
Inventory turnover	1.2	1.2	1.2	1.2	1.1	1.1
Total debt to equity	0.6	0.5	0.4	0.4	0.3	0.3
Return on equity	18%	15%	14%	12%	11%	11%
Return on assets	10%	9%	8%	8%	8%	7%

Since the corporate office uses a centralized cash management system, business segments do not have separate bank accounts and therefore do not show cash balances on their balance sheets. This distorts both the current ratio and the quick ratio, both of which include only receivables and inventory as the numerator. Asset turnover is very relevant, however, and a comparison of these ratios shows that the catalog unit makes the best use of its few assets, mostly inventory. Its high inventory turnover ratio supports this finding and could make the unit an attractive acquisition for a company able to expand the operation and generate higher profits.

The return on equity ratios for both the made-to-order business unit and the retail store are certainly adequate, although the retail store ratio should be higher to make the unit an attractive acquisition. Ratio analysis of the three business segments indicates that perhaps MULTICORP should consider disposing of its catalog unit and expanding its made-to-order unit.

As far as cash flow goes, the made-to-order line and the retail store project reasonable cash flows of $323,000 and $836,000, respectively, for the five-year period Year 2 through Year 6 (as can be seen in Figure 13-2). The catalog unit, on the other hand, has forecasted a negative cash flow of

$97,000 for the same period, draining cash from the other two units and offering nothing to support the corporate office. Unless the company has a synergistic reason for retaining the catalog unit as a loss leader, it would probably be better off closing this unit down if a buyer cannot be found.

FIGURE 13-2

MULTICORP
SUMMARY OF CASH FLOWS ($000)

	Actual			- - - - Forecasted - - - -		
	Year 1	Year 2	Year 3	Year 4	Year 5	Year 6
Annual Cash Flows						
Catalog	16	(16)	(18)	(20	(21)	(22)
Made-to-order	131	54	57	63	71	78
Retail store	891	153	162	168	173	179
TOTAL	1,039	192	201	212	223	234
Cumulative Cash Flows						
Catalog	16	1	(18)	(37)	(58)	(81)
Made-to-order	131	186	242	305	376	454
Retail store	891	1,044	1,207	1,375	1,548	1,727
TOTAL	1,039	1,230	1,431	1,643	1,866	2,100

Corporate Office Cost Center

Those expenses and assets that remain after as much as possible has been allocated to operating business units fall into the corporate office or headquarters pool. In some companies, allocating corporate expenses doesn't make sense. In others, excluding the business owners, it's possible to allocate the salaries and expenses of all management personnel except for those of the business owner. To the extent that separate facilities house different business units, the cost of buildings, improvements, and office equipment can be charged directly to the units. If all businesses occupy the same premises, however, it usually makes sense to treat common facilities as corporate office assets.

Some analysts dispute this approach, arguing that even unidentifiable buildings and support equipment should be allocated on square footage used by each business segment or some other basis, so that the corporate office cost center has zero assets. This has merit when the resultant business unit ratios are to be used for establishing product prices or other internal measures. However, it's difficult to see how an allocation of common assets or costs contributes anything to the valuation of each unit. If each business is viewed as a stand-alone entity that could be severed from the total company without endangering other business segments, clearly allocated floor space and allocated costs become meaningless.

In many small businesses the corporate office comprises the business owner/manager and supporting staff, such as a secretary, a controller, and perhaps a receptionist/office clerk. Theoretically, benefits derived from the costs incurred in running such an office arise from the sharing of certain managerial responsibilities among business units. If the units were to be run separately, each would need a general manager and support personnel, thereby increasing total administrative overhead.

In many cases, however, business units can run efficiently on their own, making a corporate office an unnecessary overhead expense that drains cash. Many small businesses find that when each business segment is valued, the corporate office stands out as a nonproductive luxury—as we'll see later in the valuation process for MULTICORP.

The following represent typical corporate office expenses that cannot logically be allocated to operating units:

- Salary, fringes, and expenses of the business owner/manager
- Salary, fringes, and expenses of secretaries, receptionists, office clerks, custodians, and so on
- Salary, fringes, and expenses of the accounting/finance function
- Property, liability, and casualty insurance
- Office rent
- Office equipment, maintenance, and telephone expense
- Professional fees: legal, accounting, consulting
- Charitable contributions, goodwill promotion and public relations expenses, companywide advertising

In certain companies, one or more of these expenses can be reasonably allocated, but in most cases they cannot be. In the MULTICORP example, it has been assumed that all these expenses remain at the corporate level. In addition, long-term debt and associated financing costs that benefit the entire company are normally kept at the corporate level, as are all cash management activities. If the business units were to be spun off, it might be necessary to include in the valuation calculation sufficient debt and associated interest payments to keep each unit financially viable.

One way to test the reasonableness of corporate office expenses is to compare the ratios of expenses to sales and expenses to equity with ratios from public companies in similar industries. Although large corporations certainly have many more levels of administrative overhead than small businesses, theoretically at least, the ratios of expenses to owner's equity and expenses to sales should be somewhat comparable. Several analytical studies of the twenty-five largest industrial companies conducted over the past ten years have indicated that the ratio of corporate overhead to owner's equity ranges from 0.3 percent all the way to 9 percent, and the ratio of corporate overhead to sales from 0.1 percent to 2.7 percent.

In the case of MULTICORP, corporate expenses for Year 1 are 6.7 percent of equity and 3.3 percent of sales. This indicates (1) that expenses are somewhat high relative to profit and (2) that this level of expenses can support substantially higher sales or, conversely, that at this sales level, corporate expenses should be reduced.

To value corporate cost centers, first calculate the present value of a future cost stream and then compare it with the present value of cost center benefits. If costs exceed benefits by a wide margin, potential investors can look at the company as a viable acquisition candidate, since immediate cash savings are achievable by trimming back corporate office expenses. MULTICORP's corporate office costs for Year 1 were $214,000, as shown in Figure 13-3, including interest expense but before tax savings. Over the next five years they are projected to be:

Year 2	$217,000
Year 3	221,000
Year 4	226,000
Year 5	231,000
Year 6	236,000
TOTAL	1,131,000

FIGURE 13-3

CORPORATE OFFICE
STATEMENT OF INCOME ($000)

	Actual			----Forecasted----		
	Year 1	Year 2	Year 3	Year 4	Year 5	Year 6
Selling expenses	75	77	80	82	84	87
Administrative expenses	100	101	104	107	110	113
Other expenses	25	25	25	25	25	25
Depreciation	3	3	3	3	3	3
Total expenses	203	207	211	217	222	228
Net income before interest and taxes	(203)	(207)	(211)	(217)	(222)	(228)
Interest expense	11	10	10	9	9	8
Net income before taxes	(214)	(217)	(221)	(226)	(231)	(236)
Taxes	(81)	(82)	(84)	(86)	(88)	(90)
Net income	(132)	(134)	(137)	(140)	(143)	(147)

CORPORATE OFFICE
BALANCE SHEET ($000)

	Actual			----Forecasted-----		
	Year 1	Year 2	Year 3	Year 4	Year 5	Year 6
Cash	1,768	1,823	1,884	1,954	2,032	2,118
Building	100	100	100	100	100	100
Equipment & vehicles	10	10	10	10	10	10
TOTAL	110	110	110	110	110	110
Accumulated depreciation	(20)	(23)	(26)	(29)	(32)	(35)
Net	90	87	84	81	78	75
Other assets	25	25	25	25	25	25
Total assets	1,883	1,935	1,993	2,060	2,135	2,218
Bank loan	70	70	70	70	70	70
Accounts payable	20	20	20	20	20	20
Accrued expenses	10	10	10	10	10	10
Total current liabilities	100	100	100	100	100	100
Due to business units	1,039	1,230	1,431	1,643	1,866	2,100
Long-term note	47	42	37	32	27	22
Total liabilities	1,186	1,372	1,568	1,775	1,993	2,222
Common stock	100	100	100	100	100	100
Retained earnings—beginning	729	597	462	325	185	42
Profit	(132)	(134)	(137)	(140)	(143)	(147)
Retained earnings—end	597	462	325	185	42	(104)
Total equity	697	562	425	285	142	(4)
Total liabilities and equity	1,883	1,935	1,993	2,060	2,135	2,218

CORPORATE OFFICE
STATEMENT OF CASH FLOW ($000)

	Actual		----Forecasted-----			
	Year 2	Year 3	Year 4	Year 5	Year 6	
CASH RECEIPTS						
Received from business units	1,039	192	201	212	223	234
CASH EXPENDITURES						
Material expenditures	5	0	0	0	0	0
Accrued expenses—beginning	0	10	10	10	10	10
Selling expenses	75	77	80	82	84	87
Administrative expenses	100	101	104	107	110	113
Other expenses	25	25	25	25	25	25
Accrued expenses—ending	(10)	(10)	(10)	(10)	(10)	(10)
Total operating expenditures	190	204	208	214	219	225
Financing costs:						
Interest	11	10	10	9	9	8
Principal	5	5	5	5	5	5
Total financing costs	16	15	15	14	14	13
Taxes	(81)	(82)	(84)	(86)	(88)	(90)
Total expenditures	129	136	139	142	145	149
NET CASH GENERATED	909	55	62	70	78	86
Cash in bank—beginning	858	1,767	1,823	1,884	1,954	2,032
Cash in bank—ending	1,767	1,823	1,884	1,954	2,032	2,118
Net present value of cost center	644					

Assume that a risk-free interest rate of 7 percent on U.S. Treasury notes will be used as a capitalization rate. Since the mathematics of discounting losses or costs produces a present value less than the actual forecast, a minimum risk factor should be added to the risk-free rate only if you believe that forecasted expenses are too high and that the cost center will actually incur less expense than is budgeted. At a 7 percent rate, the present value of the five-year stream of costs from the MULTICORP corporate office turns out to be $581,000.

Benefits derived from a corporate administrative cost center are far more difficult to calculate. Broadly speaking they fall into two categories:

1. Tax savings to the company as a whole from using losses from one business unit to offset taxable income from another unit or by leveraging the company at the corporate level, with corresponding tax deductions for interest expense (obviously, without corporate debt and interest expense, tax savings won't occur)

2. Intangible, qualitative benefits derived from vertically integrated economies of scale, overall management direction, improved communications throughout the company, relationships with external parties such as banks and the financial community, and so on. These factors clearly benefit a company; however, since they are impossible to quantify, they must be weighted subjectively.

MULTICORP's catalog business segment is the only segment running at a loss. Therefore, the present value of tax savings resulting from its forecasted loss should be included as a corporate office benefit. At a 10 percent discount rate, the present value of the stream of the catalog unit's five-year tax savings amounts to $25,000. Comparing this to the present value of the headquarters cost stream of $581,000 makes it clear that unless qualitative factors offset this wide variance, MULTICORP isn't getting much benefit from its corporate office.

Present Value Comparisons by Business Segment

Once the corporate office valuation is in hand, the next step is to value each operating business unit. Each unit should be viewed as a stand-alone company, generating its own earnings and cash flows and having its own asset base and financing requirements. Although certain business segments, such as the catalog unit for MULTICORP, have very few assets and require no outside financing, more complex segments, such as the retail store, do.

Valuing the Catalog Segment

The preparation of pro forma financial statements and cash flow forecasts should be based on prior history plus projected market growth factors and associated cost increases or decreases. Figure 13-4 shows the catalog unit's actual Year 1 financial statements and cash flow along with pro forma forecasts for five years.

The low overhead costs indicate that this business unit is very volume-sensitive. With an 11 percent gross margin, 11 cents out of every dollar increase in sales should fall to the bottom line. No external financing was required in Year 1, although the forecast shows cash contributions from the corporate office of $81,000 over the period Year 3 through Year 6. As increases in sales volume begin to generate higher profits, trade credit should take care of this unit's financing needs, although when the unit is in a loss position it clearly does not.

FIGURE 13-4

CATALOG RESALE
STATEMENT OF INCOME ($000)

| | Actual | | ----Forecasted---- | | | |
	Year 1	Year 2	Year 3	Year 4	Year 5	Year 6
Sales	1,235	1,272	1,297	1,323	1,350	1,377
Cost of sales	1,100	1,132	1,155	1,178	1,201	1,225
Gross profit	135	140	143	146	148	151
% of sales	11%	11%	11%	11%	11%	11%
Selling expenses	70	72	74	76	79	81
Administrative expenses	75	77	80	82	84	87
Other expenses	5	5	5	5	5	5
Total expenses	150	154	159	163	168	173
Net income before taxes	(15)	(14)	(16)	(18)	(20)	(22)
% of sales	-1%	-1%	-1%	-1%	-1%	-2%
Taxes	(6)	(5)	(6)	(7)	(7)	(8)
Net income	(9)	(9)	(10)	(11)	(12)	(13)
% of sales	-1%	-1%	-1%	-1%	-1%	-1%

CATALOG RESALE
BALANCE SHEET ($000)

| | Actual | | ----Forecasted---- | | | |
	Year 1	Year 2	Year 3	Year 4	Year 5	Year 6
Cash	0	0	0	0	0	0
Inventory	131	142	154	166	178	190
Total current assets	131	142	154	166	178	190
Other assets	12	12	12	12	12	12
Due from(to) corporate	16	1	(18)	(37)	(58)	(81)
Total assets	159	155	148	140	131	121
Accounts payables	139	143	146	149	152	155
Accrued expenses	14	14	15	15	15	15
Total current liabilities	153	157	160	164	167	170
Retained earnings—beginning	16	7	(2)	(12)	(23)	(36)
Profit	(9)	(9)	(10)	(11)	(12)	(13)
Retained earnings—ending	7	(2)	(12)	(23)	(36)	(49)
Total equity	7	(2)	(12)	(23)	(36)	(49)
Total liabilities and equity	159	155	148	140	131	121

CATALOG RESALE
STATEMENT OF CASH FLOW ($000)

	Actual		---- Forecasted- ----			
	Year 1	Year 2	Year 3	Year 4	Year 5	Year 6
CASH RECEIPTS						
Sales receipts	1,235	1,272	1,297	1,323	1,350	1,377
CASH EXPENDITURES						
Accounts payable—beginning	116	139	143	146	149	152
Purchases	1,111	1,143	1,166	1,190	1,213	1,238
Accounts payable—ending	(139)	(143)	(146)	(149)	(152)	(155)
Material expenditures	1,088	1,139	1,163	1,187	1,210	1,235
Accrued expenses—beginning	0	14	14	15	15	15
Selling expenses	70	72	74	76	79	81
Administrative expenses	75	77	80	82	84	87
Other expenses	5	5	5	5	5	5
Accrued expenses—ending	(14)	(14)	(15)	(15)	(15)	(15)
Total operating expenditures	136	154	159	163	168	173
Taxes	(6)	(5)	(6)	(7)	(7)	(8)
Total expenditures	1,219	1,288	1,316	1,343	1,371	1,399
NET CASH GENERATED	16	(16)	(18)	(20)	(21)	(220
Due (to)/from corporate—beginning	0	16	0	(18)	(37)	(58)
Due (to)/from corporate—ending	16	0	(18)	(37)	(58)	(81)

Valuing a troubled company—or in this case a business unit creating losses—requires creative techniques not found in traditional valuation methods. One technique that usually works well is the asset cash flow method, whereby an estimate is made of the cash flow each business asset brings in a going-concern environment.

In the case of MULTICORP's catalog unit, its only asset is inventory, which has a very rapid turnover. However, to conserve cash, the unit has stretched accounts payable beyond the inventory turn, which means that no free cash would be generated by liquidating inventory. Since neither the discounted cash flow method nor the liquidation method will yield a reasonable value for this unit, the only alternative is to look at non–balance sheet assets.

Catalog sales depend to a large extent on the composition and breadth of catalog mailing lists. The value of mailing lists cannot be recorded in the books of account, so judgment must determine their value. If a potential buyer were to view these lists as a valuable commodity and believe that extending the mailings or accelerating an advertising program would produce increased sales, perhaps MULTICORP's owners could negotiate a sale price that would liquidate payables and still net free cash to the corporate office.

As a starting point, the catalog unit does create tax savings through its net operating loss. We have already seen how an offset of this operating loss against the consolidated income of the other two units brings tax savings of $25,000. Therefore, selling price negotiations should begin with that value. To it could be added judgment values for a mailing list and any goodwill that exists.

Valuing the Made-to-Order Segment

The made-to-order business segment of MULTICORP presents an entirely different valuation challenge. This is a specialty manufacturing operation that makes small quantities of products to customer specifications. As Figure 13-5 shows, the operation produces a gross margin of 58 to 60 percent and a very handsome operating income to sales ratio of 18 percent in Year 1, forecasted to improve to 21 percent by Year 6. Such a high profit margin enables this business segment to manage an 18 percent sales growth over the forecast period without working capital borrowings. However, five years earlier, the unit incurred long-term debt of $90,000 to purchase new equipment, resulting in an annual interest charge of $4,000 in Year 1.

The return on equity and return on assets ratios turn out as expected for a business with high margins and a relatively low asset base. Receivables turnover of four times for all forecast years looks low, however, as does the inventory turnover of between 3.4 and 2.3 turns. These ratios detract from the unit's value.

On the other hand, this business segment maintains a cash-positive position throughout the forecast period, which is a healthy sign given its heavy current asset load. Cash flow in Year 1 of $131,000 was reduced in the forecast years primarily as a result of cash-draining increases in purchased materials to support sales growth, without a concurrent growth in trade credit. The poor collections record and the inability to obtain trade credit to support inventory growth detracts from the unit's value and increases the risk of not achieving the forecasted cash stream.

FIGURE 13-5

MADE TO ORDER
STATEMENT OF INCOME ($000)

	Actual		----Forecasted----			
	Year 1	Year 2	Year 3	Year 4	Year 5	Year 6
Sales	575	586	604	622	647	679
Cost of sales	240	246	248	249	259	272
Gross profit	335	340	356	373	388	408
% of sales	58%	58%	59%	60%	60%	60%
Manufacturing expenses	120	124	127	131	135	139
Selling expenses	40	41	42	44	45	46
Administrative expenses	60	62	64	66	68	70
Depreciation	10	10	10	10	10	10
Total expenses	230	237	243	250	258	265
Net income before interest and taxes	105	104	113	123	131	143
% of sales	18%	18%	19%	20%	20%	21%
Interest expense	4	3	2	2	1	0
Net income before taxes	101	100	111	121	130	143
Taxes	38	38	42	46	49	54
Net income	63	62	69	75	81	88
% of sales	11%	11%	11%	12%	12%	13%

MADE TO ORDER
BALANCE SHEET ($000)

| | Actual | | ----Forecasted---- | | | |
	Year 1	Year 2	Year 3	Year 4	Year 5	Year 6
Cash	0	0	0	0	0	0
Receivables	144	147	151	156	162	170
Inventory	70	79	89	99	110	121
Total current assets	213	226	240	255	271	290
Equipment & vehicles	100	100	100	100	100	100
Accumulated depreciation	(50)	(60)	(70)	(80)	(90)	(100)
Net	50	40	30	20	10	0
Due from corporate	131	186	242	305	376	454
Total assets	394	452	513	580	658	745
Accounts payable	104	107	107	108	112	118
Accrued expenses	52	53	54	55	56	58
Total current liabilities	156	160	161	163	169	176
Long-term note	45	36	27	18	9	0
Total liabilities	201	196	188	181	178	176
Retained earnings—beginning	131	194	256	324	400	480
Profit	63	62	69	75	81	88
Retained earnings—ending	194	256	324	400	480	569
Total equity	194	256	324	400	480	589
Total liabilities and equity	394	452	513	580	658	745

MADE TO ORDER
STATEMENT OF CASH FLOW ($00)

| | Actual | | ----Forecasted---- | | | |
	Year 1	Year 2	Year 3	Year 4	Year 5	Year 6
CASH RECEIPTS						
Receivables—beginning	140	144	147	151	156	162
Sales	575	586	604	622	647	679
Receivables—ending	(144)	(147)	(151)	(156)	(162)	(170)
Receipts from operations	571	584	600	618	641	671
CASH EXPENDITURES						
Accounts payable—beginning	45	104	107	107	108	112
Purchases	250	256	258	259	269	283
Accounts payable—ending	(104)	(107)	(107)	(108)	(112)	(118)
Material expenditures	191	253	257	258	265	277
Accrued expenses—beginning	30	52	53	54	55	56
Manufacturing expenses	120	124	127	131	135	139
Selling expenses	40	41	42	44	45	46
Administrative expenses	60	62	64	66	68	70
Accrued expenses—ending	(52)	(53)	(54)	(55)	(56)	(58)
Total operating expenditures	198	225	233	240	246	253
Financing costs:						
Interest	4	3	2	2	1	0
Principal	9	9	9	9	9	9
Total financing costs	13	12	11	11	10	9
Taxes	38	38	42	46	49	54
Total expenditures	440	529	543	555	570	593
NET CASH GENERATED	131	55	57	63	71	78
Due (to)/from corporate—beginning	0	131	186	242	305	376
Due (to)/from corporate—ending	131	186	242	305	376	454

Note: All columns do not add due to rounding.

Beginning with the same 7 percent rate for risk-free U.S. Treasuries, an analyst would probably consider a risk discount of 3 percent as adequate, producing a total capitalization rate of 10 percent. The following cash flow was forecasted in Figure 13-5:

Year 2	$55,000
Year 3	57,000
Year 4	63,000
Year 5	71,000
Year 6	78,000

Applying a 10 percent discount rate to this stream yields a present value of $241,000.

Valuing the Retail Store Segment

Accounting for 63 percent of Year 1 total company sales volume and more than 80 percent of operating income, the retail store segment must be considered the heart and soul of MULTICORP. As a percentage of sales, operating income is slightly less than that of the made-to-order segment, but high sales volume and virtually no receivables make up for the shortfall.

As can be seen in Figure 13-6, the biggest risk is the enormous inventory the store must carry relative to total assets. An inventory turnover of 1.2 is certainly nothing to brag about. Furthermore, this unit has been forced to borrow on a line of credit to support its slow-turning inventory. It wouldn't take much of a sales drop to quickly eat up the average cash flow of $167,000 over the five-year forecast period.

FIGURE 13-6

RETAIL STORE
STATEMENT OF INCOME ($000)

	Actual	----Forecasted----				
	Year 1	Year 2	Year 3	Year 4	Year 5	Year 6
Sales	2,190	2,256	2,323	2,393	2,465	2,539
Cost of sales	1,260	1,308	1,348	1,388	1,430	1,473
Gross profit	930	947	976	1,005	1,035	1,066
% of sales	42%	42%	42%	42%	42%	42%
Selling expenses	420	433	446	459	473	487
Commissions	44	45	46	48	49	51
Administrative expenses	70	72	74	76	79	81
Other expenses	20	21	21	22	23	23
Depreciation	4	4	4	4	2	0
Total expenses	558	574	592	609	625	642
Net income before interest and taxes	372	373	384	396	410	424
% of sales	17%	17%	17%	17%	17%	17%
Interest expense	54	54	54	54	54	54
Net income before taxes	318	319	330	342	356	370
Taxes	121	121	126	130	135	141
Net income	197	198	205	212	221	230
% of sales	9%	9%	9%	9%	9%	9%

RETAIL STORE
BALANCE SHEET ($000)

| | Actual | | ----Forecasted---- | | | |
	Year 1	Year 2	Year 3	Year 4	Year 5	Year 6
Cash	0	0	0	0	0	0
Receivables	91	94	97	100	103	106
Inventory	1,026	1,078	1,132	1,187	1,245	1,303
Total current assets	1,117	1,172	1,229	1,287	1,347	1,409
Equipment & vehicles	24	24	24	24	24	24
Accumulated depreciation	(10)	(14)	(18)	(22)	(24)	(24)
Net	14	10	6	2	0	0
Due from corporate	891	1,044	1,207	1,375	1,548	1,727
Total assets	2,022	2,226	2,441	2,664	2,895	3,136
Bank loan	600	600	600	600	600	600
Accounts payable	223	227	234	241	248	255
Accrued expenses	111	113	117	120	124	128
Total current liabilities	934	940	950	961	972	983
Retained earnings—beginning	891	1,088	1,286	1,491	1,703	1,924
Profit	197	198	205	212	221	230
Retained earnings—ending	1,088	1,286	1,491	1,703	1,924	2,153
Total equity	1,088	1,286	1,491	1,703	1,924	2,153
Total liabilities and equity	2,022	2,226	2,441	2,664	2,895	3,136

RETAIL STORE
STATEMENT OF CASH FLOW ($000)

| | Actual | | ----Forecasted---- | | | |
	Year 1	Year 2	Year 3	Year 4	Year 5	Year 6
CASH RECEIPTS						
Receivables—beginning	95	91	94	97	100	103
Sales	2,190	2,256	2,323	2,393	2,465	2,539
Receivables—ending	(91)	(94)	(97)	(100)	(103)	(106)
Receipts from operations	2,194	2,253	2,321	2,390	2,462	2,536
New bank loan	600	0	0	0	0	0
Total receipts	2,794	2,253	2,321	2,390	2,462	2,536
CASH EXPENDITURES						
Accounts payable—beginning	142	223	227	234	241	248
Purchases	1,336	1,361	1,401	1,444	1,487	1,531
Accounts payable—ending	(223)	(227)	(234)	(241)	(248)	(255)
Material expenditures	1,255	1,356	1,395	1,436	1,480	1,524
Accrued expenses—beginning	30	111	113	117	120	124
Selling expenses	420	433	446	459	473	487
Commissions	44	45	46	48	49	51
Administrative expenses	70	72	74	76	79	81
Other expenses	20	21	21	22	23	23
Accrued expenses—ending	(111)	(113)	(117)	(120)	(124)	(128)
Total operating expenditures	472	568	584	602	620	638
Financing costs:						
Interest	54	54	54	54	54	54
Principal	0	0	0	0	0	0
Total financing costs	54	54	54	54	54	54
Taxes	121	121	126	130	135	141
Total expenditures	1,902	2,100	2,158	2,222	2,289	2,357
NET CASH GENERATED	891	153	163	168	173	179
Due (to)/from corporate—beginning	0	891	1,044	1,207	1,375	1,548
Due (to)/from corporate—ending	891	1,044	1,207	1,375	1,548	1,727

Although the unit's current ratio remains relatively constant at 1.2 to 1 throughout the period, it reflects the high short-term debt the unit carries. Moreover, the quick ratio is virtually nonexistent. This increases the uncertainty of future cash flows and decreases this business segment's value. The debt load isn't as precarious as in some companies, however, because of the relatively high equity base. This is reflected in an average debt-to-equity ratio of approximately 0.5 to 1. The return on equity and return on assets ratios seem to be reasonably comparable to those of other retail organizations in this industry.

Determining a capitalization rate for the retail store segment is more difficult than for the other two operating units. Clearly, the profit margins are acceptable, although the unit's illiquid position makes its future uncertain. Beginning once again with a 7 percent U.S. Treasuries risk-free rate, investors might look at a risk discount of anywhere from 3 to 10 percent. Because of the segment's strong market position, we will use a 5 percent rate, making the total capitalization rate 12 percent. According to Figure 13-6, the retail store segment's forecasted cash flow is as follows:

Year 2	$153,000
Year 3	162,000
Year 4	168,000
Year 5	173,000
Year 6	179,000

Applying a 12 percent discount rate, the present value of this cash flow stream turns out to be $597,000.

Consolidated Valuation

Small companies usually reap enormous benefits from valuing their businesses as separate units. The valuation process immediately identifies where future growth efforts should be concentrated and which business lines should be sold or liquidated. It also clears the air about the positive or negative contribution of nonproductive administrative offices. More often than not, once such an exercise has been completed, it becomes obvious that corporate administrative costs should be trimmed back. And with financing becoming increasingly costly and difficult to attract, the disposal of cash-draining business units can have a dramatic effect on total company cash flow.

Our demonstration company, MULTICORP, offers a good example of how business unit valuations form the foundation for restructuring an average-performing company into a clear winner. The following summarizes the key statistics and valuations for each of MULTICORP's business segments based on the average of forecasted performance over the five-year period:

FIVE-YEAR AVERAGES ($000)

	Catalog Resale	Made-to-Order	Retail Store	Corporate Office	Total Company
Sales	1,324	628	2,395		4,347
After-tax profit	(11)	75	213	(140)	137
Total assets	142	557	2,564	2,037	5,300
Total debt	-0-	23	600	105	728
Return-on-equity	-0-	20%	13%	0	6%
Cash flow for the entire period	(97)	323	835	(711)	350
Present value	(73)*	241	597	(581)	184

*Calculated using the discounted cash flow method for consolidation purposes only.

The owners of MULTICORP have several alternatives for improving the value of their business, if and when they decide to sell it, and for increasing the cash available for distribution. The most obvious alternative is to sell or liquidate the catalog business. If a selling price based on mail order customer lists that exceeds the sum of accounts payable and accrued expenses could be negotiated, this would be the preferable route. Otherwise the owners could liquidate the inventory at cost and take a one-time cash drain of $22,000, which represents the excess of liabilities over inventory book value. Figure 13-7 shows the impact of this strategy on the total company.

FIGURE 13-7

OPTION 1: LIQUIDATE CATALOG RESALE
Five-Year Averages ($000)

	Made-to-Order	Retail Store	Corporation Office	Total Company without Catalog	Total Company with Catalog
RATIOS					
Sales	628	2,395		3,023	4,347
After-tax profit	75	213	(140)	148	137
Total assets	557	2,564	2,037	5,158	5,300
Total debt	23	600	105	728	728
Return on equity	20%	13%	0	6%	6%
CASH FLOW					
Cash flow for the entire period	323	835	(711)	447	350
Less cash shortfall on liquidating catalog segment				(22)	0
Net cash flow				425	350
PRESENT VALUE					
Present value	241	597	(581)	235	184
Less present value of tax savings from catalog operating loss				(25)	0
Net present value				210	184

A second alternative would be to reduce corporate overhead by (1) laying off the corporate sales manager (Year 1 expense of $75,000) and (2) subletting building space occupied by the catalog unit ($10,000 pretax income per year). These two steps in conjunction with the disposal of the catalog segment result in the impact on the total company shown in Figure 13-8.

By making three strategic moves—(1) disposing of the catalog business unit, (2) laying off corporate sales personnel, and (3) subletting building space previously occupied by the catalog unit—MULTICORP can more than double its value, from $184,000 to $414,000. Once the profitability, cash flow, and fair market value of each business segment are known, many alternative strategies become available. Those most commonly open to small businesses include the following options:

- Sell a business unit
- Liquidate cash-draining business segments
- Purchase a company complementary to the business unit
- Redirect advertising and other sales promotion efforts
- Redesign pricing policies
- Redirect management efforts
- Restructure the administrative organization
- Refinance debt structures for specific business segments
- Raise new equity capital
- Sell the entire company at a premium price

FIGURE 13-8

OPTION 2: REDUCE CORPORATE OVERHEAD
Five-Year Averages ($000)

	Made-to-Order	Retail Store	Corporate Office	Total Company without Catalog	Total Company with Catalog
RATIOS					
Sales	628	2,395		3,023	4,347
After-tax profit	75	213	(83)	205	137
Total assets	557	2,564	2,037	5,158	5,300
Total debt	23	600	105	728	728
Return on equity	20%	13%	0	9%	6%
CASH FLOW					
Cash flow for the entire period	323	835	(426)	732	350
Less cash shortfall on liquidating catalog segment				(22)	0
Net cash flow	323	835	(426)	710	350
PRESENT VALUE					
Present value	241	597	(399)	439	184
Less present value of tax savings from catalog operating loss				(25)	0
Net present value				414	184

The key to business segmentation is a workable cost accounting system. If your company already has a cost accounting system in place, it is a relatively simple matter to establish a chart of accounts commensurate with business segment allocation and recode transactions to accumulate costs, revenues, assets, and liabilities for each segment.

Multibusiness valuations can be accomplished without a cost accounting system, but they are much more difficult and less accurate. Therefore, regardless of how you keep your financial accounting records and whether or not your company prepares formal financial statements, I strongly urge the implementation of at least a basic cost accounting system. It is the only feasible way to track business segment profitability and cash flows, and in the long run it is well worth the money and effort to install.

Once the amount of cash flow contributed by each business segment has been established and tested over time—generally the shorter of one year or half a business cycle—alternative restructuring strategies can be evaluated. The business valuation techniques described throughout this book can be used by business owners as well as investors to evaluate alternative courses of action.

As a general rule, with the exception of micro businesses, professional practices, and companies in certain unique industries, the discounted cash flow method, asset cash flow method, or liquidation method will yield informative results in the situations appropriate for each. It's important to recognize, however, that as in the MULTICORP example, different valuation methods may be appropriate for each business segment, depending on its income, cash flow, and asset characteristics.

PART III

VALUATIONS FOR SPECIAL TYPES OF COMPANIES

CHAPTER 14

Micro Businesses

Business valuation methods that work satisfactorily for neighborhood drug stores, auto repair shops, dry cleaners, paint and wallpaper stores, magazine distributors, specialized machine shops, car washes, bakeries, and other very small businesses differ markedly from those applied to larger companies. Such micro businesses characteristically have relatively level year-to-year sales and simple cost structures, retain little control over market changes, and keep their records on a cash basis, primarily for income tax purposes.

In most cases, micro business owners mix personal expenses with business expenses, clouding the company's functional cost relationships and making ratio analysis very difficult. Comparisons with public companies are irrelevant. Market niches tend to be defined geographically. Typically, competitive businesses turn over very rapidly, with frequent new entrants to the market, many ownership changes, and a high percentage of bankruptcies and liquidations.

Although there is no clear-cut distinction between small businesses and micro businesses, I arbitrarily define the latter as having annual sales of less than $1 million. It should be noted that many of the preliminary steps in valuing micro businesses are identical to those used for larger companies. The actual valuation calculations described in this chapter, however, relate primarily to micro businesses.

One caveat for micro business owners/investors reading this book: The nature of these businesses makes any valuation method less precise than those used for larger companies. Much of the investigative work is judgmental. Without meaningful financial ratios, traditional comparative and risk analyses won't work. And in most buy/sell transactions, the price must be negotiated from a very meager base of financial data. There are, however, acceptable methods that can be used to at least get a starting point from which to negotiate, and those are the ones discussed in this chapter.

Valuation Alternatives

Aside from the use of cash basis accounting, one of the most troublesome matters confronting micro business buyers is that sellers frequently value their businesses higher than the market does. Even if the business fits perfectly into a buyer's strategic plans and the seller desperately wants to sell, unrealistic asking prices nearly always kill the deal before negotiations can begin.

The most prevalent misconception is that a business should be valued at the replacement cost of its hard assets—namely, inventory, machinery, vehicles, furniture and fixtures, and real estate. This method ignores the depreciated state of these assets, potential inventory obsolescence or damage, and the improbability of finding another facility in exactly the same location and condition. In addition, replacement cost is not a valuation method generally accepted by the IRS or financial institutions. And finally, the replacement cost method ignores intangibles or non–balance sheet assets, which in micro businesses can be more valuable than recorded assets.

Every operating business is more than a collection of assets. It is a going concern, represented by a dynamic collection of people, products, suppliers, and customers. A going concern creates profits, and profits are converted to cash. And, as with valuation techniques applied to larger companies, future cash benefits are the prime ingredient that attracts investors.

To reflect value as a going concern, micro businesses commonly use one or a combination of four valuation methods:

1. Book value
2. Historical cash flow
3. Discounted future cash flow
4. Price/earnings comparisons

Book Value Method

The *book value method* continues to be a favorite of many micro business owners. Despite its many drawbacks, book value is easy to understand, it can be readily calculated from the most basic records, and in certain cases it can yield a reasonable approximation of business value at a specific point in time. This method does have serious disadvantages, however, and those who use it should be on the lookout for potential traps. Its major shortcomings are discussed below.

Book value seldom reflects the fair market value of assets. The net cost of buildings, machinery, or equipment, recorded at original cost and depreciated by one of many acceptable methods, only coincidentally represents market value. Moreover, it is quite common for companies to own and use fully depreciated assets that are not even shown on financial statements. Inventory written off by auditors as obsolete but still usable in the business is another example of an asset that is not reflected in book value. Slow-paying or disputed accounts receivable that have been written off but are still collectible is yet another example.

A second difficulty with the book value method is that it does not take into account the company's ability to generate future profits as a going concern. It represents the condition of a business at a fixed point in time and ignores the benefits that assets generate over time. It is a static, not a dynamic, measurement and therefore confuses the accounting measurement of assets with the value of the company as a going business.

Nevertheless, many people still consider book value a viable micro business valuation method. In addition to providing some measure of value and being readily accessible, book value does offer a measure of consistency for comparative analysis with other companies. To achieve meaningful comparisons, however, adjustments should be made to the accounting records to bring book value into line with accrual accounting standards.

Only those balance sheet accounts reflecting assets that are expected to generate earnings for buyers should be included in the calculation. Since accounts such as prepaid expenses or unamortized organization expenses add nothing to the future earnings potential of the business, they should be excluded. One might argue that goodwill does contribute to future earnings; however, generally accepted accounting principles allow only purchased goodwill that arises from the premium paid for the acquisition of a going business to be recorded as an asset. Such an amount has little value to an investor unless the operations of the two businesses have been combined.

The exclusion of nonproducing assets makes book value for valuation purposes somewhat different from the owner's equity recorded in the books of account or shown on a balance sheet. Theoretically, however, such adjustments are necessary to reflect only the assets of value to potential investors.

Certain micro businesses with very low ratios of net worth to earnings might be valued at a multiple of book value, such as two times or 2.5 times. However, in most cases, unfactored book value is preferable as a negotiating base for buy/sell transactions.

The majority of micro businesses are operated as sole proprietorships, family partnerships, or S corporations. Since income taxes are never recorded in the books of account for any of these structures, the question of including taxes in valuation calculations or excluding them never arises. C corporations are different, however. In C corporations, corporate income taxes are a normal operating expense. In this case, the exclusion of taxes would make year-to-year comparisons similar to matching apples with oranges, as it were, unless you went all the way back to the original formation of the corporation, which in most cases would be impractical. Furthermore, since taxes cannot logically be excluded from book value, comparing the financial performance of C corporations with that of S corporations, partnerships, or proprietorships would be meaningless anyway.

Historical Cash Flow Method

The *historical cash flow method* bases a valuation on the actual cash generated by the business in prior years. This certainly gives a much better picture of the productivity of business assets than the book value method. In fact, since most micro business buyers are interested in the amount of cash the business can throw off, not in its intrinsic characteristics, they would argue that the historical cash flow method is the only reasonable way to fix the company's current value. The theory is that at a minimum the business should be able to generate as much cash in the future as in the past. Therefore, it makes sense to base a purchase price on historical achievement rather than on predicted future results.

This approach has merit in that the success or failure of a micro business depends to a large extent on the individual abilities of its owner/manager. Very few are large enough to hire skilled supervisors. Few can afford to pay top wage rates. And hardly any can afford to spend much on new advertising campaigns, sales promotions, or other marketing tactics to increase their business base. Placing such high reliance on a single owner puts the future performance of micro businesses in jeopardy when the present owner leaves and, theoretically, makes the future very uncertain.

The main reason buyers are willing to take such a high risk and still pay a reasonable price for the business has to do with ego: Most of us firmly believe that we can run a business as well as or better than anyone else, including the previous owner. At least a price based on historical cash flow somewhat reduces the price of failure.

Typically, this method uses cash flows from the most recent three years. Anything prior to three years ago is ancient history and probably does not reflect the current condition of the company. Also, three years should be enough to smooth out unusual, short-term sales dips or splurges.

From the Seller's Perspective

Although the historical cash flow method makes sense for business buyers, sellers find this approach less than satisfactory. The two objections frequently voiced are:

1. Certain decisions and actions in prior years have laid the groundwork for greater cash flows in the future. Therefore, forecasted benefits that reflect these improvements give a more accurate picture of the company's true value. Investors are, after all, purchasing a right to receive these future benefits, and therefore the price should be based on those benefits, not on historical cash flows, which will be exceeded in the future.

2. At a minimum, owners are entitled to recoup their original investment plus an amount for the risk they have taken in developing the business. Historical cash flow does not compensate for either, and therefore a premium should be added.

These are valid arguments; they can be addressed either by using a different valuation method or by negotiating an add-on premium to historical cash flow. One way to arrive at an add-on premium is by using a multiplier, typically applied to an average of the prior three years' cash flows. Although this multiplier should be negotiated for each transaction, precedents can be used as guidelines.

For example, thirty years ago, multipliers ranging from six- to eight-times average annual cash flow were frequently used for most companies other than those engaged in high-tech industries, which ran in the ten- to twelve-times range. For the last decade, with market interest rates running about 3 to 4 percent, multiples of four or five have been quite common.

Owner's Compensation

The question of owner's compensation invariably arises when a company's historical performance is analyzed. Some analysts argue convincingly that if the owner is paid a reasonable salary for management services, it should be included as a normal operating expense. Although this has merit in larger companies, the elimination of all owners' compensation paints a more accurate picture for micro businesses.

The reason is relatively simple, especially for a buy/sell valuation. When a new owner takes over, the company's free cash should be used first to repay borrowed money or deferred payments for the purchase of the business, then to pay a return on the buyer's investment, and only after that to compensate the new owners for management services.

If the sequence is reversed, all too often there isn't enough free cash to meet debt service payments and provide an investment return. Furthermore, in nearly all cases, a new owner will require a compensation structure different from the seller's. This makes calculating the purchase price and the potential return on investment net of a seller's draw a meaningless exercise.

As an example of a typical micro business, we will use another fictitious company, this time called MICRO, Inc. MICRO's financial statements for the previous three years, shown in Figure 14-1, have been restated to eliminate owner's compensation.

FIGURE 14-1

MICRO, INC.
STATEMENT OF INCOME ($000)

	Year 1-2	Year 1-1	Year 1
Sales	500	510	490
Cost of sales	300	306	294
Gross profit	200	204	196
% of sales	40%	40%	40%
Selling expenses	47	48	50
Administrative expenses	55	57	58
Other expenses	5	5	5
Depreciation	9	9	9
TOTAL	116	119	122
Net income before taxes	84	85	74
% of sales	17%	17%	15%
Taxes	32	32	28
Net income	52	53	46
% of sales	10%	10%	9%

MICRO, INC.
BALANCE SHEET ($000)

	Year 1-2	Year 1-1	Year 1
Cash	57	150	235
Receivables	42	42	41
Inventory	38	38	37
Total current assets	136	231	313
Vehicles	45	45	45
Accumulated depreciation	(18)	(27)	(36)
Net	37	18	9
Total assets	163	249	322
Accounts payable	8	8	7
Common stock	10	10	10
Retained earnings—beginning	62	146	231
Profit	52	53	46
Tax adjustment	32	32	28
Retained earnings—ending	146	231	305
Total equity	156	241	315
Total liabilities and equity	163	249	322

MICRO, INC.
STATEMENT OF CASH FLOW ($000)

	Year 1-2	Year 1-1	Year 1
CASH RECEIPTS			
Accounts receivable—beginning	38	42	42
Sales	500	510	490
Accounts receivable—ending	(42)	(42)	(41)
Total cash receipts	496	509	492
CASH EXPENDITURES			
Accounts payable—beginning	6	8	8
Material purchases	300	306	293
Selling expenses	47	48	50
Administrative expenses	55	57	58
Other expenses	5	5	5
Accounts payable—ending	(8)	(8)	(7)
Total expenditures	405	416	407
NET CASH GENERATED	91	93	85
Bank balance—beginning	(34)	57	150
Bank balance—ending	57	150	235

As seen in the cash flow statement, MICRO generated cash for each of the last three years of $91,000, $93,000, and $85,000, for an average of $90,000. By applying a multiple of four to this average, the company's value turns out to be:

Average cash flow for three years	$90,000
Multiple	4
Business value	$360,000

Future Cash Flow Method

Just as business buyers prefer to value a company on historic cash flow, business owners typically look to future growth opportunities. Believing a business will do better in the future is such a natural assumption that such optimism flourishes even in companies suffering deep financial problems. Moreover, since the whole purpose of investing in advertising promotions, new equipment, or personnel training is to build a business to greater heights in the future, it would be unreasonable not to expect an improvement over past performance.

This argument has as much merit from the perspective of business owners as the historical cash flow method does for business buyers. It makes little sense to consider investing in a business of any size unless you believe that future benefits will surpass past performance.

Goodwill

Goodwill is another off–balance sheet asset that tends to be more pronounced in micro businesses than in larger companies. Benefits derived from goodwill that has been built up over a period of years by the business owner and employees can frequently be a better measure of a company's value than any numerical calculation based on recorded assets. It's hard to argue against the concept that customer loyalty, industry reputation, and personnel efficiency make a company worth more than one with twice the assets but with a tarnished image in the marketplace. In service businesses, and also in retail and manufacturing industries, the smaller the company, the more important are personal relationships with customers.

Several polls taken over the last two decades revealed that consumers overwhelmingly rated personal attention by business owners as the single most important reason for frequenting a particular establishment. It seems probable that at least in micro businesses, unrecorded goodwill could be worth more than the entire pool of buildings, equipment, receivables, inventory, and other recorded assets.

If these arguments hold, then logic would dictate that the future cash flow method is the most viable approach to valuing micro businesses, just as it is for most larger companies. The major difference, however, is that in micro businesses the stream of future cash flows may derive more from unrecorded assets than from balance sheet assets.

To recognize such unrecorded assets as customer loyalty and industry or neighborhood reputation, a reverse capitalization rate rather than a discount rate should be applied to future cash flows. Conversely, when valuing micro businesses for buy/sell transactions, to the extent that future cash flows are dependent on the relationships established by the present owner, the risk of achieving forecasted performance in the absence of the previous owner dictates an offsetting discount rate.

To demonstrate the process, we'll use the MICRO, Inc. financial statements from Figure 14-1 as the starting point in preparing pro forma forecasts. Since larger companies have the luxury of looking much farther into the future than micro businesses, mainly because the smaller the company, the less control it has over market and cost fluctuations, Figure 14-2 shows pro forma forecasts for three years, rather than the customary five to eight years.

FIGURE 14-2

MICRO, INC.
STATEMENT OF INCOME ($000)

	Actual		----Forecasted----	
	Year 1	Year 2	Year 3	Year 4
Sales	$490	505	520	535
Cost of sales	294	303	302	300
Gross profit	196	202	218	236
% of sales	40%	40%	42%	44%
Selling expenses	50	51	53	54
Administrative expenses	58	60	62	64
Other expenses	5	5	5	5
Depreciation	9	9	0	0
TOTAL	122	126	120	124
Net income before taxes	74	76	98	112
% of sales	15%	15%	19%	21%
Taxes	28	29	37	43
Net income	46	47	61	69
% of sales	9%	9%	12%	13%

MICRO, INC.
BALANCE SHEET ($000)

| | Actual | | ----Forecasted---- | |
	Year 1	Year 2	Year 3	Year 4
Cash	235	319	416	527
Receivables	41	42	43	45
Inventory	37	38	38	37
Total current assets	313	399	497	609
Vehicles	45	45	45	45
Accumulated depreciation	(36)	(45)	(45)	(45)
Net	9	0	0	0
Total assets	322	399	497	609
Accounts payable	7	8	8	7
Common stock	10	10	10	10
Retained Earnings—beginning	231	305	381	479
Profit	46	47	61	69
Tax adjustment	28	29	37	43
Retained earnings—ending	305	382	479	591
Total equity	315	392	489	601
Total liabilities and equity	322	399	497	609

MICRO, INC.
STATEMENT OF CASH FLOW ($000)

| | Actual | | ----Forecasted---- | |
	Year 1	Year 2	Year 3	Year 4
CASH RECEIPTS				
Accounts receivable—beginning	42	41	42	43
Sales	490	505	520	535
Accounts receivable—ending	(41)	(42)	(43)	(45)
Total cash receipts	492	503	519	534
CASH EXPENDITURES				
Accounts payable—beginning	8	7	8	8
Material purchases	293	303	302	300
Selling expenses	50	51	53	54
Administrative expenses	58	60	62	64
Other expenses	5	5	5	5
Accounts payable—ending	(7)	(8)	(8)	(7)
Total expenditures	407	419	422	424
NET CASH GENERATED	85	84	97	111
Bank balance—beginning	150	235	319	416
Bank balance—ending	235	319	416	527

The sum of forecasted cash flows for Year 2 through Year 4 ($84,000, $97,000, and $111,000) is $292,000. A reverse capitalization rate can be used to calculate the present value of a premium for the sum of goodwill, prior years' sales promotions, employee training, investment in equipment, and other valuable assets not appearing on the balance sheet.

Unlike discount rates, which measure the risk of not receiving forecasted future benefits, a premium rate measures the probability of receiving these benefits or more. This probability may be 5 percent, 10 percent, or any other rate. Since there are no market rates against which to measure comparable premiums, a mutually agreeable rate must be negotiated.

In the MICRO example, an 8 percent premium applied to forecasted cash flows yields a value of $348,000; a 10 percent premium produces a value of $365,000; a 12 percent premium a value of $383,000; and a 15 percent premium a value of $413,000.

As an offset to this premium, we must take into account diminishing goodwill as a result of losing the personal relationships developed by the selling owner. This has merit because without the owner's personal efforts, the uncertainty of actually achieving the forecasted cash flow increases. Discounting can be accomplished by applying a present value rate to future cash flows. Once again, since no comparable market rates measure this type of uncertainty, a discount rate must be negotiated along with the premium rate.

In the MICRO example, an 8 percent discount rate yields a present value of future cash flows totaling $249,000; a 10 percent rate produces $240,000; a 12 percent rate, $231,000; and a 15 percent rate, $219,000. These discounted present values should then be compared with the premiums previously calculated and a weighting negotiated. One method for weighting premiums and discounts is by taking straight arithmetic averages and then averaging the averages, as in the following:

Capitalization Rates	Premium Present Value	Discount Present Value
8%	$348,000	$249,000
10%	365,000	240,000
12%	383,000	231,000
15%	413,000	219,000
Average	377,000	235,000

The average of the averages comes out to $306,000. This simplistic compromise assumes that equal weighting is given to the factors creating the premium and those causing the discount. Of course, any weighting other than arithmetic averages will tilt the result in one direction or the other. Since the entire forecasting exercise is merely a best guess at the future, it usually doesn't pay to get too elaborate. The absence of measurable financial ratios in most micro businesses makes more sophisticated valuation techniques unreasonable.

Another, less complex method can also be used as a shortcut to get at a negotiating base. Like the historical cash flow method, this approach applies a multiplier to the average of the forecasted cash flows.

The average of the three years' forecasted cash flows for MICRO works out to $97,000. Applying the same multiple used in the historical cash flow method, we get:

Average forecasted cash flow	$97,000
Multiple	× 4
Business Value	$388,000

The multiplier of four times is arbitrary and should be a topic for negotiation. However, as in the historical method, current practice in buying and selling micro businesses is generally to use a multiplier of four to five times.

Price/Earnings Method

There is nothing very sophisticated about the *price/earnings method*, which is why it remains one of the most popular bases for negotiating buy/sell prices. This method matches a company's prior–year profits with an average stock market price/earnings ratio derived from published trading records of public companies in similar industries. As an alternative, average price/earnings ratios from broad-based stock indexes, such as the Dow Jones Industrial Average, can be used.

For example, in MICRO's case, Year 1 net income before taxes was $74,000. Assume that the average P/E ratio on the New York Stock Exchange at the end of Year 1 was eighteen times. Merely multiply $74,000 by eighteen to arrive at a value of $1,332,000. Some analysts, however, prefer to use after-tax profit as more comparable with public company earnings. This has merit because in public companies taxes are regarded as a normal business expense. Multiplying the Year 1 after-tax income for MICRO, Inc. of $46,000 by eighteen yields a value of $828,000.

Those who advocate this method ignore the fact that earnings of multibillion-dollar conglomerates operating in a wide range of industries bear little similarity to the earnings of a micro business. Nevertheless, whenever we have a buoyant stock market that pushes P/E ratios to unrealistic levels, there will be some business owners who continue to argue that this method is the only realistic way to value their businesses.

Comparing Results

The four methods commonly used to value micro businesses—that is, book value, historical cash flow, discounted future cash flow, and the price/earnings method—yield widely different results. This can be seen in the following summary of results for MICRO, Inc.:

Book value	$223,000
Historic cash flow	360,000
Discounted future cash flow (average)	306,000
Future cash flow using multiplier	388,000
Price/earnings method (after tax)	828,000

As expected, the price/earnings method produces the highest value by far, even using after-tax profits. The book value method might have come closer to both cash flow methods if it had been possible to restate book value on a pretax basis. The three cash flow methods produce remarkably similar results, considering the wide range of multiplier and discount assumptions. However, this is relatively common when valuing micro businesses. As long as sales volume and cost structures do not materially change from year to year—and in micro businesses they seldom do—virtually all valuations based on cash flow should produce similar results.

Reconstructing Cash Flows and Asset Values

In certain micro businesses, record keeping is so sparse that constructing financial statements is impractical. Despite IRS enforcement efforts, many business owners have neither the time nor the inclination to keep formal records. Typically, receipts are recorded on cash register tapes. Vendor invoices are paid in cash. At tax time, these informal records serve as documentation for bookkeepers or tax accountants preparing tax returns. Without financial statements, none of the previously described valuation methods is practical, and more creative techniques must be concocted.

In most businesses, sales are usually fairly well documented, either on cash register tapes or in bank deposits. But accounting for expenses on a cash basis makes analyzing cost structures virtually impossible. Arriving at previous years' profits is equally impractical.

To compound the difficulty, personal expenses are very often mingled with business transactions. If it's a food store, restaurant, or small hotel, the business supplies food for the family table. In real estate agencies, insurance agencies, pharmacies, and computer stores, the business frequently pays for automobiles and related expenses, insurance premiums, and personal entertainment expenditures. With a hardware store or lumber yard, it's not uncommon to find the owner's home repairs, remodeling costs, and appliances expensed by the store. Obviously, these practices are contrary to the tax laws, but many micro-business owners consider them an entrepreneurial fringe benefit.

Pragmatically, the only logical measure of value is the amount of cash available for withdrawal from the business and the market value of business assets. The analyst must work with the available records, usually tax returns and bank statements, to determine the amount of sales, and then apply common sense to reconstruct abbreviated cash flow projections and a conservative estimate of asset market value. The following calculation demonstrates the procedure for a small restaurant:

Cash Sales

Bank deposits		$180,000
Less: Loan proceeds from bank	15,000	
Repayment of owner's loan	3,000	18,000
Net cash sales (reconcile this to cash register tapes and tax returns)		162,000

Cash Expenditures

Food and other resale purchases—from major supplier invoices (reconcile to tax return cost of sales)	50,000
Rent—from lease	7,500
Electricity, gas, fuel oil—from utility bills	10,000
Payroll—from payroll tax returns	30,000
Sales tax, use tax, payroll taxes, and licenses—from tax returns filed	3,000
Miscellaneous expenses—estimate	3,000
Total expenditures	103,500
Net cash flow	58,500

Theoretically, this net cash flow represents the excess cash generated in one year that can be either withdrawn by the business owner or reinvested in vehicles, fixtures, and other hard assets. In some cases that's as far as one can go in establishing a starting point for negotiating a buy/sell price. Since the value was calculated from current operating receipts and expenditures, it can be assumed to include any goodwill associated with the business and all other intangible assets that contribute to profitability.

On the other hand, if it can be established that the business is in a strong growth mode or that advertising and other sales promotion programs begun in the current year will benefit future performance, it might be necessary to quantify this goodwill by negotiating a multiplier to be applied to the current year's cash flow. In micro retail businesses it is not uncommon to use multiples of 1.5 to two times. In the above example, this would produce a business value range of $87,750 ($58,500 x 1.5) to $117,000 ($58,500 x 2).

The disadvantage of stopping with a reconstructed cash flow is that the market value of hard assets has not been recognized. If vehicles, fixtures, office equipment, or inventory are used in the business, these assets also carry a value and should be included in the calculation.

In businesses with a high inventory turnover, current inventory can be valued at the most recent invoice price and reconciled with the amount shown on the most recent tax return. Older inventory should be factored down by approximately 20 percent for each year it has been held. Store fixtures, office equipment, furniture, and vehicles can be valued at depreciated value as shown on a tax return depreciation schedule.

In those companies that carry receivables, normal practice is to exclude them from the valuation on the basis that the selling owner will keep the collections. However, if most sales are on credit, receivables can be a major asset and should be included. In that case, the receivables balance is usually discounted by some factor, typically 5 to 10 percent, to account for collection risk.

To continue with the previous example, assume that the following asset costs are included in the valuation:

Inventory	$4,000
Store fixtures, net book value	10,000
Equipment, such as freezers, scales, computer	10,000
Total asset value	24,000

Making the assumption that a true measure of goodwill equates to two years' cash flow, the total business valuation would then be:

Two years' cash flow	$117,000
Asset value	24,000
Total business valuation	141,000

A value of $141,000 is probably reasonable for a retail store with $150,000 annual sales. A cash flow of $58,500 means that an investor who is willing to pay $141,000 for the business will recover the investment in approximately 2.5 years, exclusive of any salary draw. This seems to be an acceptable standard in today's market. However, to conserve part of the cash flow for a salary draw, payment terms would have to include the deferral of a relatively high percentage of the purchase price.

Valuation Effects of Stock or Asset Sale

In addition to numerical calculations, several qualitative factors enter into a micro business valuation. In buy/sell transactions, one of the most important considerations is whether the transaction will be a sale of common shares or assets. The choice has a major impact on how to value the business.

In a sale of common shares, the corporation remains intact and the new owner assumes responsibility for paying the company's debt obligations, including accounts payable, taxes, and bank loans. When calculating the value of the future cash flows or the market value of assets, it is necessary to deduct all corporate obligations. When an owner has invested very little capital and has withdrawn most or all of the company's profits over the years, shareholders' equity will be near zero or negative. In that case the company's liabilities could equal or exceed the market value of its assets, making it necessary for a buyer to immediately obtain new bank loans for working capital.

This substantially decreases the value of the business from what it would be if the company were purchased free and clear of all obligations.

Buyers also usually need new working capital if they buy assets. On the one hand, since buyers acquire only productive assets, the value of the transaction and hence the purchase price is usually much higher than with a stock sale. From a seller's perspective, this has merit because the price and the cash down payment must be sufficient to liquidate all of the company's obligations; otherwise it wouldn't make any sense to sell.

On the other hand, if receivables are not included in the transaction, buyers are faced with the same working capital shortage as in a stock sale. And from their perspective, the need to get a bank loan immediately detracts from the business's value.

The tax code also comes into play. When common shares are sold, sellers report a capital gain on the full amount of the buy/sell price. The buyer's cost basis in the shares equals the full amount of the purchase price. Asset sales are more complicated, however. Since the corporation sells its assets, it must report all gains and pay appropriate taxes. Gains on net receivables and inventory are ordinary income; gains on hard assets are considered capital gains.

On the buyer's side, the entire purchase price can be allocated to the assets acquired. This means that any premium paid in excess of the book value of the assets can be added to the cost basis of inventory or hard assets, thereby reducing taxes in future years. Obviously, the tax impact on both sellers and buyers plays a major role in establishing the final negotiated business value, either increasing the calculated value or decreasing it.

Valuing Deferred Payments

A second qualitative consideration is the terms of payment. Experience has shown that few if any micro businesses are sold for 100 percent cash. Seldom do buyers have sufficient cash to handle the transaction, and even if they do, the uncertainty of the future success of the business in the absence of the selling owner virtually requires deferred payment of part or even all of the purchase price. Deferred payments may involve one or a combination of the following:

- A promissory note to make a specific number of monthly, quarterly, or annual payments
- A contingency contract, specifying that the occurrence of certain future events will trigger a series of monthly, quarterly, or annual payments
- An earn-out contract, whereby seller and buyer share predetermined percentages of company profits over a defined time period until the purchase price plus interest has been paid in full

It is very difficult to attach a value to an earn-out contract, since the discount required to compensate for the extreme uncertainty of future performance would make the present value negligible. For this reason, sellers who agree to earn-out payments attempt to recoup at least part of the risk by injecting a high interest rate. Even with that, however, the earn-out time period is usually so long—often up to ten years—that compensation for the entire risk cannot be logically calculated.

A similar problem, although not as severe, arises with a contingency contract. If sellers can be reasonably assured that the contingency will be triggered as planned, such as with a major new order or a service contract renewal, then the contract valuation can be calculated in the same manner as a normal debt obligation. Without such assurance, sellers run the same risk as they do with an earn-out contract.

A promissory note to pay a fixed amount over a defined period is the cleanest arrangement and the one most sellers demand. Such an obligation can be valued and the amount incorporated into the value of the entire transaction. The methods for valuing debt securities described in Chapter 11 also apply to deferred payment contracts. The following examples put these methods into perspective for a micro business buy/sell transaction.

An auto repair shop is sold for a price of $125,000. The buyer agrees to pay $25,000 cash down payment and the balance in equal monthly installments over ten years, including an interest rate of 6 percent. The first step is to compute the amount of monthly payments. For that you can use a set of annuity tables or the annuity function in a computer spreadsheet program. The monthly payment under these terms would be $1,110.

The next step is to convert this stream of monthly payments into its present value. For that we need a capitalization rate that reflects the current market rate of interest. Banks normally make secured loans to micro businesses at approximately 2.5 to 3 percent over the prime rate. We'll assume 3 percent. If the prime rate is 6 percent, the capitalization rate becomes 9 percent (prime plus 3 percent), and the present value of this stream of payments is $87,641. If the buyer pays $25,000 as a cash down payment, the seller is actually selling the business for $112,641.46 ($25,000 plus $87,641), $12,358 less than the $125,000 expected.

To turn this calculation around, the actual selling price would have to be $140,000 with a $25,000 down payment and monthly payments at 6 percent interest to yield a present value of $125,000. In that case, the buyer's monthly payments would increase to $1,276. If the capitalization rate were increased to reflect a perceived risk of receiving this payment stream—say to 12 percent instead of 9 percent—the actual selling price would have to be $155,000 to net a present value of $125,000. Monthly payments would then be $1,443.

Another variation on deferred payments might be a consulting contract for the seller. If no services were expected, the calculation of the present value of this contract would be identical to that of receiving a promissory note with monthly payments. When actual consulting services are expected to be rendered, however, the market price of such services should be excluded from the contract and only the excess discounted to present value.

CHAPTER

Professional Practices and Personal Service Companies

Goodwill is the cornerstone upon which the valuation of both professional practices and personal service companies rests. Without careful nurturing, customers/patients/clients would soon take their business elsewhere. Without a high-standing reputation in the marketplace, these businesses could not attract new customers. Goodwill in these types of businesses is developed and sustained by the specialized expertise of individuals. Whether from a law office or a medical practice, a literary agency or a consulting business, an architectural firm or an appliance repair service, an accounting practice or a market research service, customers buy expertise that they do not have. They buy specialized knowledge, not products.

However, the purchase of products may be a peripheral reason attracting customers, as in personal service agencies (e.g., insurance agencies, real estate agencies, securities brokers, and so on). This makes the line between personal service companies and other service businesses very murky. The distinction between professional practices and personal service companies has also become blurred as common usage of the term *professional* has been extended to businesses not requiring licensing, certification, or specialized formal education, such as management consulting and financial planning.

Nevertheless, for valuation purposes, the single common element that separates both professional practices and personal service companies from other types of businesses is their overwhelming dependence on goodwill to build and sustain a customer base. It is the value of goodwill that makes up the major portion of the fair market value of the business. Some such businesses may use a modest collection of hard assets to perform services, such as dental equipment, computers, testing paraphernalia, or office equipment. In that case the fair market value of these assets must be added to the value of goodwill to arrive at a total business valuation.

To simplify the following discussions, the terms *business* or *firm* will be used to designate both professional practices and personal service companies. Emphasis will be placed on determining a fair market value for goodwill, to be used either for buy/sell transactions or for establishing a settlement in a divorce proceeding.

Since the valuation techniques in this chapter will be limited to small professional and personal service businesses, many of which are one-person businesses, readers involved with multipartner businesses should refer to the methods described in Chapter 12 for valuing buy/sell agreements. Large multioffice law firms, accounting practices, or agencies should be valued using the same methods described in earlier chapters for valuing non–personal service businesses.

The Uniqueness of Professional Practices and Personal Service Companies

When taken together, several features of professional practices and personal service businesses make these firms distinctly different from other small or micro businesses, thereby requiring special valuation techniques. Although the emphasis on one or another of the following characteristics may vary with specific types of businesses, in general they hold for nearly any type of profession, whether medicine, law, dentistry, accounting, consulting, architecture, or engineering:

1. Services provided are not price sensitive. When we shop for a car of a specific make, model, and year, we compare the offerings of various dealers to get the best price. However, when we have been sued or need an operation, we seek out the most qualified professional, often regardless of price.

2. Services are generally performed by the business owner or by a few employees under close supervision. Dentists may hire technicians to perform perfunctory examinations or services, but the practitioner approves the diagnosis and work performed. A real estate agency may hire appraisers, lawyers, and clerical help, but the head of the agency approves all activities and interfaces directly with the customer. Customer loyalty flows to the individual business owner more than to the business.

3. The level of trust that customers have in the integrity and expertise of the service provider determines the success and longevity of the business. As long as this trust is maintained, customers will continue to return or will refer other customers to the business. It is this trust that builds and sustains goodwill.

4. Services are relatively uniform among businesses. When businesses require licensing or certification, customers can be assured that all such businesses will possess approximately the same level of competence. This makes product differentiation difficult and reinforces

the elements of trust and reputation as crucial to sustaining the business. It is the individual skills of the owner and employees that make one firm preferable to another.

5. Typically, markets are geographically restricted. Physicians, lawyers, CPAs, real estate agents, and insurance agents generally attract clientele within a relatively small area. There are exceptions, however. Specialized management consultants, literary agents, highly respected trial lawyers, and financial advisers, for example, may service national markets.

6. Advertising, sales promotions, and other marketing tactics are minimal, and most new business comes from referrals. However, under certain circumstances, the location of a business attracts new customers, as with insurance and real estate agencies, optometrists, dentists, and veterinarians. In other cases, affiliations attract customers, such as literary agents affiliated with New York publishing houses or medical specialists affiliated with hospitals or clinics. In most cases, however, referrals from satisfied customers and other professionals or agencies are the main source of new business.

7. Transactions are usually recorded on a cash basis: Revenues are booked as cash is received and expenses are incurred when bills are paid. Formal financial statements are seldom prepared for other than income tax or banking reasons.

8. The customer base comprises many small clients/patients/customers, in contrast to companies that serve a handful of large customers. This creates a high volume of billings, each contributing little to the overall profitability of the business. The loss of a few customers caused by a change in ownership will have little bearing on the valuation of the business.

9. Few, if any, tangible assets are required to operate the business. A few pieces of equipment, a reference library, and an inventory of operating supplies generally constitute the total asset base. Many firms do carry unrecorded receivables, however, which represent unrealized income until they are collected. Tangible assets and receivables that are required to operate the business represent a very small percentage of the firm's market value

The main asset of a professional or personal services business, goodwill, is never recorded on the books; yet it is what generates cash flow, and hence value. For business valuation purposes, goodwill constitutes the amount of the business's purchase price in excess of the fair market value of its identifiable assets, net of liabilities. Another way of looking at goodwill is that it represents the premium paid for the purchase of a business.

Goodwill

Goodwill is probably the most misunderstood asset of a professional or personal service business. Too often, professionals or business owners believe that such goodwill cannot have any value because once they are gone, the goodwill will dissipate. This is a major mistake and causes substantial losses for many business owners who lock the doors and sell off equipment and other hard assets when they retire, die, become disabled, or otherwise decide to get out. In most cases, with careful planning and the right buy/sell structure, a large portion of goodwill can be transferred to a new owner and therefore has significant value.

It's important to note the difference between two types of goodwill present in nearly every professional or personal service business:

1. Business goodwill, which is derived from the business itself, such as that generated because of location, advertising, and the market reputation of the firm's name
2. Personal goodwill, which is derived from the expertise and reputation of the business owner

Business goodwill exists because of the entity and is very similar to the goodwill present in any type of business. It has value because the entity is a going concern that has a proven record of generating cash flows from an established customer base.

The collection of office equipment, personnel, facilities, and client/customer files or records gives the entity form and substance. Bank accounts and contracts are in the name of the entity. If a corporation, the entity pays taxes and can sue or be sued. A corporation also enjoys an unlimited life; it will continue in existence after shareholders depart.

These elements generate value over and above the value of the entity's recorded net assets, and this extra value is called business goodwill. Such value can be measured using any of the business valuation methods previously discussed in this book. Theoretically, business goodwill is derived from the operations of the firm and will continue as long as the company remains in operation, regardless of ownership.

Personal goodwill is a different story. This type of goodwill is related solely to the reputation and expertise of the individual practitioner. Litigation lawyers, tax-proficient CPAs, automobile mechanics, or investment advisers attract and retain customers because of their special expertise and reputation, not because a business entity exists in a particular location. This ability to attract and retain customers is personal goodwill.

It may appear on the surface that personal goodwill has no market value because it cannot be transferred to another person. Clearly, personal knowledge, experience, and technical skill developed over years of study and practice cannot be transferred. But to a customer, the goodwill that this knowledge and skill engenders can be transferred through a weaning process aimed at shifting customer allegiance from one party to another. The process requires cooperation between buyer and seller, it must be done over a period of time, and, obviously, the customer must agree to transfer allegiance.

The most difficult situation arises when the seller obtains new business through referrals from other professionals or business persons. This occurs very frequently in certain types of management consulting businesses. Repeat business may be nonexistent. To get referrals for new jobs, the consultant relies exclusively on a network of personal contacts with bankers, lawyers, CPAs, community organizations, and government officials that has been built up over a period of years.

A similar problem confronts bankruptcy lawyers and certain other specialists in the legal profession. Repeat business is very rare, and new business nearly always comes through referrals from other lawyers, CPAs, management consultants, and financial institutions.

Despite such difficulties, several steps can be taken by both buyer and seller to ensure the transfer of at least a large portion of personal goodwill. The best way to ensure the transfer of customer trust, which, of course, is the foundation of personal goodwill, is to form a succession partnership between buyer and seller for a defined period of time. During this period, customers can get to know the new partner. Through a gradual weaning process they can be encouraged to use the new partner's services in lieu of the seller's. Concurrent with the formation of such a partnership, announcements should be sent to all repeat customers informing them of the new partner's credentials, including education, experience, and technical qualifications.

Notices should also be sent to all referral leads, asking for their cooperation in referring customers to the new partner. This normally won't happen unless the referral contacts have previously known the new partner. Therefore, it's important to let them know that the seller will also participate in any engagements with new customers. Over time, referral contacts will develop confidence in the new partner, completing the weaning process.

Under certain circumstances it also pays to run small advertisements in local newspapers, announcing the formation of the partnership. The buyer's credentials should be couched in terms that clearly give the impression of high qualifications without specifically identifying them, other than technical certification. Personal introductions to important members of the community or local practitioners also help.

Measuring Goodwill

Both business goodwill and personal goodwill are difficult enough to define; they are even harder to measure. Yet some yardstick must be used to determine whether goodwill exists at all, and if so, whether it is worth considering in a business valuation. In general, the same qualitative criteria used to evaluate the market demand for any business can be applied to professional practices and personal service businesses.

Competitive Market Position

How many similar businesses compete for the same market? In rural communities, professionals of almost any class are scarce. However, Manhattan has thousands of lawyers, CPAs, doctors, and dentists. Qualified computer repair services are nonexistent in many small towns, yet companies compete fiercely in concentrated commercial developments in and around metropolitan areas. Certain businesses have become extremely difficult to start from scratch. Many metropolitan areas have an overabundance of medical doctors, making the purchase of an existing practice the only viable way to enter the market.

Demographics, location, the number of similar businesses, and commercial/industrial concentration can all have a bearing on the level of competition, and the less competition, the more valuable a business.

Referral Base

If a business depends on referrals for most or all of its new customers, the size and quality of the referral base bear heavily on its value. A business whose referrals come from a large number of current customers will have greater value than one with fewer customers. Similarly, for businesses that rely on third-party referrals, say from lawyers, CPAs, bankers, other agencies, or government officials, the greater the number and the better the quality of such referral contacts, the higher the value of the business.

Certain type of businesses, such as medical and dental practices, rely on government or insurance payments or reimbursements. These will have less value than firms whose customers pay their own bills, primarily because collection from the government and/or insurance companies takes much longer and requires more paperwork.

Synergies Between Buyer and Seller

Synergistic objectives and work habits can in many ways be the most important determinants of a seller's ability to transfer goodwill. Take the case of a real estate agent who gets new business by making under-the-table deals with financial institutions or cutting commissions. A buyer who regarded such practices as unethical would have a hard time either keeping the referral contacts or getting repeat business from previous customers. Or a dentist who encouraged late night and weekend appointments and played golf three days a week would have difficulty transferring personal goodwill to a buyer who refused to work nights or weekends and encouraged early morning appointments. In both cases, the value of goodwill to buyers could be practically zero.

Fee Structure

Does the business charge fees comparable to, above, or below those of competitors? A business with a low fee base relative to competition and a large customer base is probably "buying" customers—that is, earning less for longer working hours than other firms. This reflects on the owner's expertise and reputation, and diminishes business value. Conversely, a business with higher-than-average fees and a large customer base probably has proven expertise and an excellent reputation, both adding immeasurably to the value of the business.

Marketability

The greater the marketability of a business, the higher its value. If the profession or industry is easy to enter, chances are good that the marketability of a business is low. When the entrance of new firms is difficult, either because of a saturated market or because of the high expense of acquiring new equipment and other assets, the marketability of an existing business should be high. Although marketability can be difficult to determine, it is an essential ingredient of a complete valuation.

Financial Analysis

Once the level of goodwill has been established and its transferability confirmed, an analysis of the firm's accounting records can begin. Be alert to two frequently encountered obstacles, however: (1) the absence or inaccuracy of accounting records because transactions are recorded on a cash basis, with just enough detail to satisfy the IRS, and (2) intangible assets, such as customer files, that carry a higher value than balance sheet assets. It takes a fair amount of digging to uncover sufficient financial data for a meaningful valuation. Nevertheless, perseverance and a healthy dose of common sense usually win out. A good place to begin is with billings, cash receipts, and receivables.

Billings, Cash Receipts, and Receivables

A rule of thumb for professional practices and personal service businesses is that the longer the firm has been in operation, the higher the percentage of sales that are made on open account, thereby creating accounts receivable. Using cash basis accounting, however, few firms formally record receivables as an asset.

One-person businesses usually maintain an informal customer card file or notebook to keep track of billings, collections, and unpaid accounts. Slightly larger firms may keep track with an elementary bookkeeping software program. When the business has many small customers, such rudimentary systems can become very cumbersome, especially when there are hundreds of small open accounts. Sole practitioner professional businesses are notorious for losing track of customer accounts that remain open beyond sixty days.

About the only practical way to ferret out unpaid accounts is to match billing records with collections recorded as bank deposits. Be especially alert to open accounts from government agencies such as Medicare and Medicaid and from insurance companies. In both cases these paying agencies may have adjusted the amounts billed. Whether adjusted or not, these accounts tend to stretch well beyond normal trade credit terms; in fact, they are frequently outstanding for ninety days or more. If significant discrepancies arise, it may be desirable to confirm major open accounts directly with customers, as auditors do.

Billing systems vary all over the lot but generally reflect an accurate accounting of charges. Most small businesses use formal invoices, prepared in duplicate or triplicate on a typewriter or computer, and maintain at least one copy on file until the customer pays. Personal service businesses tend to do a better job of tracking collections than professionals. All too often, lawyers and physicians, for instance, feel self-conscious about asking customers for payment and allow past-due accounts to build.

For valuation purposes, any account from a customer other than a government agency or insurance company that remains open more than sixty days should be excluded. Government and insurance accounts older than ninety days should be excluded as well.

Although an examination of individual customer payment histories is probably the most reliable method for ascertaining the collectibility of accounts, this can be a very time-consuming job and is usually not worth the effort. In most cases, satisfactory analyses can be performed from a simple listing of accounts, aged by invoice date. When reviewing receivable accounts at the end of a year, it's a good idea to remain alert to tax-savings manipulations. Not infrequently, business owners hold customer checks in drawers until after the first of the year as a means of deferring income to the next year.

Inventory

Cash-basis businesses do not generally record inventory of any type. Yet, in certain cases, inventory can be a very sizable and valuable asset. Three types of inventory need to be analyzed:

1. Expensive operating supplies such as drugs, valuable tools, major office supplies, disposable high-cost materials, and so on
2. Items held for resale, such as parts, small assemblies, and so on for repair-type businesses; ointments and accessories for personal care businesses; bandages, crutches, braces, and so on for certain health care businesses
3. Work in process, typically unbilled services by lawyers, CPAs, consultants, and other professionals

Verifying the value of inventories of supplies and resale items is relatively simple. Start by taking a physical count of all major items. Then price each item from the latest supplier invoice. Only major or high-priced items need to be included. Inexpensive, disposable items such as letterhead, computer paper, accounting forms, rubber gloves, and so on won't add to the business value.

Work-in-process inventory is more difficult to quantify but can also account for a significant portion of business assets. Most work in process arises in businesses that charge by the hour or the day for services performed. Such charges are normally called *unbilled receivables* and include completed but unbilled work as well as time expensed on a percentage-of-completion engagement.

Any business that bills by the hour or day must maintain some type of time records. Time may be formally recorded, as on a computer time-keeping system, or informally recorded, as on time cards or work papers. Regardless of the time-keeping method, however, it is usually possible to determine the current amount of unbilled receivables.

Conversely, it is normally impossible to reconstruct unbilled receivables for more than one or two prior months. For example, in June, few businesses can determine what the unbilled hours were on the previous December 31, although they should be able to calculate unbilled hours on May 31. Several methods of calculating the value of unbilled receivables may be used, but the following represents one of the most common:

Unbilled work-in-process	120 hours
Billing rate	× $75 per hour
Gross value of unbilled hours	$9,000
Less: Value of hours to be written-off based on historical average of 10%	($900)
Less: Portion billed but uncollectible based on historical average of 5%	($450)
Value of unbilled receivables before discounting to present value	$7,650

Historical averages of hours written off and uncollectible accounts should be derived from an analysis of previous years' billing records, time-keeping records, and collections. At the same time, an analysis of the paying record of repeat customers gives an indication of the risk in future collections and should be part of the determination of a discount rate.

Customer Files, Working Papers, and Libraries

Although neither the IRS nor the accounting profession permits the value of customer files and/or working papers to be included as a balance sheet asset, these are very real assets that are required if the business is to continue operating as a going concern. Some analysts argue that these assets are part of goodwill, and in certain businesses this has merit. To the extent that customers return to the business for additional services primarily because it maintains the customer's prior records, such as tax returns and tax preparation working papers, those files certainly generate goodwill.

On the other hand, customer files may also have intrinsic value. For instance, customer mailing lists that can be used for direct mail advertising could have a very high value to the business. Or such lists could be sold to other companies for their use in direct mail solicitations and advertising.

One convenient way to value such files is by analyzing the price of similar-size customer lists sold by mailing list companies. Another, more indirect approach is to estimate for each customer account the potential for repeat business that is likely to occur because the customer's prior history is retained in the files. A third, although less satisfactory method, is to calculate the amount of revenue generated by each customer over the prior three years and assign an estimated revenue percentage to the files.

Law offices, medical practices, CPA firms, and other professional businesses rely heavily on libraries of technical reference material to perform continuing services. Without extensive, up-to-date libraries covering court cases, tax laws, diagnostic techniques, medications, and so on, these professionals would be out of business. Therefore, although they never show up as balance sheet assets, current reference works are an integral asset of the business.

This is one of the rare exceptions where assets should be valued at replacement cost. Since reference works do not depreciate in value, current libraries should be valued at the current cost to replace them: out-of-date libraries carry no value.

Equipment

The choice of a method for valuing equipment depends on the relative importance of the equipment to the continuance of the business. Dental offices, laboratories, repair businesses, and so on have significant investments in various types of equipment that they depend on in performing services. Newly acquired equipment can be valued at invoice price. Certain types of equipment can easily be valued at published market values, such as those found in the Kelley Blue Book for automobiles. Older equipment with values not found in readily accessible catalogs or reference works should be valued by an independent equipment appraiser who maintains a computer database of used equipment sales.

Many personal service businesses do not use any equipment to perform their services but still maintain offices. Office furniture and fixtures, computers, copying machines, fax machines, typewriters, and telephone answering equipment all have value, although in some businesses this value is very low. To the extent that office furniture and equipment is new, high-priced, or unique to the business, it should be valued at the original invoice price less depreciation calculated on a three-year useful life. If these assets don't fall into this category, it's usually best to value them at zero or an estimated amount approximating zero.

Liabilities

Regardless of accounting method, every business owes something to someone. These liabilities might be for purchases of supplies on open account, equipment or office lease payments, mortgage debt or bank loans, earned vacation time for employees, property taxes, sales taxes, income taxes, or any number of other possibilities. When records are maintained on a cash basis, the chances are good that none of these liabilities will be recorded, except for mortgages and bank loans.

When constructing financial statements, it is extremely important to include all debts owed by the business as offsets to asset values. This is not a difficult task. Just make a list of all unpaid invoices, lease contracts, and tax bills; review employee personnel practices; obtain clearances from latest tax audits; and confirm open loan balances and terms with lenders.

If the business has outstanding loans to be assumed by a buyer, their present value should be calculated using one of the methods described in Chapter 11. For all current liabilities, use the face amount of the invoices as offsets to asset values.

Be alert for contingent liabilities that may arise in the future but are unsupported by invoices, notices, or contracts. Although most professional businesses carry adequate liability insurance, many small personal service businesses do not. This makes future product liability claims arising from past services a distinct possibility. Tax claims, employee claims, and other hidden liabilities may also arise. Despite efforts to uncover these hidden future costs, chances are good that some will be missed. Therefore, the perceived risk of future liabilities arising from prior actions should be included as a reduction in business value.

Valuation Calculations

No single valuation method yields the best results for all professional practices and personal service businesses. Each case includes special considerations unique to that business. Each business has procedures and policies best suited to the personal goals and objectives of the owner. In nine out of ten cases, income tax laws play a major role in the caliber of record keeping and the use of business cash for personal expenses. Furthermore, each type of professional practice has peculiarities that do not apply to the others. And the wide variation in personal service businesses makes uniform valuation methods impractical.

Nevertheless, over the years, several valuation methods have become generally accepted techniques for use in buy/sell transactions, and successor partnership arrangements. The following discussions relate primarily to methods commonly used for buy/sell transactions.

Capitalization of Earnings Method

The capitalization of earnings method appeals to both buyer and sellers of professional practices and personal service businesses because it is based on the expectation that future earnings will duplicate prior years' earnings, which can be reasonably determined. Also, this method establishes one value for the business, inclusive of goodwill, tangible assets, and intangible assets. Disputes over the value of customer files, work in process, and depreciated equipment are eliminated. Negotiations over the potential loss of customers caused by the seller's absence can also be omitted.

The major disadvantage of this method is the difficulty of determining the capitalization rate. Sellers and buyers invariably see risk differently, making the capitalization rate a negotiated item. Still, there are broad-based standards to fall back on. The capitalization rate for most professional practices, for instance, falls between 18 and 40 percent, depending on location, the type of customer base, and other variables previously discussed. The capitalization rate for many personal service businesses can be reasonably set at 15 to 20 percent for those in a competitive environment and 12 to 15 percent for businesses that encounter less competition.

In this context, the term *capitalization rate* means the percentage by which a constant income stream is divided in order to arrive at its value. A capitalization rate can also be stated as a multiple of earnings simply by using its reciprocal. For instance, a 25 percent capitalization rate is equal to a multiple of four times earnings, arrived at by dividing one by 0.25.

The use of a capitalization rate in this context differs from using it to discount a future stream of variable cash flows to present value. For present value calculations, the capitalization rate is often referred to as a discount rate. For professional practices and personal service businesses, however, the capitalization of earnings method relates to the extrapolation of one year's earnings to the future and does *not* involve present value formulas.

A simple example of this method is as follows:

Normalized earnings of last year	$50,000
Divide by capitalization rate of	25%
Business value	$200,000

It should be noted that with this method, as with others using earnings as a base, the term *normalized earnings* means that all nonrecurring or unusual items of income and expense have been eliminated. It should also be noted that the standard capitalization rates previously quoted relate to earnings after a deduction for owner's salary and benefits.

When owner's salary and benefits are added back to the firm's earnings to arrive at a pure cash flow estimate, a much higher capitalization rate should be used—in many cases as high as 100 percent. Since most small business owners tend to withdraw all available cash in either salary or benefits, this add-back usually provides a more meaningful valuation base.

Excess Earnings Method

Although the excess earnings method is fraught with error and usually produces very misleading valuation results, many people still find it an acceptable method. Divorce courts particularly like this method, probably because it appears to be based on more or less scientific assumptions. In realty, however, the excess earnings method is difficult to apply, its base assumptions can be totally erroneous, and it produces widely conflicting results for businesses with differing hard asset bases, even though they are in the same industry and of the same size.

Chapter 3 explains the detailed procedure for calculating value using the excess earnings method, and there is no need to repeat the full description here. Briefly stated, however, the calculation involves:

- An estimated value of net tangible assets
- A determination of normalized earnings
- A return on net tangible assets based on presumed industry standards
- A deduction of these earnings from normalized earnings
- The capitalization of the difference between normalized earnings and the return on net assets at an arbitrary capitalization rate

Typically, an average of five years of historical earnings is used to determine normalized earnings, after eliminating nonrecurring items of income and expense, of course.

Although this method is widely used, it is frequently misapplied, especially when so many judgments must be made by outsiders unfamiliar with the business. It nearly always overstates goodwill by ignoring marketability deterrents. And, because it is based so heavily on estimated hard asset market values, it understates the value of firms without hard assets or with very few.

Declining Goodwill Method

The declining goodwill method, at times referred to as the *depreciating goodwill method*, recognizes a very logical fact: Once the sale has closed and the seller has departed, the business's goodwill created by the seller will decline over time. How fast it will decline is anyone's guess, but it will certainly decline. The declining goodwill method is based on the same calculations used in the excess earnings method, with one important exception.

Instead of capitalizing excess earnings at a constant rate, establish a period over which the excess earnings created by goodwill will diminish to zero. This might be three years, five years, or some other purely arbitrary period. The determination of the period of decline is the Achilles heel of this method. Who can say whether goodwill from the previous owner will last six months or six years?

Once the period of decline has been established, the same capitalization rate used in the excess earnings method is applied to arrive at the present value of the stream of declining goodwill values. This is the second major weakness in this method. The capitalization rate applied to excess earnings recognizes the perceived risk of not achieving these earnings in the future. The further out one goes, the higher the risk. This is exactly the opposite of the declining goodwill theory, in which the risk of not benefiting from seller goodwill actually decreases with time as the goodwill is written off.

Leveraged Buyout Method

The leveraged buyout (or LBO) method, variously called the *self-finance method*, the *cash flow measurement method*, and the *net return on invested capital method* applies the same leveraging principles as used in the leveraged buyout of a manufacturing, retail, or distribution company. A buyer uses the assets of the business plus personal assets to secure an acquisition loan and then uses the cash generated by the business to repay it.

Pragmatically, if outside financing is required to buy a business, this method makes more sense than any of the others. Even if outside financing is not required, the debt service calculation can be viewed as a return on the buyer's investment and therefore compared to returns of alternative investment options.

This is how the LBO method works. Assume that you wish to purchase an accounting practice that currently nets $160,000 before owner's salary and benefits. Further assume that you can get a bank loan amortized over five years at 10 percent interest, with equal monthly payments of interest and principal. You are willing to draw a maximum salary of $50,000 for a few years to ensure free cash sufficient to meet debt service. The following calculation demonstrates maximum prices that you could afford to pay for the practice with varying down payments:

Annual cash flow	$160,000
Annual salary draw	$50,000
Free cash	$110,000
Less: Contingency reserve	$20,000
Available for debt service	$90,000
Maximum monthly payment	$7,500
Maximum amount of loan	$352,990

	Down Payment Options			
	10%	20%	25%	30%
Maximum amount of loan	$352,990	$352,990	$352,990	$352,990
Plus cash down payment	$39,221	$88,248	$117,664	$151,282
Maximum value of practice	$392,211	$441,238	$470,654	$504,272

Although it is a somewhat backhanded way to arrive at the fair market value of a business, this calculation does give buyers a method of determining the amount that they can afford to pay and still meet LBO debt service requirements. It is also a handy gauge for sellers willing to finance the acquisition with deferred payments. With this model, you can vary any or all of the terms quickly to test various assumptions concerning price and payment terms.

Multiples of Revenue

Multiples of revenue also serve as a rough guide for determining the approximate market value of professional practices and, in certain cases, personal service businesses. The big advantage is that this method does not require any analysis of expenses, only revenues. The biggest disadvantage is that it ignores the basic principle of business valuations: value a business based on a stream of future benefits discounted to recognize investment risk.

Over the years, sales of practices in several professions have resulted in broad-based multiples that can be used in lieu of pure guesswork. Here are some of the more common ones:

Medical practices: Multiples of 25 to 60 percent of revenues include the fair market value of equipment, inventory, and goodwill. Practices located in highly competitive areas might go for as little as 25 percent of revenues for goodwill only, plus the appraised value of equipment and supplies. More desirable practices sell for as much as 60 percent of revenues for goodwill, plus an amount for equipment and inventory.

Optometric practices: 50 to 60 percent of revenues, including all book assets.

Veterinary practices: Those in good locations have been selling for prices ranging between 75 and 125 percent of revenues, everything included.

Health care labs: Those involved in drug testing sell for from 100 to 150 percent of revenues; labs that handle blood tests, pregnancy tests, and other standard procedures have been running much lower, in the 30 to 50 percent of revenues range, including all supplies and equipment.

Accounting practices: Three classes of client revenues are valued separately: tax clients, 40 percent of one year's revenues; bookkeeping clients, 40 to 50 percent of revenues; audit and management consulting clients, 100 to 200 percent of revenues. These percentages relate only to goodwill. Net asset values go at appraised value. To the extent that payment is based on the collection of fees over one, two, or three years from the seller's clients, the goodwill values should be increased by approximately 50 percent.

Law practices: Most outright sales are priced at net asset value, including libraries and supplies. Valuations of practices with repeat clients tend to use future referrals to compensate for ethical conflicts arising from the transfer of goodwill.

Real estate agencies: Depending on location and competition, the values of single owner/manager agencies range from 10 percent of revenues to 80 percent.

Insurance agencies: Again depending on location and competition, but also on the proportion of policies attributable to different types of insurance, recent sales have been as little as 10 percent and as much as 100 percent of revenues. Agencies with steady repeat business and low-risk policies (e.g., homeowners' policies in safe areas, automobile insurance in certain states, and life insurance) top the list. Agencies concentrating on business insurance fall in the middle range; those with a high turnover of policyholders, a weak carrier base, or high-risk policies tend to be valued at the low end.

Literary agencies: 40 to 50 percent of contracted revenues seems to be the norm, although those with well-known authors or with contracts involving television or movie rights can skyrocket to five or six times revenues.

CHAPTER

Real Estate–Based Businesses

In good times and bad, real estate–based businesses have been regarded as prime assets in long-term investment portfolios. Entrepreneurs are also drawn to these high-asset-value businesses, correctly recognizing that lending institutions view real estate as superior loan collateral. Retirees and individuals seeking a more offbeat lifestyle/workstyle continue to be attracted to bed and breakfast businesses, small vacation resorts, RV campgrounds, and roadside hotels/motels. Indeed, many types of investors have been drawn to real estate–based businesses as a viable long-term investment alternative to securities.

A wide variety of businesses can be grouped as real estate–based businesses: hotels, resorts, shopping centers, apartment complexes, sports stadiums, and so on. All real estate–based businesses have several common features. They are easily leveraged, illiquid, adaptable to investment groups, and enjoy long-term appreciation. However, since hotels and resorts are the most complex to value, this chapter explores valuation methods applicable to them as representative of all real estate–based businesses.

It should be noted that two types of valuations are commonly performed in the hotel industry: development valuations, for buying land and constructing a hotel, and valuations of hotel properties that are already in business. The latter may be used for buy/sell transactions, divorce settlements, estate planning, minority interest investments, dissolutions, and so on, just as with other closely held businesses.

Determining the potential investment return for hotel developments is a complex undertaking, similar to calculations applicable to other construction projects. Methods of valuing hotels and other real estate–based businesses for purposes of estate planning, divorce settlements, minority interests, and so on, are identical to those described in previous chapters for closely held businesses in general. Therefore, the balance of this chapter is primarily limited to a discussion of valuation methods for buy/sell transactions.

Investments in hotels, motels, and small resorts are considered by many to be high-risk ventures. And rightly so. Not only does the real property that comprises the major business asset experience highly volatile market values; the business itself may include several diverse business segments. Depending on the type of establishment and the location, business segments may include lodging accommodations, restaurants, bars, banquet facilities, recreational facilities, health clubs, and perhaps a night club and gambling casino, all of which are service-oriented businesses.

A characteristic that is even more difficult to manage is that by their nature, hotels, like all real estate–based businesses, have a finite capacity to increase sales. The business has a fixed supply of product to generate sales, such as a fixed number of rooms, a fixed number of restaurant or bar seats, a fixed number of banquet facilities, a fixed number of apartments to rent, a fixed number of offices to lease, and so on. Furthermore, many real estate–based businesses, especially hotels, experience radical changes in revenues caused by variations in both occupancy and prices. This may result from national and regional economic cycles or competition or both.

On the plus side, hotel industry groups compile a wealth of statistics that cover occupancies, room rates, and room expense ratios; restaurant, bar, and banquet revenue-to-expense ratios; leverage ratios; hotel operating expenses; and a variety of other financial and business data. This, of course, makes comparative analyses much easier for hotel valuations than for valuations of other small businesses. In fact, the hotel industry compiles far more financial and operating statistics than apartments, shopping centers, office buildings, or any other real estate-based industry.

Furthermore, many larger hotels are owned by publicly traded limited partnerships, providing an excellent comparative measure of equity market value. And finally, mainly because of the large number of hotels that have been built and subsequently sold, selling prices for most configurations are readily available and can be tapped to verify valuations.

Market and Competitive Factors

The first step in analyzing a hotel's future market outlook is to examine the long-term growth potential of the area. Hotel sales are extremely sensitive to the characteristics of the property's immediate location. A hotel located in a declining neighborhood or city, whether commercial, industrial, or residential, will inevitably suffer from declining sales over the long run, even though there may be periodic spurts. Similarly, a suburban hotel near rapidly growing commercial and industrial parks or tourist attractions should look forward to occupancy and room-rate increases commensurate with the success of these periphery businesses.

However, the economics of the immediate area may not have as strong an impact on sales as the economic/demographic circumstances of the main source of paying guests. For instance, hotels located near an airport that is primarily a transit stop for airline networks, such as Memphis, Charlotte, or Raleigh-Durham, will not attract overnight guests as readily as hotels located near a terminal airport, such as Minneapolis-St. Paul International, Chicago's O'Hare, or Newark International. The value of a hotel that enjoys a steady source of traffic will be higher than that of one whose sales depend on less constant traffic sources.

It's important to view hotel markets as long-term, since the economic life of a lodging facility typically ranges from twenty to sixty years, with the median falling between thirty-five and forty years. This is a crucial factor in judging investment value, since plans may be afoot to renovate a dying neighborhood, close or open an airport, revitalize or abandon vacation facilities, and so on. It is the long-term outlook that affects hotel values, not short-term circumstances. Examples of major long-term trends that affect a hotel's location include the following:

- An aging population, with many retirees enjoying company-paid pensions, will create an increased market demand for moderately priced tourist facilities, both roadside hotels and resorts.
- Continued intense competition in the airline industry coupled with bigger and faster aircraft will keep prices competitive on the one hand and encourage longer distance domestic and overseas trips for both commercial travelers and vacationers on the other. This will further increase market demand for hotels in destination locations that attract long-distance travelers, such as New York, Los Angeles, and Anchorage domestically, and Singapore, Rio de Janeiro, and Moscow overseas. On the other hand, many domestic business flights that in the past required overnight stays, such as the New York-to-Chicago junket, have now become short one-day hops. This, of course, will decrease market demand for hotels that previously counted on overnight business guests.
- A continued growth in high-tech and service industries should mean increased business for hotels located in areas where these companies predominate.
- An increasing percentage of the world's population will have money to spend on travel, and this will help hotels in major metropolitan areas, vacation locations, and rapidly growing commercial centers.
- Longer stays for business travel will continue to encourage construction of new suite-type facilities that will take business from traditional hotels catering to business travelers.
- Increasing global competitiveness in a variety of industries will make corporate travelers more cost conscious and lead to even greater downward pressure on room rates

This means high-cost-per-room hotels will be at a severe competitive disadvantage.

In addition, competition among the various classes of hotels, as well as among hotels catering to the same clientele, has a major impact on hotel values. In the hospitality industry, the supply of rooms changes only when new hotels are constructed or old ones are torn down. The number of new hotels being built has been increasing at a fairly constant rate; however, very few old hotels are ever torn down. This means that while the supply of products—specifically hotel rooms—has been steadily increasing, demand for rooms fluctuates with a wide range of factors ranging from weather conditions to national economic growth patterns.

The analysis of market supply and demand factors is a crucial step in any real estate–based valuation. In the hotel industry, supply comprises all the competitive lodging facilities in the area while demand represents the number and nature of travelers visiting the area who will use these facilities. When supply and demand achieve a reasonable balance, hotels maintain a level of occupancy sufficient to yield a continuing profit. More than any other factor, the supply of rooms and demand from travelers influence the long-term value of hotels. When the supply of lodging accommodations exceeds demand, hotels lose money. In the reverse situation, they can become cash cows.

Hotel values increase under the following market conditions:

- *A shortage of lodging accommodations relative to burgeoning customer demand.* The opening of Disney World near Orlando and the Mall of America in Bloomington, Minnesota, legislation permitting gambling casinos in Atlantic City and on Native American reservations, slot machine parlors, river-boat gambling and the onslaught of Latin American traders and financiers in Miami created significant imbalances in the demand/supply curve for hotels rooms.
- *Cyclical trends in local areas.* Hotels situated in areas that are susceptible to wide economic swings—Seattle's reliance on the Boeing Corporation, Microsoft, and Starbucks, Houston's focus on NASA and the oil industry, Los Angeles' dependence on the defense industry and the movie business, Boston's emphasis on computer companies—experience significant swings in demand and a relatively constant supply of accommodations. When dependent factors are on the downside of a cycle, hotels in those markets decline in value; when these factors are on the upswing, hotel values increase. However, since the hospitality industry requires, by its nature, long-term investments, too much reliance on short-term vacillations in demand can cause distorted results.

- *Barriers to the entrance of new hotels.* Zoning restrictions, the lack of available land, and environmental regulations are common barriers to new market entrants. Since the supply of rooms is fixed, hotels in these areas should prosper over the long term, assuming local economic conditions remain healthy.
- *Diversity of demand.* Hotels that cater to several sources of demand, such as air travel, business travel, vacationers, automobile travel, conventions, and so on, find their market base far more stable than those concentrating on one or two market segments. And this increases their value.

Product diversity is also important. Hotels that offer a wide range of products that can be adjusted to changing market demand will be worth more than those restricted to one or two products. For example, hotels with banquet facilities can attract conventions; those with formal dining facilities attract wedding receptions and holiday parties; those with health club facilities can sell memberships. Hotels with a combination of single rooms, suites, permanent apartments, and penthouse accommodations, and the ability to shift emphasis from one type of accommodation to another, are better situated to meet changing demand than those with sparse, fixed facilities. This same type of diversity applies to any real estate–based business.

A second product feature that strongly affects a hotel's value is the room rate structure. Amenity creep has elevated many low-rate hotels with flags from chains like Hampton and Fairfield to mid-rate facilities, opening the door to new low-rate entrants. Many of those in the mid-rate range rose to first-class status. Traditional top-of-the-line hotels such as Hilton, Sheraton, Marriott, and Hyatt found these newcomers knocking at their doors.

A truism in the hotel industry is that the addition of amenities to justify increased prices is relatively easy, but the reverse tactic of reducing amenities to lower rates is nearly impossible. You can go up, but the public won't allow you to come down. Since hotel rates are very sensitive to regional and national economic fluctuations, those properties with low-to-mid-range price structures generally fare better than those with high rates.

Price structure affects value in those situations where future earnings are susceptible to economic swings. Conversely, price structures for properties in Manhattan, for example, have little bearing on either attracting more business or losing business. Security, location, and amenities have a stronger impact.

Product niches play a very large role in determining value. The major niche markets created over the last several years include the following:

- *Extended-stay hotels:* Marriott's Residence Inn Chain is a prime example.
- *All-suite hotels:* Embassy Suites and Guest Quarters are two examples.
- *Budget hotels:* The Microtel brand has downsized motel-type units with prices 15 to 25 percent less than traditional economy rates and without restaurants, bars, meeting rooms, swimming pools, lobby areas, or other amenities.
- *Full-service resorts:* These resorts offer complete facilities for vacationers, including a variety of restaurants, boutique shops, convenience stores, bars, pools, entertainment, golf courses, tennis courts, and laundry facilities. Many are located in or near theme parks (e.g., Disney World) or in remote vacation areas (e.g., Caribbean islands, mountain ski areas, or desert sites).

The highest-value hotels are those that offer good price/value relationships. First-class all-suite hotels are a good example. They offer comfortable long-term living accommodations with living room, bedroom, and kitchen as well as a full complement of hotel services such as health club, pool, meeting rooms, restaurants, and so on. Another good example is the residence-type hotel that, for a modest price, offers commercial travelers comfortable long-term accommodations with no frills. In evaluating the prospects for a hotel, shopping center, apartment complex, or any real estate-based investment, one of the most important criteria is the proper matching of the property's price structure and amenities with market demand. The right match nearly always brings high occupancy rates. An improper match leads to empty rooms.

Competitive Analysis

Thus far we have considered qualitative alternatives related to market position and product offering. It's important to establish such factors at the beginning of a valuation; if a given property's market position and product offering don't appear to afford sufficient long-term potential, going further in the analysis would be a waste of time. However, if the hotel seems to be reasonably positioned, the next step is the quantification of this position. And that requires comparisons against competitive facilities, in terms of (1) market share, (2) occupancy rates, and (3) average room rates. Based on a competitive analysis, it's possible to forecast future cash benefits.

Although several methods can be used to evaluate competitive position, the two most widely accepted are (1) the market penetration method and (2) the competitive index method.

Market Penetration Method

The term *market penetration* as used in the hospitality industry has a very narrow definition, as opposed to its use in a rather broad sense for other industries. Market penetration means a comparison of the percentage relationship between a property's actual market share and its fair market share. Actual market share is calculated as the number of rooms occupied per day divided by the total number or rooms occupied per day in the property's competitive market. Its fair market share is calculated as the property's total number of rooms available divided by the total number of rooms available in the market. Market penetration is then measured by dividing the actual market share by the fair market share.

To demonstrate this calculation, assume that in a given market, say near a busy airport, five hotels compete for airline travelers—a Holiday Inn, a Hampton, a Ramada Inn, a Hilton, and a Marriott Residence Inn—each having between 100 and 300 rooms available for sale. The following table shows the actual market share of each.

	Number of Rooms	Percent Occupancy	Number of Occupied Rooms	Actual Percent Market Share
Holiday Inn	250	60	150	20.95
Hampton	175	55	96	13.41
Ramada	300	80	240	33.52
Hilton	225	70	158	22.07
Marriott Residence Inn	110	65	72	10.06
TOTALS	1,060		716	100.00*

*Does not add due to rounding.

The fair market shares shown in the following table are calculated by dividing each hotel's available rooms by the total number of rooms in the market (1,060). The market penetration is then calculated by dividing actual market shares by fair market shares.

	Number of Rooms	Actual Market Share Percent	Fair Market Share Percent	Market Penetration
Holiday Inn	250	20.95	23.58	0.89
Hampton	175	13.41	16.51	0.81
Ramada	300	33.52	28.30	1.18
Hilton	225	22.07	21.23	1.04
Marriott Residence Inn	110	10.06	10.38	.97
TOTALS	1,060	100.00*	100.00	

*Does not add due to rounding.

To interpret market penetration, subtract these amounts from 1.00; the difference is the over- or under-achievement of market penetration. In this instance, Holiday Inn has achieved 11 percent less than its fair market share (1.00 – 0.89 = 0.11); Hampton has achieved 19 percent less than its fair market share (1.00 – 0.81); Ramada has achieved 18 percent more than its fair market share (1.00 – 1.18 = -0.18); Hilton has achieved 4 percent more than its fair market share; and Marriott Residence Inn has achieved 3 percent less than its fair market share. From the perspective of current performance, it appears that Ramada Inn would be the best investment and Hampton the worst; however, other factors described later in this chapter also enter the valuation process.

Competitive Index Method

Using a much simpler calculation, the competitive index method yields the same results as the market penetration method. This method reflects the number of days in a year that one room in a hotel is rented and is calculated by multiplying the annual percentage occupancy by 365 days, as follows:

	Percent Occupancy	Days/Year	Competitive Index
Holiday Inn	60	365	219
Hampton	55	365	201
Ramada	80	365	292
Hilton	70	365	256
Marriott Residence Inn	65	365	237

The second step is to determine the relative competitiveness of each hotel. As can be seen from the following calculation for the Holiday Inn, the relative competitiveness determined by the competitive index method is exactly the same as the results of the market penetration method:

	Competitive Index	Market Penetration
Holiday Inn	219	0.89
Hampton	201	0.81
Relative competitiveness of Holiday Inn to Hampton	1.09	1.09

This shows that Holiday Inn is 9 percent more competitive than Hampton. The comparative analysis can be made even more meaningful by breaking down room occupancy rates by class of guest. For example, assume that Holiday Inn and Hampton each experienced the following occupancy rates:

Class of Guest	Holiday Inn	Hampton
Leisure/vacation	40%	60%
Business travelers	30%	25%
Meeting rooms	20%	15%
Conventions	10%	0%

If these occupancies are evaluated with the competitive index method by multiplying each occupancy by 365 days, the comparative market segment results would be:

Class of Guest	Holiday Inn	Hampton
Leisure/vacation	146	219
Business travelers	109	91
Meeting rooms	73	55
Conventions	36	0

A relative competitive analysis would give Holiday Inn the edge for business travelers (+20 percent), meeting rooms (+33 percent), and conventions. Conversely, Holiday Inn performs only two-thirds as well as Hampton in the leisure/vacation segment.

Competitive indexes are also helpful for determining the percentage of each market segment. Assume the following actual occupancy by market segment:

Class of Guest	Holiday Inn	Hampton	Ramada	Hilton	Marriott Residence Inn
Leisure/vacation	40%	60%	50%	20%	40%
Business travelers	30%	25%	40%	50%	50%
Meeting rooms	20%	15%	0%	10%	10%
Conventions	10%	0%	10%	20%	0%

To calculate market share, multiply each hotel's total room count by its competitive index, which is arrived at by multiplying each market segment's occupancy by 365 days. The result is referred to as the *market share adjuster*. The corresponding market share percent for the five hotels by market segment is shown in Figure 16-1.

Forecasting Market Share and Occupancy

The ultimate objective in the valuation of a business or business interest is to establish a reasonable projection of future cash benefits, and that requires the preparation of a cash flow forecast. But before beginning a forecast, it's necessary to make a judgment about the future sales potential of the business.

In the hotel industry, future sales potential means increases or decreases in room occupancy and room rates, which to a large extent are affected by the actions of competing hotels in the area. One way to measure such impact is to project market share for each of the hotel's market segments (e.g. leisure/vacation guests, business travelers, meeting room sales, and conventions).

FIGURE 16-1: Current Market Share by Hotel by Market Segment

LEISURE/VACATION MARKET SEGMENT

	Number of Rooms	Competitive Index	Market Share Adjuster	Market Share Percent
Holiday Inn	250	146	36,500	22.5
Hampton	175	219	38,325	23.6
Ramada	300	183	54,900	33.9
Hilton	225	73	16,425	10.1
Marriott Residence Inn	110	146	16,060	9.9
TOTAL	1,060		162,210	100.0

BUSINESS TRAVELERS MARKET SEGMENT

	Number of Rooms	Competitive Index	Market Share Adjuster	Market Share Percent
Holiday Inn	250	110	27,500	18.5
Hampton	175	91	15,925	10.7
Ramada	300	146	43,800	29.5
Hilton	225	183	41,175	27.7
Marriott Residence Inn	110	183	20,130	13.6
TOTAL	1,060		148,530	100.0

MEETING ROOMS MARKET SEGMENT

	Number of Rooms	Competitive Index	Market Share Adjuster	Market Share Percent
Holiday Inn	250	73	18,250	45.3
Hampton	175	55	9,625	23.9
Ramada	300	-0-	-0-	-0-
Hilton	225	37	8,325	20.7
Marriott Residence Inn	110	37	4,070	10.1
TOTAL	1,060		40,270	100.0

CONVENTIONS MARKET SEGMENT

	Number of Rooms	Competitive Index	Market Share Adjuster	Market Share Percent
Holiday Inn	250	37	9,250	25.2
Hampton	175	-0-	-0-	-0-
Ramada	300	37	11,100	30.2
Hilton	225	73	16,425	44.6
Marriott Residence Inn	110	-0-	-0-	-0-
TOTAL	1,060		36,775	100.0

This process is not unlike the segregation and independent valuation of diverse business lines in nonhotel multibusiness companies, described in Chapter 13. The idea is to quantify market share for each segment based on current occupancy rates and then to forecast future segment demand and market share changes. However, there are two significant differences between multibusiness valuations for real estate–based businesses and those for companies in other industries.

The main difference is that businesses in other industries can adjust their supply of products or services with market demand, either up or down. Since real estate–based businesses have a fixed supply of product they have substantially less flexibility. Deliberate marketing policies may change the mix of product sold, but the total number of units sold during a period cannot exceed the number of units available for sale.

The second difference is that real estate–based businesses have coined a vocabulary to describe various features of the market that in many respects have no counterparts in other businesses. For example, in the hotel industry, occupancy, room-nights, room-nights captured, accommodated room-night demand, and latent demand.

Market demand and a specific property's share of that demand as reflected in occupancy rates determine the character of a sales forecast. Market demand must be built up through a series of calculations, beginning with current markets and then extending future years' sales based on forecasted growth curves.

It should be noted that accommodated demand means the demand for rooms that is met by existing lodgings in the area. Latent demand is demand that potentially exists, but that for any number of reasons is not accommodated by existing lodging supply. Examples of latent demand include:

- Unaccommodated demand during peak periods, such as high season for vacation resorts or Monday through Thursday for commercially oriented hotels, when demand for rooms is greater than the number of rooms available from all competing properties
- Alternative accommodations outside the immediate market area that travelers will frequent when all hotels are at 100 percent occupancy
- New hotels that provide amenities not previously available (e.g., golf course, marina, health spa, and so on)
- Special promotions from one or more hotels in a market area
- The opening of a convention center, sports arena, or major retail complex

Figure 16-2 lays out the calculation of accommodated demand for the five hotels used in previous examples. When forecasting from accommodated room-night demand, a percentage of room-nights should be added to compensate for latent demand. Normally, latent demand is very small relative to accommodated demand, and a factor such as 2 or 3 percent could be used. If latent demand were substantial, new properties would undoubtedly be developed to absorb it.

FIGURE 16-2: Calculation of Accommodated Demand

	Holiday Inn	Hampton	Ramada	Hilton	Marriott Residence Inn
Total rooms	250	175	300	225	110
Annual days	365	365	365	365	365
Total rooms available	91,250	63,875	109,500	82,125	40,150
Annual occupancy	60%	55%	80%	70%	65%
Total rooms sold	54,750	35,131	87,600	57,522	26,098
BY MARKET SEGMENT					
Leisure/vacation	40%	60%	50%	20%	40%
Room-nights	21,900	21,078	43,800	11,504	10,439
Total room-nights occupied per year for all hotels: 108,721					
Business travelers	30%	25%	40%	50%	50%
Room-nights	16,425	8,783	35,040	28,761	13,049
Total room-nights occupied per year for all hotels: 181,158					
Meeting rooms	20%	15%	-0-	10%	10%
Room-nights	10,950	5,270	-0-	5,752	2,610
Total room-nights occupied per year for all hotels: 24,582					
Conventions	10%	-0-	10%	20%	-0-
Room-nights	5,475	-0-	8,760	11,504	-0-
Total room-nights occupied per year for all hotels: 25,739					

TOTAL ROOM-NIGHTS CAPTURED FROM ACCOMMODATED ROOM-NIGHT DEMAND

	Leisure/ Vacation	Business	Meetings	Conventions	Total	Occupancy
Holiday Inn	21,900	16,425	10,950	5,475	54,750	60%
Hampton	21,078	8,783	5,270	-0-	35,131	55%
Ramada	43,800	35,040	-0-	8,760	87,600	80%
Hilton	11,504	28,761	5,752	11,504	57,521	70%
Marriott Residence Inn	10,439	13,049	2,610	-0-	26,098	65%
TOTAL	108,721	181,158	24,582	25,739	340,200	

Forecasting Average Room Rate per Occupied Room

Average room rate is a key ingredient for forecasting cash flow and hence for making hotel valuations. The calculation of average room rates is also one of the most misunderstood aspects of hotel valuations. The average room rate is not an arithmetic average of posted rates. Nor is it necessarily arrived at by applying standard discounts for corporate accounts, elderly guests, children, and so on. The formula for calculating average room rates is standard throughout the industry and sanctioned by the *Uniform System of Accounts for the Lodging Industry*, published by the American Hotel and Motel Association. It is:

$$\frac{\text{Net room revenue}}{\text{Number of paid rooms occupied}} = \text{Average rate}$$

The term *net room revenue* means the total revenues received for all rooms, less allowances. *Allowances* are rebates and overcharges, revenues not known at the time of the room sales but adjusted at a later date, and forgone revenues resulting from promotions and complimentary services. *Paid rooms occupied* means all rooms occupied by paying guests and excludes complimentary rooms.

In most businesses, unit price trends tend to reflect inflation rates in the region and/or nationally. This is generally not true of hotel room rates. Except in special locations, such as Manhattan, downtown Chicago, or locations with enforced barriers to new entrants, room rates react to occupancy levels and competition much more than to inflationary pressures. When occupancy reaches levels beyond 80 percent, the average room rate increases, as more high-rate rooms can be sold and fewer discounts need to be granted to attract guests. As occupancy decreases, say to below 50 percent, or when competitors offer special promotions, defensive tactics cause room rates to plummet.

Product mix also affects average room rates. For instance, airlines, bus tours, conventions, and large corporate accounts usually pay the lowest rate, called a *contract rate*. As this type of business increases, it will drive down the average rate. *Commercial rates* charged business travelers are the next highest, also pulling the average rate downward. *Published rates* are higher than commercial rates and appear in hotel publications, directories, and travel agency computer bases, usually quoted in ranges, such as $150 to $200 for a single room.

The *rack rate* is the highest rate charged and is usually posted on the door of each room. When occupancy approaches 100 percent, desk clerks will sell rooms at the rack rate rather than at a discounted rate. A preponderance of high-occupancy nights will substantially boost the overall average rate.

In forecasting hotel revenues, it's important to relate the average room rate to the assumptions made concerning occupancy levels and product mix. The starting point, of course, is the historical experience of a hotel. It usually pays to correlate occupancy, product mix, and average room rates over a three-to-five-year period. Barring any major changes in the economics of the market or competition, the annual trend of such a correlation should be the basis for projecting growth, or decline, in future room sales.

Forecasting Expenses

Nearly all hotels maintain their accounting records according to the *Uniform System of Accounts for the Lodging Industry*. Smaller hotels may use only a fraction of the accounts needed for large properties, but even microtels usually find it easier to use this system than to keep cash register tapes and invoices in shoe boxes. The general industry acceptance of the *Uniform System of Accounts for the Lodging Industry* has enabled the accumulation of vast amounts of industry data over a long time period. Such data is available through hotel consulting firms or trade associations. Reams of hotel statistics can be found in many libraries, although the most recent year is usually two to three years out of date.

These accumulated statistics are extremely helpful in forecasting average expense levels and should be correlated with a hotel's actual expense experience whenever possible. A characteristic of hotel operating expenses is that some are occupancy-sensitive but many are fixed; they do not vary with fluctuating levels of room sales. Examples of expenses that are sensitive to variable occupancy levels include:

- Laundry expenses
- Room supplies
- Commissions to travel agencies
- Reservation expenses
- Certain payroll expenses, such as overload maids, banquet waiters and waitresses, and extra bellhops

The *Uniform System of Accounts for the Lodging Industry* breaks out the following room expenses, indicating their variability and showing their average ratios to total expenses:

	Percent of Total	Occupancy Sensitivity
Salaries and wages	50–70	Moderate
Employee benefits	5–15	Moderate
China, glassware, and linen	3–8	Slight
Commissions	0–3	High
Contract cleaning	1–3	Fixed
Laundry and dry cleaning	7–12	Slight
Operating supplies	1–4	Very slight
Other operating expenses	1–4	Very slight
Reservation expenses	0–8	High
Uniforms	1–3	Very slight
	100	

The room expense ratio—that is, the ratio of room expense to room revenue—is an important indicator of a property's profitability and hence its value. Barring an unusually low occupancy level, room expenses should not exceed 25 percent of net room revenue. When forecasting room expenses, bear in mind that of the total, approximately 50 to 70 percent should be fixed and 30 to 50 percent variable with occupancy levels. Family-operated hotels generally have a higher percentage of fixed expenses; expenses of high-priced resorts tend to be more occupancy-variable.

The same proliferation of statistics is available for hotels with food and beverage amenities as for those without. The *Uniform System of Accounts for the Lodging Industry* categorizes food and beverage expenses as follows:

	Percent of Total	Food and Beverage Sales Sensitivity
Cost of food sales	35–45	High
Cost of employee meals	1–4	Moderate
Cost of beverage sales	20–30	High
Salaries and wages	25–35	Moderate
Employee benefits	2–9	Very slight
Contract cleaning	0–3	Fixed
Laundry and dry cleaning	1–2	Slight
Licenses	1–2	Fixed
Music and other entertainment	2–7	Moderate
Operating supplies	1–3	Very slight
Other operating expenses	1–3	Very slight
Uniforms	1–2	Very slight
	100	

Properties with normal food and beverage revenues in relation to room revenues should not allow food and beverage expenses to exceed 80 to 83 percent of food and beverage revenues. Generally, for forecasting purposes, one can assume that 35 to 55 percent of food and beverage expenses are fixed and 45 to 65 percent are variable with revenues. Clearly, these ratios will differ drastically between a first-class metropolitan hotel or resort and a roadside motel.

Although large hotels account for telephone expenses as a separate department, like rooms or food and beverage, modern communications equipment enables most properties to automate their system and treat telephone expenses like any other operating expense. The following shows the average percentage of each nondepartmental expense category considered fixed and the typically largest expense account within each category:

	Percent Fixed	Largest Expense
Telephone	55–75	Phone service
Administrative	65–85	Salaries
Management fee	-0-	Percent of revenues
Marketing	65–85	Advertising/promotion
Property operations and maintenance	55–75	Salaries
Energy	80–95	All
Property tax	100	N/A
Insurance	100	N/A
Reserve for replacement	-0-	2–4% of revenues

Income Capitalization Valuation

Although comparisons with sales of other properties in the area provide reasonable parameters within which the valuation should fall, the complexities engendered by hotel product mix, flag identification, types of amenities, and, probably most important, the caliber of employees makes absolute value comparisons with other properties suspect. Differences in product mix, amenities, and location make valuations of shopping centers, office complexes, and most other real estate–based businesses based on comparative analyses equally difficult. Nevertheless, as a rough measure, comparing hotel values with sale prices of other properties is a popular approach, especially for microtels, roadside motels, and bed and breakfast properties.

For larger properties, traditional valuation procedures, such as the discounted earnings method, yield better results. Unlike most other businesses, hotel earnings equate closely with cash flow, provided earnings before depreciation and debt service are used. The reason is relatively simple. Hotel receivables are primarily composed of credit card receivables and a handful of accounts of large corporations, such as airlines. Receivables turnover is relatively constant month-to-month and year-to-year, so that credit sales closely approximate cash sales. Moreover, hotel inventories, such as linens, glassware, food and beverages, and so on are high-turnover items, usually expensed as purchased.

Since earnings before depreciation and debt service should be reasonably similar to cash flow, there is virtually no difference between the discounted earnings method and the discounted cash flow method. The industry prefers to use discounted earnings mainly because the *Uniform System of Accounts for the Lodging Industry* makes comparative statistics reasonably reliable for ratio and risk analyses. Therefore, although the following discussion relates to the discounted earnings method, it applies equally to the discounted cash flow method.

Typically, the pro forma financial statements of hotels and other real estate–based companies cover a ten-year period instead of the three to eight years customary for most other businesses. Also, the last forecast year is normally assumed to be representative of every year thereafter for purposes of determining continuing value. Depending on the location and nature of the property, continuing value forecast periods stretch from fifty to 100 years.

Once an income stream has been forecasted, the high leveragability of real estate–based businesses requires the allocation of income before depreciation and debt service to debtholders first, then, after debt service, to equity interests. The sum of mortgage value and equity value equals the total value of the property. As seen in the following descriptions, hotel valuations employ a slightly different approach to the valuation of equity than do other businesses, primarily because buyers typically finance a high percentage of equity capital. Equity investors, quite naturally, tend to base their investment decisions on projected returns on investment, not unlike debtholders.

In both economic growth periods and recessions, thirty-year mortgages have been the instrument of choice of long-term lenders such as insurance companies and pension funds for financing real estate–based businesses, especially hotels. This makes the market rate of interest easily obtainable from any commercial mortgage house. With market interest rates and payment terms in hand, a cash flow stream for mortgage holders can be forecasted and discounted to present value. The next step is to calculate the present value of the future stream of benefits to equity investors.

Passive investors in hotel equities typically demand a guaranteed dividend return over at least a five-year period, and generally over ten years. Not infrequently, this involves cumulative dividend rights on preferred stock, not common stock. The dividend rate may also be incorporated as a fixed annual return in a limited partnership agreement. Moreover, investors generally expect to be able to cash in their investment at an appreciated value. The sum of this appreciated value and the dividend returns equals the value of equity interests.

Of course, the difficulty of determining a reasonable capitalization rate applies to hotels just as it does to other businesses. Although the perceived risk of not receiving forecasted returns must be weighted in the discounting equation, the application of the extensive quantitative market analysis procedures described previously in this chapter should mitigate such uncertainty. Furthermore, a cumulative equity return tied to preferred stock agreements creates a legal liability to pay, further reducing risk.

As an offset, many local markets are currently overdeveloped. Too many rooms are chasing too few guests. As new hotels come on line and offer amenities suited to specific market niches, such as budget prices, long-term residence accommodations, and so on, the occupancy and room rates of older full-service hotels will undoubtedly suffer. This, of course, increases investment risk.

Internal Rate of Return Method

As an alternative to the traditional debtholder/equity holder income capitalization method, the *internal rate of return method* combined with the discounting to present value of a future stream of cash flows has attracted an increasing number of investors as a more expedient valuation method. It offers a handy reference method to establish:

- The present value of a long-term loan
- The present value of a highly leveraged equity investment
- An investment rate of return for investors to use in comparative analyses against returns from alternative investments
- A discounted value to use in negotiating a buy/sell price

Pragmatically, the internal rate of return method has more appeal for investors in shopping centers, office buildings, and apartment complexes, but it also applies to hotels, motels, and resorts. The following example demonstrates how the method works.

Assume the following for a hotel on the market at an asking price of $4 million:

1. Leveraging with a mortgage loan can go as high as 75 percent of the purchase price. Market rates of 8 percent and monthly payments of principal and interest over a thirty-year term are available. The monthly payment on such a mortgage is $22,013. The loan balance after ten years will be $2,631,741.
2. With a $3 million mortgage, equity of $1 million must be raised. Equity will be raised through a venture capital fund whose members want a rate of return ranging from 30 to 40 percent over a ten-year period, including appreciation gain on their investment in the

eleventh year when the property will be sold and the balance of the mortgage loan repaid.

3. A recent pro forma financial statement projected for ten years indicates the following net income before depreciation, taxes, and debt service:

	Net income
Year 1	$504,000
Year 2	524,000
Year 3	532,000
Year 4	540,000
Year 5	548,000
Year 6	557,000
Year 7	566,000
Year 8	575,000
Year 9	584,000
Year 10	6,707,000*

*10th year net income of $594,000 plus sale proceeds to equity holders of $6,113,000.

4. To calculate the selling price of the property in Year 11, make the assumption that the income for that year will increase by the same proportion as between Year 9 and Year 10. This yields an income for Year 11 of $611,321. Although the capitalization rate applied to this income will vary with investors' perception of uncertainty, it is not unreasonable in this case to assume a rate of 10 percent. Dividing income for Year 11 by 10 percent gives a gross selling price of $6,113,208. Subtracting the loan balance of $2,631,741 at the end of Year 10, we arrive at net proceeds to be paid to equity holders of $3,481,485. The following summary shows these calculations:

Net income in Year 11	$611,321
Capitalization rate	10%
Gross selling price	$6,113,208
Less: Outstanding mortgage balance to be repaid	($2,631,741)
Net to equity investors	$3,481,485

5. Figure 16-3 shows the internal rate of return calculations for each class of investor for each of the ten years. Note that in Year 10, the total debt service payment of $2,895,896 includes the regular payment made that year plus the balance of the loan paid off in Year 11. Similarly, the total cash flow to equity holders in Year 10 includes the net income for that year plus the net proceeds of the sale of the property ($3,481,465); and the total company net income stream in Year 10 includes the net income for that year plus the gross proceeds from the sale ($6,113,208).

The following summarizes the investment and projected rate of return for each class of investor, and the total company, that resulted from these cash flow and earnings streams.

	Investment*	Projected Internal Rate of Return
Debtholders	$3,000,000	8.0%
Equity holders	$1,000,000	32.1
Total company	$4,000,000	16.0

*Rounded

The internal rates of return were calculated using an embedded macro function in a spreadsheet program. Calculations can also be done manually using complex algebraic formulas, but that's more work than it's worth.

The internal rates of return were then used as capitalization (discount) factors and applied to forecasted cash flow streams for equity holders and the total company to arrive at the discounted present values.

It's interesting to note the wide variation in internal rates of return for the different classes of investors—8 percent for debtholders and 32.1 percent for equity investors. This would indicate that as long as market projections hold and new competition doesn't destroy occupancy or room rate forecasts, this investment is probably as good as can be found at the moment. The average rate of return normally demanded by hotel equity investors ranges from 8 to 12 percent, although it should be expected that a small hotel producing this level of profits could return a much higher return on leveraged capital.

Despite the ease of using this method, investors should be warned that the mathematics embedded in internal rate of return formulas can be manipulated easily by changing estimated return factors. This tends to leave the door open for divergent views when negotiating a buy/sell price. In the end, most knowledgeable investors, either lenders or equity investors, prefer the income capitalization method.

FIGURE 16.3: Internal Rate of Return for Each Class of Investor

Yield to Debtholders

Year	Debt Service (in dollars)	Present Value Factor @ 8%	Discounted Cash Flow (in dollars)
Year 1	264,155	0.92593	244,589
Year 2	264,155	0.87534	226,471
Year 3	264,155	0.79383	209,694
Year 4	264,155	0.73503	194,162
Year 5	264,155	0.68058	179,779
Year 6	264,155	0.63017	166,463
Year 7	264,155	0.58349	154,132
Year 8	264,155	0.54027	142,715
Year 9	264,155	0.50025	132,144
Year 10	2,895,896	0.46319	1,341,350
		Total	2,991,499
		Rounded	3,000,000

Yield to Equity Holders

Year	Net Income After Debt Service (in dollars)	Present Value Factor @ 32.1%	Discounted Cash Flow (in dollars)
Investment	(1,000,000)		
Year 1	240,000	0.75700	181,681
Year 2	260,000	0.57305	148,994
Year 3	267,800	0.43380	116,172
Year 4	275,834	0.32839	90,581
Year 5	284,109	0.24859	70,627
Year 6	292,632	0.18818	55,069
Year 7	301,411	0.14246	42,938
Year 8	310,454	0.10784	33,479
Year 9	319,767	0.08163	26,104
Year 10	3,810,825	0.06180	235,500
		Total	1,001,144
		rounded	1,000,000
		IRR	32.1%

Yield for Total Property

Year	Net Income Before Debt Service (in dollars)	Present Value Factor @ 16%	Discounted Cash Flow (in dollars)
Investment	(4,000,000)		
Year 1	504,155	0.84551	426,270
Year 2	524,155	0.71632	375,464
Year 3	531,955	0.61258	325,867
Year 4	539,989	0.52731	284,743
Year 5	548,264	0.45672	250,406
Year 6	556,788	0.39787	221,531
Year 7	565,567	0.34845	197,070
Year 8	574,609	0.30663	176,194
Year 9	583,922	0.27101	158,248
Year 10	6,706,721	0.23511	1,576,850
		Total	3,992,643
		Rounded	4,000,000
		IRR	16.0%

CHAPTER 17

Start-Up Businesses

Previous chapters dealt with a variety of methods for valuing almost any type of business. From capitalized earnings calculations to the much less sophisticated multiple of revenue approach, these methods were used to value the nebulous goodwill generated from years of satisfied customers and clients. Each had one element in common: They relied on historical earnings or revenues as a base for projecting future streams of cash flow. Even when financial statements needed to be restated to take into account an owner's personal draws and expenses, by and large they could be used as a starting point. Start-up businesses, on the other hand, lack such historical data. These businesses are too new to generate operating results that show any type of trend, making traditional valuation methods susceptible to controversy. How can you forecast revenues and costs without historical trends to point the way?

Before proceeding I should define what I mean by a start-up business. A start-up business is a company that has been in operation for less than three years. Beyond three years, a business becomes entrenched in its markets and can be considered a going concern. The business may be a CPA practice begun by an accountant who recently qualified for a certification license. It may be an auto repair shop in a mechanic's home garage. Or a computer whiz may start a business by designing and selling a new software program. Start-ups may be new companies selling products or services that are similar to those of competitors. Or they may involve newly invented products or services. They may be professional practices, manufacturing companies, retail establishments, distributors, or service businesses.

The type of business is incidental. And whether the product or service is truly original or similar to others in the marketplace is irrelevant. Start-ups are defined strictly by how long they have been in business. We are only concerned with those companies that have begun operations within the past thirty-six months. The single thread common to all start-ups is that they have not been in business long enough to generate trend-setting financial data. How then can such a business have market value? That is what we shall discuss in this chapter.

Virtually all valuation authorities ignore start-up businesses, probably for good reason. Of what possible use is the market value of such a business? Certainly the company cannot be sold. Partnerships are unlikely to breakup in such a short time period. Although divorce is always possible at any time, the amount of settlement arising from a start-up is probably not large enough to be concerned about. For some, such reasoning may be accurate. However, I have known several partnerships that did break up during the first year or two. As for a divorce, the value of a new business might indeed be sufficient to warrant a settlement. And several clients have sold start-ups. In fact, I sold two of my own start-up businesses—Accounting Associates, Inc., a bookkeeping practice, and Latin America/Caribbean Productions, a seminar production company.

All businesses begin with an idea. It may be an idea for a product no one else has thought of. Or it may be an idea of how to do something better than anyone else. The trick is to express the market worth of these ideas in monetary terms.

Valuing Ideas

When one normally thinks of new ideas in a business sense, one conjures up images of new technology, new services, or new patented products. In the 1980s and 1990s California's Silicon Valley saw a plethora of dot-com start-ups blossom like a field of wild flowers. Creative new software, personal computer gadgetry, telecom gizmos, and many other high-tech products were conceived during this period, giving birth to thousands of start-up businesses. Venture capitalists recognized the potential of many of them and poured millions of dollars into businesses with little or no history. Traditional valuation techniques were thrown to the wind. Entrepreneurial ideas interested these financiers, not because the ideas had produced earnings in the past but because they believed that substantial cash could be generated from them in the future.

Dot-coms weren't the only type of start-up business breeding off the high-tech revolution of the '90s. Creative ideas for performing old services in new ways also popped up. Using the Internet as a marketing tool, Mr. Jeff Bezos, of Amazon.com fame, conceived a new way to sell books, bypassing the entire retail-bookstore industry.

The millennium saw the application of a new technology to the established Internet search engine industry and Google, Inc. was born. The use of this new idea "to organize the world's information and make it universally accessible and useful," according to Google's mission statement, was offered free to the public. Although the company had no history to draw from, investors were so excited by the future potential of this start-up business that an IPO was quickly arranged—which, as we all know, was eminently successful.

These are a few examples of investors attaching value to creative ideas with very little or no historical data from which to forecast future returns. Were these values predicated on realistic formulae or acceptable valuation procedures? No, they were not. Were they justified? History has shown that the investing public certainly thought they were.

How then did underwriters who handled initial public offerings (IPOs) for these start-ups determine equitable offering prices for the shares? Forecasting future cash flow without historical data to draw from requires a fair bit of ingenuity. Why, for example, should investors believe that the business will enjoy a 25 percent growth rate when it struggled to survive the first six months of its existence? The answer lies in promotional efforts that convince the market to expect superior performance from the start-up and hence burgeoning future sales and cash flow. And this points to three value-building criteria.

Three Value-Building Criteria

Strong market demand, assured continuity of the business, and market-driven ideas are the three criteria that start-ups must have to create market value. Although from a buyer's perspective, the value of a start-up may be only in the eye of the beholder and no market-value calculations will yield an answer that is any more definitive, some type of authoritative valuation should be applied to satisfy the needs of money lenders, potential partners, the IRS, and the courts.

The quantifying of future market demand is always the basic ingredient in a start-up valuation. Of the three value-building characteristics, future demand for the product or service is the most difficult to judge and frequently the most controversial. Everyone has the best estimate of how well the market will accept the innovation. Everyone seems to be clairvoyant in judging customer tastes. Yet no one has developed a generally acceptable method for evaluating future market growth for start-ups. The best that can be done is to base forecasts on the performance of companies with similar products or services or, lacking information about that, on the expected growth of an industry or industry segment.

Although the certainty of future market demand for new products or services is at best questionable, steps can be taken to validate an entrepreneur's estimate. Factors influencing market demand, such as demographic shifts, macroeconomic trends, financial market predictions, and globalization all cast shadows over the likelihood of future revenues. Fortunately, these factors can be quantified, probabilities of occurrence can be assigned, and dollar values can be computed.

Several other conditions centering more on the specific business must be analyzed. Competition from companies offering similar or substitutable products or services will certainly impact future market demand. Ease of market entry for potentially competitive products will affect the likelihood of others coming up with the same or similar ideas. Government regulations will impact market demand for certain types of products or even new ideas. One could speculate about many other factors affecting future demand and such speculation should, in fact, be thoroughly explored during the valuation process.

Continuity of the Business

In addition to market demand, one must look at the likelihood of the continuity of the company. Many start-ups begin as one-person businesses. At first glance one might assume that a one-person start-up could not continue to operate after that person leaves. The entity may continue to exist, as with a corporation, but the goodwill of the business evaporates like fog in the morning sun. Until the entrepreneur solves the succession problem, valuing the business is meaningless.

Fortunately, the continuity of a one-person start-up can be assured. Arrangements can be made to bring a partner into the business, ensuring management succession in the event of the death or incapacity of the original founder. Perhaps the entrepreneur's daughter or a son could take over in an emergency. Maybe it's the type of business that a spouse could easily step into to run, if necessary. The structure of the business notwithstanding, the problem of succession management must be addressed. If it is adequately addressed, the continuity question no longer affects the valuation process.

Market-Driven Ideas

From the perspective of business valuations, estimating future market demand and ensuring the continuity of the business are meaningless unless the start-up idea is market driven. Inventing a new buggy whip won't attract many customers, except perhaps in Amish country. A new way to categorize archived documents won't generate many sales, except perhaps from professional archivists. Although new ideas and new products may have benefits in and of themselves, they are not market driven unless the market accepts them, thereby creating sales and cash flow. Until that happens, the business remains merely a dream of the founder.

Far too often, entrepreneurs get carried away with their innovations. Brake drums for intercity high-speed monorail trains, toothpaste that guarantees no cavities for life, rocket-propelled harnesses for individual flight, self-steering automobiles, and energy from sea water to light a city are real inventions that my clients have concocted. None were market driven, however, and all faded like shadows in the night.

Nearly all start-up businesses based on ideas that are not market driven inevitably fail and are therefore worth nothing. However, given enough cash to stay afloat for an extended period of time, some seemingly worthless creations may eventually find a market, albeit the wait might be measured in years or even decades. Videoconferencing is a good example. In the late 1950s the Western Electric Labs, then part of American Telephone and Telegraph Company (the old AT&T), did in fact develop the technology for cost-effective videoconferencing. AT&T tried to sell the technology but the market wasn't ready for such a high-tech invention. Not until the 1980s did videoconferencing become a viable, marketable technology, primarily for use in specialized surgical procedures. And not until this century did it find a home in corporate America. Obviously, prior to the 1980s a start-up business producing videoconferencing equipment would have no value.

In addition to dealing with these three value-building characteristics, you need to get a handle on costs, primarily those costs incurred in building a customer base.

Building a Customer Base

Without customers you have no business. That's obvious. So you need to build a customer base quickly and economically. That might involve advertising, publicity campaigns, trade shows, or other types of sales promotions. It might mean hiring a publicist or an advertising agency. Maybe you should run a promotional give-away in the local newspaper. Some talented entrepreneurs write magazine articles or even a book to describe the benefits of their new product or idea. Each of these steps costs money. And you need to get a good approximation of that cost before proceeding to calculate a market value for your business. The cost of acquiring customers is then added to the expected internal ongoing costs of running the business and this total cost, along with expected revenues, is used to forecast cash flow.

Advertising, publicity, and trade shows are the main types of promotions used by start-ups to acquire new customers. Each has its particular use and cost. Advertising builds product acceptance. Publicity establishes a company's reputation and brand recognition. Trade shows introduce your new product or service to a captive audience.

You probably can't afford to spend a lot this early in the game so it's important to choose the promotion that will be the most cost-effective for your specific business. Also, speed is essential. Waiting too long to build a customer base increases the cost of doing so.

Trade Shows

Displaying your new product at industry trade shows is certainly the easiest and the least costly way to introduce it to the marketplace. This is also an excellent way to get a firsthand glimpse of your competition. And it's a convenient arena in which to meet potential customers as well as distributors and sales agents should you decide to employ such professionals in the future. At the same time you can get a feel for market acceptance and hence future demand for your product.

Every trade show is different. The bigger ones tend to be more expensive but attract much larger audiences. Regional shows give you better coverage from local buyers and tend to be less expensive than national shows. Trade shows sponsored by development agencies are the least attractive and also the least expensive. They tend to draw more tire kickers than legitimate customers. Also, trade shows for industries different from yours will most likely be a waste of money and time. Some generic trade shows, however, such as the big national computer shows in Las Vegas or the huge national automotive shows, cross many industry lines and could provide good coverage. These are much more expensive than the smaller ones, however, ranging from about $8,000 to $15,000 for a small booth. Compare this to about $2,000 to $4,000 for a booth at a smaller, regional show.

You might also consider sharing a booth with other entrepreneurs from your area. You don't have to be in the same industry to do so. As a matter of fact, you'll do better by sharing with someone who sells an entirely different product. Here are some key questions to resolve before signing up for a trade show booth:

- What is the expected number of attendees?
- How many exhibitors will be at the show?
- From how large a region will the show draw exhibitors and attendees?
- What type of facility houses the show and where is it located relative to major hotels and airports?
- What type of pipe and drape configurations are used?
- Are booth dimensions metric? What are the maximum, minimum, and customary sizes?
- How are booths constructed? Modular components, hard walls, curtains?

If you decide to promote through a trade show, do it right. Get advice from experts. It goes without saying that you must indoctrinate those experts with the unique design qualities of your new products or the advantages in using your new services. If they don't know what you are trying to sell, they won't know how to help design your booth.

Publicity

A dynamic publicity campaign may be more effective for your start-up business than either trade shows or advertising. If you are already in business with other products, you have a built-in customer base to tap. However, if you don't have an established business, it's doubtful that the marketplace has heard anything about you, your company, or your new innovation. Since markets regard unknown products or companies with skepticism, you must create a favorable, recognizable identity as soon as possible. Such a reputation can best be developed through a publicity campaign that stresses your high–quality, competitively priced products; outstanding customer service; and long-term staying power.

One of the biggest hurdles a start-up business must overcome is the fear on the part of potential customers that it will be here today and gone tomorrow. You must convince the market that your new company will remain competitive over the long haul and that it will stand behind its products for many years to come.

It doesn't pay to embark on a publicity campaign on your own. Much better is hiring a quality publicist and including its fees as part of your estimated cost of acquiring new customers. Expect to pay a retainer of about $5,000 to $10,000 plus an hourly rate and expenses. Professional publicists run the gamut from superb to charlatan, and from one-person businesses to multinational companies with offices throughout the world. The choice of one over another should be based on the firm's experience in your particular market and its fee structure.

A contract with a publicist may be structured either for a single, time-limited project, or on a continuing basis. But regardless of which approach is taken, it's important to rely on the publicist's professional judgment as to which promotions will work and which will not. After all, it doesn't make sense to pay for expertise and then ignore it. A publicist should be able to design an appropriate image-building program and make all arrangements for its implementation, including multimedia coverage. Here are a few examples of very low-cost ideas that have worked well for my clients trying to launch new products and services:

- Participate in radio interviews about your new product or service (National Public Radio frequently does this type of interview).
- Invite a local newspaper to write an article on the uniqueness of your product or service or company.
- Ask television reporters to cover a special event that highlights the benefits of your new product.
- Do television interviews on business-oriented talk shows (MSNBC and other cable channels are your best bet).

- Support a young people's athletic team with your company's name on the uniforms.
- Sponsor an entrant in a local parade.
- Donate materials, space, or services to community groups.

Good publicity can do more to help you reach your projected future growth than almost anything else. And it costs less than advertising. Conversely, bad publicity can kill your new innovation before it's out of the gate.

Advertising

Of the three main approaches for promoting your new business, chances are good that advertising will be the most expensive. Whether you choose radio, television, billboards, or print media, the cost will far exceed what you would spend on trade shows and will certainly outpace a reasonably priced publicity campaign. Expect to pay up to $25,000 or more depending on your choice of media. For certain products and services in certain industries, however, you can't beat advertising for attracting new customers, regardless of cost. Here are a few guidelines to help keep expenditures under control:

- Focus your ads on attracting customers to your product, not on creating a public image.
- Retain control over the format design of your ads and be sure to monitor the agency's expenditures against an agreed-to budget.
- Establish a schedule for the advertising agency to follow, including progress milestones that can be measured.
- Devise a follow-up procedure to monitor the agency against these milestones.
- Define targeted recipients (e.g., types of customers, geographic coverage, specific competitors) before starting the advertising campaign.
- Explain why your new products or services are better than those of your competitors.
- Define the time frame within which results can be expected.

Selecting an Advertising Agency

Don't try to handle advertising on your own. This is always a big mistake, resulting in high expenditures and minimal results. Difficult as it may be for an established business to conduct an advertising campaign without help from an agency, it's virtually impossible for start-ups to do so. A quality agency can advise you on which media will bring the best results, tricks for minimizing the cost of each media, and a variety of cost-effective ways to promote your products.

Try to interview at least two or three agencies. You need to find one that understands your objectives and will promise to keep costs under control. It's far better to conduct several interviews to be sure you're getting an agency you can count on than to be sorry later on, after you have committed expenditures.

Cooperative Advertising

Cooperative advertising has become a popular way for small businesses to keep expenses in line. Two of the best ways to participate in cooperative programs are: (1) through group advertising sponsored by your trade association (especially if you decide to advertise your booth at upcoming trade shows) and (2) with shared advertising sponsored by chambers of commerce and trade promotion groups.

Cooperative advertising costs significantly less per individual member than going alone. Also, since advertising agencies have a bigger budget with which to work, they tend to be more enthusiastic. On the downside, with shared advertising you lose control over content and choice of media.

Cooperative advertising is a viable alternative, however, and can be very productive under certain circumstances. It is definitely cheaper than going alone. The combined budgets of companies with related but noncompeting products can produce more elaborate and far-reaching advertising campaigns than any of them could afford to do individually. Furthermore, the increased sales of complimentary products may, in fact, boost sales of your new product as well.

Calculating Business Value

Based on a reasonable estimate of incremental selling costs and thorough research of customer demand, you should be able to approximate future cash flow. This forecast won't be as accurate as one based on historical performance, but lenders, buyers, partners, and everyone else know that and will make allowances. Maybe five years is too long a period over which to forecast. Perhaps you should settle on three or four years. Granted, a cash flow forecast of three to four years isn't much to base a company's value on, but it may be the best you can do.

Assuming your forecast of future sales growth and cash flow looks reasonable, the next step is to assign a probability of occurrence to it. Measuring risk is always hit or miss. With a start-up it is doubly difficult. Still, an estimate of risk must be part of your valuation.

How sure are you that the 15 percent growth rate you have forecasted will actually occur? Are you 90 percent certain, 50 percent, 25 percent, 10 percent? Anything less than 75 to 80 percent certainty means that a high discount rate, probably in the 25 to 30 percent range, should be applied to future cash flows. This could make many of the methods discussed in this book meaningless. It does not mean your business is worthless, however. It merely implies that fair market value must be determined by other means. Comparing a calculated value with recent selling prices of companies producing similar products or services would be a good start and certainly add credence to your calculation. By and large, however, when the owner of a start-up is less than 75 percent certain of attaining a pro forma cash flow forecast, any value used in buy/sell or partnership agreements must, of necessity, be one based on negotiation between the parties rather than on a definitive calculation.

CONCLUSION

This book has set out a wide range of valuation methods currently in use by professional appraisers. No one method will work in all cases. Each valuation must be arrived at by using those tools best suited to a company's unique characteristics.

As pointed out at the beginning of this book, valuing a business is an art form, not a science. In the end, a business appraiser can only give you a reasonable approximation of the worth of your business. Anyone who claims that the value he or she has calculated is the only accurate one is missing the boat.

On one hand, it is wrong to believe the myth that the fair market value of a business is always in the eye of the beholder. On the other hand, it may be that this is the only way to determine a particular company's market worth. No valuation method currently accepted as reasonable by the trade will fit every circumstance. We can only do our best with the information available to us.

Index

ABOUT THE AUTHOR

Lawrence W. Tuller has owned and operated fifteen companies. He is a graduate of Harvard University and the Wharton School and holds a CPA certificate. He is the author of thirty books. His other books relevant to small business owners include:

Secrets of Buying/Selling a Business
Finance for the Non-Financial Manager, 2nd Edition
Entrepreneurial Growth Strategies
The Complete Book of Raising Capital
Buying In: A Complete Guide to Acquiring a Business or Professional Practice
Getting Out: A Step-by-Step Guide to Selling a Business or Professional Practice
Tap the Hidden Wealth in Your Business
Financing the Small Business

Made in United States
Orlando, FL
25 February 2023